Social Issues of Advertising

Social Issues of Advertising

Kara Chan

CITY UNIVERSITY OF
HONG KONG PRESS
香港城市大學出版社

ISBN: 978-962-937-283-5

Published by
City University of Hong Kong Press
Tat Chee Avenue
Kowloon, Hong Kong
Website: www.cityu.edu.hk/upress
E-mail: upress@cityu.edu.hk

Printed in Hong Kong

Contents

List of Illustrations

Tables

Figures

Foreword

Social Issues of Advertising is one of the most updated anthologies in the field of advertising in Hong Kong. The book addresses the most important and controversial advertising issues in Hong Kong with contributions from academics and practitioners in the field. Besides mainstream topics such as the regulation of advertising, issues surrounding commercials and the effects of advertising on children, the book also touches upon some newly emerging topics in relation to gaming and political communication in Hong Kong. This book is perhaps the first in Hong Kong that bridges advertising as an academic field and advertising as a profession. I would like to hereby congratulate Professor Kara Chan who gathered these experts and intellectuals and put together this volume for all advertising students in Hong Kong.

Anthony Fung
Director and Professor
School of Journalism and Communication
The Chinese University of Hong Kong

Preface

Advertising has become a part of our daily lives. Whenever people learn that I teach advertising, they always have something to say on the subject. Some people recall advertisements they found interesting or sometimes they share a story of how an advertisement impacted them emotionally. Once, a sales agent shared with me a Thai commercial about a handicapped girl struggling for success, and told me that whenever he felt down or stressed at work, he would watch the commercial to gain encouragement.

This book is a textbook designed for a senior level course about advertising and society. The basic question that we ask is: does advertising improve society? This question is especially relevant for students who intend to pursue careers in advertising, marketing or public relations. We want our students to be aware of the social impact of advertising. The knowledge and the attitudes they gain through a deep understanding of the social responsibility of advertising will prepare them to be ethical communicators.

The chapters in this book cover the major social issues of advertising, from the perspectives of advertisers and marketers, as well as consumers and special groups such as children and youth. The first two chapters provide a framework of the advertising production system. Chapter 1 introduces various indicators that measure the performance of advertising messages through production, distribution and reception. Chapter 2 discusses market trends as well as the economic and social environment in which advertising operates. Chapter 3 explains advertising creativity from the perspective of practitioners. Chapters 4 and 5 focus on branded content and controversial advertising. In order to communicate effectively with consumers, advertising can touch on controversial issues or images; consumers' responses to these forms of advertising are elaborated upon. Chapter 6 discusses the regulation of advertising in Hong Kong and the ethical issues involved. This chapter is useful for practitioners to learn how to stay within legal and ethical boundaries when creating advertising messages.

In exploring society's reaction to advertisements it becomes apparent that they carry symbolic meaning. Chapter 7 elaborates on the use of semiotic analysis in exposing the deeper meanings embedded in advertisements. Three personal loan advertisements were selected to illustrate the process. Chapters 8 and 9 deal with the criticism that advertising enhances gender stereotypes. Chapter 8 reports a content analysis of the portrayal of women in magazine advertising, while Chapter 9 examines a qualitative study of how young people respond to the characterization of women in advertisements. Through these two chapters, readers will learn how advertisements may enhance certain stereotypes. Content analysis methodology can be used to analyze other stereotypes regarding minority groups. Chapter 10 focuses on children's understanding of advertising and in particular public services advertisements. Recent empirical evidence of children and advertising are presented. Many social marketing campaigns attempt to influence the attitudes and behavior of children and youth; in this chapter, readers will learn about persuasive skills used to target younger generations.

The last three chapters deal with more specialized areas of advertising. Chapter 11 examines the advertising of medical services. Before 2008, medical doctors in Hong Kong were not allowed to advertise, but a change in their code of practice has allowed them to advertise in print media. This chapter discusses the results of a public opinion survey about beliefs regarding the advertising of medical services. This can provide a foundation for future policies on the advertising of medical services. Chapter 12 investigates how video games can be used to promote health communication. As many young people nowadays play video games, this could be used to advance social causes such as health. Chapter 13 examines public service advertisements in Hong Kong. With free airtime, the Hong Kong SAR government is a prominent advertiser of social causes; the strategies they use are investigated in this chapter.

Most of the contributors to this book are teachers of advertising and marketing in Hong Kong. I am blessed to be able to bring together their expertise to serve our teaching needs. I am grateful to Mr Edmund Chan of City University of Hong Kong Press for his support and insightful comments. I would also like to thank Ms Joanna Pierce, Mr Laying Tam and Mr Dickson Yeung for helping us in editing the manuscript. I dedicate this book to the students at Hong Kong Baptist University. Their eagerness to learn and participate in classroom discussion fuels our teaching and learning journey.

List of Contributors

Dr. Fanny Fong Yee Chan (PhD, University of Kent) is Assistant Professor at the School of Business, Hang Seng Management College, Hong Kong. She was previously a senior executive and a part-time lecturer in the School of Communication, Hong Kong Baptist University. She also taught at the University of Kent and the School of Continuing and Professional Studies, Chinese University of Hong Kong. Her work has been published in *International Marketing Review, Marketing Intelligence and Planning, Journal of Promotion Management, Journal of Marketing Communications, Journal of Product and Brand Management, Asian Journal of Communication, The Marketing Review* and others. Her research interests include marketing communications, culture and consumer psychology.

Dr. Kara Chan (PhD, City University of Hong Kong) is a Professor at the School of Communication, Hong Kong Baptist University. She worked in the advertising business and as a statistician for the Hong Kong Government before she moved into academia. Her research areas are cross-cultural consumer studies and health communication. She has published seven books as well as over 140 journal articles and book chapters. She was a Fulbright scholar at Bradley University, Illinois as well as a Visiting Professor at Copenhagen Business School, Aarhus University and Klagenfurt University. Her journal articles have won five Emerald Literati Network Awards for Excellence. She received awards for Outstanding Performance in Scholarly Work at Hong Kong Baptist University in 2006 and 2014.

Dr. Hong Cheng (PhD, Pennsylvania State University) is a Professor and the Director of the Richard T. Robertson School of Media and Culture, Virginia Commonwealth University. His research interests center on international and cross-cultural advertising and social marketing. His articles have appeared in more than ten journals and as many books. He co-authored (with Guofang Wan) *Becoming a Media Savvy Student* and co-edited (with Kara Chan) *Advertising and Chinese Society: Issues and Impacts* and (with Philip Kotler and Nancy Lee) *Social Marketing for Public Health: Global Trends and Success Stories*. He also edited *The Handbook of International Advertising Research*. He is an associate editor of *Journalism and Mass Communication Quarterly* and the chair of the American Advertising Federation's National Education Executive Committee.

Ms. Yolanda Cheng (BSSc in Communication, Hong Kong Baptist University) is an artist and a Master of Science student in Visualization at Texas A&M University. She is currently working for Reel FX in Dallas, Texas for their new feature film, which is targeted for an early 2018 release. She worked as a student research assistant at Hong Kong Baptist University in 2009. She also worked as a freelance artist while she was living in the U.S. and New Zealand. Her research interests are gender studies and multicultural studies.

Dr. William Dezheng Feng (PhD, National University of Singapore), is a Research Assistant Professor at the Department of English, The Hong Kong Polytechnic University. His research interests include multimodal discourse analysis, and media and communication studies. He has published over twenty articles in journals such as the *Journal of Pragmatics*, *Visual Communication*, *Semiotica*, *Review of Cognitive Linguistics* and *Narrative Inquiry*. He is currently working on a project which analyzes public service advertisements in Hong Kong from analyzing discourse and cross-cultural perspectives.

Ms. Anqi Huang (MA in Communication, Hong Kong Baptist University) worked at the Department of Communication Studies, Hong Kong Baptist University as a research assistant, preparing book manuscripts as well as assisting in data collection and analysis. She participated in several research projects in advertising and public relations areas and is the co-author of several journal articles and book chapters. She is now working in public relations in the financial industry.

Dr. Annisa Lee (PhD, University of North Carolina at Chapel Hill) is an Associate Professor and Director of MSSc in Advertising and Coordinator of Public Relations/Advertising Concentration at the School of Journalism and Communication at The Chinese University of Hong Kong. Her research interest is advertising in its broadest sense, ranging from the promotion of products and services to social issues and nations. She has published on topics related to advertising, health communication and nation branding. When studying as an undergraduate law student at the University of Hong Kong, she developed a concern for social issues.

Dr. Vincie Pui Yuen Lee (PhD, University of Edinburgh) is an Assistant Professor of Advertising Design at the School of Design in The Hong Kong Polytechnic University. She holds a BA and an MSc degree in advertising and marketing from The Hong Kong Polytechnic University. Her research focuses on advertising creativity and new media. She is interested to investigate the roles creative professionals play in society; and how digital and virtual technology inform contemporary advertising creative practices. She possesses both industrial and academic experience in advertising through working in diverse multinational advertising agencies (HK4As) and various universities. She has published research papers in international journals and edited books.

Dr. Vivienne Leung (PhD, Hong Kong Baptist University) is a Senior Lecturer and the Programme Director of Advertising and Public Relations major at Hong Kong Baptist University. Previously she held positions at Grey Advertising and Fallon Asia/Hong Kong as a strategic planner. Her clients included United Airlines, P&G, Wrigley, Audi, PCCW, McDonald's and the Bank of China. Her research interests include advertising, the role of celebrities in advertising health communication and social service marketing. Her work has been published in *Service Marketing Quarterly*, *Journal of Nonprofit and Public Sector Marketing*, *Intercultural Communication Studies*, *Asian Journal of Business Research*, *Journal of Consumer Marketing*, *Chinese Journal of Communication* and *Journal of Communication in Healthcare*.

Mr. Yu Leung Ng (BSSc in Psychology, City University of Hong Kong) is a PhD student at the School of Communication, Hong Kong Baptist University. His research interests are micro-level (intrapersonal and interpersonal level) media effects, as well as behavioral and social health science. He has published over fifteen journal articles across several social science disciplines.

Mr. Lennon Tsang (MBA and MSSc, Chinese University of Hong Kong) is a Lecturer at the School of Communication, Hong Kong Baptist University. He has worked in the communication field in various sectors, including media, higher education, public utility and fast moving consumer goods (FMCG). While working as a communication practitioner, he taught at several higher educational institutions in Hong Kong as well as their continuing education arms, including The Chinese University of Hong Kong and City University of Hong Kong. In 2015, he co-authored a Chinese textbook about public relations and crisis management.

Ms. Hety Hei Ting Wong (MA in Ethnomusicology, University of Pittsburgh) is a PhD student in Ethnomusicology at the University of Pittsburgh. Her research interests are Chinese popular music in relation to identity construction media and new media development, political influences in postcolonial Hong Kong and educational issues. She was involved in several research projects as a research assistant in Hong Kong universities, most recently at the Academy of Film of the School of Communication, Hong Kong Baptist University. She is now a scholar-in-residence at the David C. Lam Institute for East-West Studies, Hong Kong Baptist University.

Mr. Jason Wong (BSSc in Integrated Communication Management, Hong Kong Baptist University) is Platform Manager at OMD International. He is a veteran multi-skilled digital marketer who worked in different HK4As agencies, including McCann Worldgroup and Ogilvy Hong Kong before joining Omnicom Media Group. At OMD, he specializes in performance media strategy and data analysis. He has worked with large-scale clients on the global and regional levels across industries such as hospitality, luxury, insurance, airline, technology, logistics, toys and games. He has been a Google certified partner since 2012. He won the Campaign Asia-Pacific MediaWorks in 2015.

Mr. Dickson Yeung is a student at Emory University. He currently edits research papers for professors at Hong Kong Baptist University's School of Communication. He has translated and proofread articles by various institutions, such as the Hong Kong Baptist University and the Red Cross. He has also transcribed interviews for these parties. He interned at the David C. Lam Institute for East-West Studies, Hong Kong Baptist University.

Ms. Melannie Zhan (MSSc in Media Management, Hong Kong Baptist University) is a PhD student at the School of Communication at Hong Kong Baptist University. Prior to her doctoral study, she worked as an account manager in Hong Kong Asia Television Limited and JCDecaux Group, both in the field of advertising.

Dedicated to

the Students of Hong Kong Baptist University

Chapter 1

An Overview of the Indicators of Advertising Performance

Fanny Fong Yee Chan

Introduction

Advertising, as a form of communication, has a process which is very similar to that described in the traditional human communication model (Arens et al., 2013). In the traditional human communication model, there are a total of six components: the source/sender, the encoding process, the message, the channel, the decoding process and the receiver (Peter and Olsen, 1994). Applying this model to advertising communication, the source is equivalent to the advertisers/creatives who are involved in the creation and production of advertising and promotional messages (the encoding process). These advertisements and commercials (the message) are then carried by different advertising media (the channel) to the general audience/consumers (the receiver) who may actively and/or passively engage in the interpretation exercise (the decoding process). Therefore in analyzing the effectiveness of advertising communication, we can focus on examining three key indicators: the production, the distribution and the reception (Chan and Lee, 1992). This chapter centers the discussion around these indicators in order to reveal the big picture of advertising communication in Hong Kong.

Production of Advertising Messages

Advertising production can be measured by examining three areas. The first indicator of productivity is the investment in advertising production; this can be seen in the level of advertising expenditure in different commercial sectors. The second productivity indicator is the capability of advertising production which is reflected by the manpower engaged in the advertising industry. The quality of advertising production represents the third productivity indicator.

Investment in Advertising Production

Nielsen (2015), the world's leading provider of marketing research, compiles figures of advertising expenditure by different product categories. In the past, reports on advertising expenditure by product category and by brand were prepared in hard-copy format on a monthly basis. However, as the advertising market is becoming increasingly competitive, clients require timely reports on an interactive platform: admanGo was founded in 1999 to provide such a service. It works closely with major advertisers, advertising agencies and media to develop an extensive online advertising archive. Its advertising intelligence database documents advertising creatives and spending data over more than fifteen years. Its competitive advertising monitoring service is updated on a daily basis. A wide range of media types are covered including television, newspapers and magazines, radio, outdoor and in-transit displays, digital and mobile advertising, among others. Detailed reports about advertising expenditure by different product categories, media, brands and campaigns are available by subscription. By clicking on the thumbnails of advertisements on the platform, subscribed users can see the two-dimensional print advertisements, can hear the radio spots, as well as watch the television or digital commercials. Users may also subscribe for enhanced features to keep track of new media types and their adoption levels in the market.

Capability of Advertising Production

In addition to advertising expenditure, the hardware of advertising production lies in the manpower engaged in the advertising industry. The first survey of advertising and public relations manpower was conducted in 1987 by the Vocational Training Council. It covered all advertising agencies, public relations agencies, media agencies and selected in-house advertising and public relations departments in Hong Kong. The manpower of the advertising and public relations industries were surveyed every two years and figures were reported. The formal training requirements and qualifications were also examined. However, the statistics were reported by job level (i.e. managerial, supervisory, executional and supporting/technical) instead of by function (e.g., account servicing, creative, media planning). Other than advertising manpower, the number of advertising programs offered by local institutions and the respective intakes every year can also serve as an indicator of the capability of advertising production. This information indicates the potential supply of advertising manpower and the amount of formal training that individuals receive before joining the advertising profession. Moreover, the analysis of relationship dynamics between advertisers and advertising agencies may also signal the capacity of advertising production (So, 2005).

Quality of Advertising Production

Another indicator of advertising productivity is the quality of production which is reflected in the number of awards and the recognition and complaints received by the industry. In Hong Kong, no official bodies are designated to censor advertising production. In other words, the advertising industry is largely self-regulated. The Association of Accredited Advertising Agents of Hong Kong (HK4As) has published a code of practice for its members to follow in order to preserve standards and ethics in the advertising profession. The high quality of advertising production was illustrated in the number of awards and positive recognition earned both locally and internationally. These include the Most Popular Television Commercials Award organized by local television broadcasters and the Hong Kong Advertisers Association (HK2A), and the Kam Fan Awards (formerly known as the HK4As Creative Awards) organized by the HK4As every year. Some creative advertisements also received renowned international awards such as the Cannes Lions International Advertising Awards, the Effie Awards and the Clio Awards, among others. Chapter 3 discusses the encoding process of advertising creativity.

Some substandard advertisements or advertisements expressing bad taste or inappropriate values were punished by the Communications Authority (formerly known as the Broadcasting Authority). These advertisements received advice, warnings or even fines from the Authority. When a member of the public feels annoyed by an advertisement, they can lodge a complaint with the Communications Authority. The Authority will then launch an investigation and file the case into an online archive which documents all the complaint cases since 2012 (Communications Authority, 2015a). Currently, there is no official body to deal with complaints on print or outdoor advertising in Hong Kong. The media themselves are responsible for the quality of advertisements that they carry.

In summary, investment, capability and quality are the three key indicators of advertising productivity. Together, they determine the distribution of advertising messages and the volume of advertising carried by different media which are discussed in the next section.

Distribution of Advertising Messages

The available channels for the distribution of advertising messages have proliferated over the past decade. They include the traditional media outlets (e.g. television, radio, newspapers, magazines, transit vehicles, outdoor billboards) as well as the unconventional platforms for advertising such as applications on smart phones and various digital formats. Audiences are becoming more fragmented nowadays and it is increasingly hard to reach audiences with a single medium. It is envisaged that more and more advertising channels will appear which will certainly drive fierce intramedia and intermedia competition. Indeed, marketers have gradually shifted their advertising budget from traditional media outlets to new media as shown by admanGo. It shows a 7% growth in television advertising expenditure in 2014, while advertising revenue from online and mobile media recorded increments of 12% and 105% respectively (Perez, 2015).

Traditional Media Outlets

Although new media channels keep evolving, currently traditional media outlets still account for a large proportion of the advertising revenue pie in Hong Kong. According to admanGo, a total of HK$49.9 billion was spent on advertising across different media in 2014, in which the following traditional mass media took up 90% (Perez, 2015).

Television

Television, a traditional advertising medium, was once the main entertainment staple of people in Hong Kong. There were originally two domestic free television program service providers in Hong Kong, Asia Television Limited (ATV) and Television Broadcast Limited (TVB), and one government-funded public service broadcaster, Radio Television Hong Kong (RTHK) (Information Services Department 2014). The government did not renew ATV's license, and it stopped broadcasting in April 2016. However, a free-to-air license was granted to HK Television Entertainment Company Limited (Viu TV). Currently the three operators broadcast a variety of programs in analog format as well as the newly introduced digital format. A one-hour television program usually embeds four commercial breaks and each commercial break contains five to eight advertisements. There are also three domestic subscription-based television program service providers: Hong Kong Cable Television Limited (Cable TV), Pacific Century CyberWorks Media Limited (now TV) and TVB Network Vision Limited (Information Services Department, 2014).

Various television advertising possibilities are available including spot television commercials, product sponsorship, title sponsorship and product placement (Chan, 2012). There are altogether four types of product sponsorship: prop sponsorship, which means the product is displayed in a program; scene sponsorship, which means a particular scene of a program is specifically built for a product; character sponsorship which means a particular character in a program is closely associated with the product; and theme sponsorship, which means the key theme of the program is tailor-made to tie in with the product (Television Broadcasts Limited, 2015). According to admanGo, television advertising accounted for 32% (equivalent to HK$15.97 billion) of the total advertising expenditure in 2014 (Perez, 2015).

Radio

Radio is a less costly platform for advertisers compared to television. Advertisers can choose to place their advertising messages in either analog or digital radio channels (Communications Authority, 2015b). Currently, there are thirteen analog radio channels in Hong Kong including three operated by Hong Kong Commercial Broadcasting Company Limited (Commercial Radio), three by Metro Broadcast Corporation Limited (Metro Radio), and seven by RTHK. RTHK is funded by the government and does not accept commercial advertisements. There are a total of eighteen digital radio channels operated by four digital audio broadcasting service providers. In March 2011, the government granted licenses to Digital Broadcasting Corporation Hong Kong Limited (DBC) to operate eight channels, Metro Radio to operate three and Phoenix U Radio Limited (U Radio) to operate two channels. In September 2012, RTHK also launched five digital channels. U Radio stopped its services in September 2015 because of consistently low ratings. Radio advertising accounts for a very small proportion of the total advertising expenditure.

Newspapers and Magazines

Hong Kong is a hotbed of publications. There are two English newspapers (the *South China Morning Post* and *The Standard,* which has now become a free newspaper) and more than fourteen Chinese daily newspapers. They include newspapers such as *Apple Daily, Oriental Daily, Ming Pao* and *Wen Wei Po,* among others. *Hong Kong Daily News* ceased publication in 2015. There are also free tabloid newspapers such as *AM730, Headline Daily* and *Metro Daily,* which have attracted many advertisers because of their growing readerships. Full-page advertisements or inserts are frequently seen in these free newspapers.

There are more than fifty magazines published in Hong Kong. They can be classified into different subcategories: business, cars, children, IT, fashion, food and cooking, health and fitness, etc. Advertisers may choose to place advertisements in magazines of a relevant subject area. Some familiar titles include *Next Magazine, East Week, Yazhou Zhoukan* and *Cosmopolitan HK.* Some freely distributed magazines like *Recruit* and *Jiujik* also provide avenues for advertising messages.

Outdoor and Transit Advertising

A lot of outdoor advertising spaces are available in Hong Kong such as around shopping malls, on high-rise buildings and above tunnel entrances. Transit advertising is also very popular. Many transportation vehicles such as the MTR, taxis, buses and minibuses are platforms for advertising. Advertisers can choose to purchase the interior or exterior advertising spaces of buses or advertise on bus-TV. RoadShow, which is owned by Kowloon Motor Bus, broadcasts on over 5,000 buses and minibuses. Likewise, M-Channel, owned by StarEast Limited since 2001, broadcasts on New World buses and in some shopping malls. These advertising platforms keep expanding and have extended to unconventional outlets, for instance, Roadshow has created the HK2gather app.

Digital Media Outlets

The Internet has changed the advertising paradigm by offering advertisers cheaper and more targeted varieties of communication. Advertisers can tailor-make advertising messages to specific audiences via the platforms of webpages, emails, search engines, social media or mobile applications. Cheung (2006) discusses some of the successful Internet advertising strategies. The distinct capability of digital media outlets lies in their interactivity. Unlike traditional media outlets, audiences are able to respond immediately to advertising messages carried by the unconventional channels below. AdmanGo forecast that digital media will overtake television to be the major outlet for advertising by 2020 (Perez, 2015).

Webpages and Emails

Many advertisers choose to post promotional messages on webpages. There are many varieties such as banners, pop-ups, pop-unders and rich media advertisements. Advertising on popular webpages such as Yahoo!HK, SinaHK and MSN can reach millions of Internet users, but is relatively costly. Alternatively, advertisers may opt for a low cost and convenient channel—email. Email direct marketing (EDM) is increasingly popular with marketers.

Search Engines

Google and Yahoo are the big players of search-engine advertising, or more specifically, keyword advertising. Advertisers buy keywords from the search engines and their advertising messages will be brought up on the pages of the search engine when specific words or phrases are entered. The ranking of ad appearance is subject to the amount placed by the advertiser and the quality of the advertisement. For instance, Google uses a quality scoring system (to estimate the quality of ads or keywords) to decide its ad rank (order of advertisements shown). Keyword advertising is popular with advertisers because it reaches consumers who have relevant needs. It also helps to feed back to advertisers the readiness of customers to partake of the product. Customers looking for comments, reviews or ratings of a particular product may represent different buying stages (i.e. searching, reviewing or comparing stages).

Social Media and Sharing Sites

Social media is another trend in advertising development. Some of the popular social media networks include Facebook, Twitter, Instagram and LinkedIn, among others. These networks, once used mainly for connecting people, have now become tools for matching advertisers to their potential buyers. Likewise, YouTube, once a video-sharing site, has now become an alternative advertising platform to reach young consumers. It also serves as a test bed for television commercials for advertisers. There are many popular YouTubers such as Bomba, Hayhay and Szeto. Inviting these YouTubers to shoot a promotional video for a product/service may cost more than HK$100,000. Other emerging advertising platforms include video games, mobile apps and product placements, to name but a few (see Chapter 4).

In summary, evaluating the utilization and performance of the above media outlets serves as a key indicator of advertising distribution. Regulation could be another indicator of advertising distribution. The restrictions put on some product categories affect the possible distribution outlets of their advertising messages. For instance, tobacco advertisements have not been allowed on broadcast media in Hong Kong since 1991. Some products, such as alcoholic drinks and condoms, are allowed to be advertised on broadcast media but have to be outside prime-time hours (see Chapter 6 for advertising regulations). Gao (2005) compared the advertising regulations in Hong Kong, Taiwan and China and revealed some regulatory congruence within the greater China region.

Reception of Advertising Messages

The third set of indicators of the effectiveness of advertising communication are the reception indicators, which include audiences' perception and evaluation of advertising messages. More than forty studies have been conducted to examine advertising messages in Hong Kong and public opinion toward them. Some of these studies have compared advertising in Hong Kong to other countries. Various research methodologies have been adopted in the studies. Content analysis and sometimes discourse analysis were employed to examine advertising messages, and surveys and experimental studies were frequently used to map individuals' cognitive, affective and behavioral responses toward advertising.

Content of Advertising Messages

Advertising messages, mainly print and television, were analyzed with respect to their appeals, language usage, information content and gender portrayal. A few studies also examined the cultural values embedded in advertising and the symbolic meanings.

Appeals and Language Usage

Studies were conducted to examine the appeals adopted by and the language used in advertisements. Ha (1998) content analyzed print advertisements in *Next* magazine (published in Hong Kong) and *Time* magazine (published in the U.S.) to compare the advertising appeals adopted by service advertisements in these two countries. The results were further examined with regard to different services types such as experience and credence services. Wu and Chan (2007) also conducted a content analysis of advertisements in *Next* magazine but their study focused on the language used before and after 1997 (i.e. before and after the return of sovereignty to China). A more recent study attempted to map the usage of humor in television advertising (Chan, 2011a). A total of 356 Hong

Kong television commercials were content analyzed and 20% of the sample were found to utilize humor devices to a certain extent.

Information Content

The first analysis of information content of television commercials in Hong Kong was conducted in 1986 using Resnick and Stern's (1977) evaluation criteria. Commercials were analyzed to see if they contained one of fourteen information cues including availability, performance and price, among others (Chan, 1986). The study also examined whether the presence of information cues depended on the type of product advertised, the duration of the commercials, and the day, time and channel of broadcasting. Altogether, 235 commercials were studied and 47% were found to contain one or more information cues. A replicate study analyzing 341 commercials was conducted a few years later (Chan, 1995b). There are also studies examining the information content of corporate advertising (Kwok, 1994; Tse, 2004) and subway advertisements (Lewis, 2003).

Gender Portrayal

Advertising is sometimes accused of creating and reinforcing gender stereotypes in society. A few content analysis studies were conducted to investigate the existence of gender stereotyping in advertising. Various items were coded, such as the frequency of males or females portrayed as central figures in the advertisement, the roles played by the central figures and the estimated price of the product (Siu 1996). Yik (1999) and Moon and Chan (2002) have conducted similar studies but with a focus on how television advertising targets children. Furnham and Li (2008) also investigated gender portrayal in advertising but focused specifically on food and beverage commercials. A recent study examined the portrayal of female figures in advertisements appearing in *Next* magazine (Chan and Cheng, 2012). The latest study on gender portrayal is from Prieler et al. (2015) and analyzed gender representations in television advertising in East Asian societies including Hong Kong, Japan and South Korea. Chapters 8 and 9 discuss gender issues in advertising.

Embedded Cultural Values

Advertising is said to reflect cultural values. Chan (1999) explored the set of cultural values embedded in newspaper advertising in Hong Kong from 1946 to 1996. A total of 580 advertisements were examined to check whether they contained any of the thirty-two cultural values including adventure, beauty, quality and safety, among others. The same coding frame was employed to compare cultural values embedded in Hong Kong and mainland Chinese television commercials (Chan and Cheng, 2003). Other cross-cultural comparisons include So (2004) which analyzed cultural values embedded in print advertisements in Hong Kong and Australia, and Moon and Chan (2005) which contrasted Hong Kong and Korean television commercials.

Layers of Meaning

Some scholars attempted to "undress" advertisements by conducting textual or discourse analysis. Frith (1997) argued that in order to comprehend an advertisement in detail, we have to deconstruct it. This enables one to identify what the advertisement states and how exactly it operates. This deconstructive reading and interpretation help to reveal the hidden motives in advertisements. In the deconstruction process, three levels of meaning that may emerge include the surface meaning, the advertisers' intended meaning and the cultural or ideological meaning (see Chapter 7 for details). Several studies were conducted to reveal the symbolic meaning of Hong Kong advertising. These included deconstructing the text and visuals of television commercials targeting children (Wong, 1997), advertisements on slimming products or services (Fung, 2006), banking commercials (Wong, 2000; Ma, 2001) as well as public services announcements (Cuklanz and Wong, 1999; see also Chapter 13).

Cognitive Responses to Advertising

Individuals' cognitive responses toward advertising mainly depend on the amount of exposure and attention paid to advertising, their understanding of advertising, especially by children, and whether one believes in what advertisements claim.

Exposure and Attention

Exposure and attention to advertising is the first step to examine in the hierarchy of effects. In order for an advertisement to be effective, one needs to have sufficient exposure and attention to it. Questions such as "What do you usually do when advertisements are on?" may be used to check audience's exposure and attentiveness to advertising (Chan, 1995a). Attention to advertising could also be reflected in the capacity to recall or recognize advertisements that they have been exposed to. For example, Prendergast and Chan (2005) surveyed the Hong Kong public about their exposure to and recall of cinema advertising and noticed significant differences across demographic groups.

Understanding

Advertising is sometimes criticized because of its manipulative effect on children (Gerbner and Gross, 1976). Advocate groups and educators are generally concerned that advertising may take advantage of children's inability to fully understand ads. Research has been conducted to investigate children's understanding of advertising and promotional messages. Chan (2000) employed three questions to examine children's understanding of television advertising: "When we are watching television, sometimes the program stops and there are other messages coming up, what are these?", "What do commercials want you to do?" and "Why do television stations carry such messages?" In another study, children were asked to recall their favorite television commercials and to describe what the commercials said by reading advertising storyboards (see Chapter 10 for details). Sin and Cheng (1984) surveyed the public's views on the impact of advertising on children with the statement, "Advertising has a bad influence on children".

Perceived Credibility

In addition to understanding, trust toward advertising is another frequently studied topic in exploring individuals' cognitive perception of advertising. Statements such as "Products don't perform as well as the ads claim" (Martin et al., 1994) and "In general, advertisements do not present a true picture of the product advertised" (Sin and Cheng, 1984) were employed to check whether people believe in advertising claims. A study was conducted to examine the credibility of advertisements of different product types and of advertisements carried by various media channels (Prendergast et al., 2009). The credibility issue is particularly controversial in relation to children because they generally lack the ability to detect exaggeration in advertising claims. Indeed, Chan (2001) interviewed 448 children regarding the truthfulness of television advertising and found that younger children were more likely to perceive advertising as truthful.

Affective and Behavioral Responses to Advertising

The higher order effects of advertising include the effects on people's attitudes and behavior toward advertising, which are frequently examined. Opinions toward advertising in general, advertising on specific products or services and different types of advertising have been investigated.

General Opinions

Many studies have been carried out to map public opinion toward advertising in general (e.g. Chan, 1995a; Martin et al., 1994; Sin and Cheng, 1984). Two recent studies focused on youth and young adults. Andersen et al. (2008) surveyed youth in Denmark and Hong Kong and found significant differences in their perception of and reactions to advertising. Jozsa et al. (2010) examined young adults' views toward television advertising by asking them to discuss three advertisements that they liked and three they did not like and the reasons for their opinions. Studies have also been conducted to explore particular sectors about their opinions toward advertising. For instance, Yau and Wong (1990) interviewed eighty professionals from CPA firms regarding their views toward the relaxation of restrictions on advertising (see also Yau et al., 1995).

Unacceptable Products and Services

Offensive advertising is another topical issue in advertising reception. Consumers were surveyed to identify product/service advertisements that they found offensive and their reactions toward these advertisements. In one study, MDR Technology Limited (1994) used the question, "Do you think it is necessary to prohibit the broadcast of commercials of female sanitary products during family viewing hours?" to check audiences' acceptance of advertising these products. In another study, respondents were asked to indicate the level of offensiveness they felt toward advertisements for products/services such as chatline services, gambling, condoms, underwear and funeral services (Prendergast et al., 2002). The reasons for finding these advertisements offensive, the level of tolerance of offensive advertisements and the impact on purchase intentions were also examined (see Chapter 5 for details).

Perceptions of Different Advertising Types/Appeals

In addition to examining opinions toward advertising in general, studies have also been conducted to explore the views of the public toward specific types of advertising. Prendergast and Chan (1999) interviewed over 100 consumers about their involvement with and attitudes toward exterior bus advertising. Au (2000) surveyed individuals' attitudes toward religion and church advertising in Hong Kong. Chan (2011b) conducted an experimental study to examine young adults' perception of humorous advertising and its effectiveness. Celebrity endorsements are very common in advertisements appearing in Hong Kong; Chan et al. (2013) conducted a focus group study to explore adolescents' interpretations of celebrities in television commercials. A similar study focused on the interpretation of images of female figures in particular (Ng and Chan, 2015). Public attitudes toward other types of advertising were also considered, such as public service announcements (Chan and Chang, 2013), product placements (see Chapter 4) and advergames (see Chapter 12).

Conclusion

In summary, the three sets of indicators—production, distribution and reception—discussed above are important in displaying the development of advertising communication in a society. Table 1.1 summarizes the different sets of indicators of the success of advertising communication. The production, distribution and reception of advertising can be viewed as three intertwined paths (see Figure 1.1). The capacity of production exerts pressures on the method of distribution which further influences the reception of messages. Meanwhile, the state of message reception also feeds back to and shapes message production and distribution. In other words, the investment in

Table 1.1

Summary of Indicators Showing the Effectiveness of Advertising Communication

Production indicators	Distribution indicators	Reception indicators
Investment in advertising production	*Traditional media outlets*	*Advertising message content*
Capability of advertising production	Television	Appeals and language usage
Quality of advertising production	Radio	Information content
	Newspapers and magazines	Gender portrayal
	Outdoor billboards and transit vehicles	Embedded cultural values
		Symbolic meaning
	Digital media outlets	*Cognitive responses to advertising*
	Webpages and emails	Exposure and attention
	Search engines	Understanding
	Social media and sharing sites	Perceived credibility
		Affective and behavioral responses to advertising
		General opinions
		Unacceptable products and services
		Perception of different advertising types/appeals

Figure 1.1

The Three Interactive States: Production, Distribution and Reception

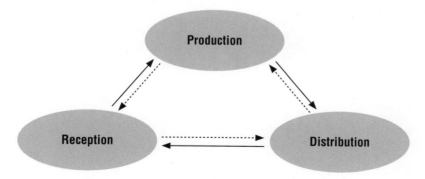

advertising production and creative manpower determines the available outlets for distributing advertisements. This further influences people's perceptions of the advertisements they are exposed to, which in turn gives suggestions for the creative execution and distribution of advertising messages. Therefore the production, distribution and reception of advertising messages are a dynamic interactive process.

Creative advertising production together with diversified and well-developed media outlets color social communication. Advancements in technology and transformation in lifestyles necessitate the timely monitoring and researching of the advertising paradigm. This chapter shows that indicators of the effectiveness of advertising communication in Hong Kong are well researched with continuous efforts being made to explore the reception of advertising messages. To succeed in the fast-growing as well as complex markets, simply knowing what products and services people are consuming is not enough, we must know why. The reception indicators help to reveal not only what people are interested in, but also why are they interested in it. Although advertising messages are increasingly carried by unconventional media outlets, most of the research on advertising reception in Hong Kong is still concentrated on traditional media platforms. In addition, little effort has been devoted to specifically researching the difficulties and challenges that advertising practitioners encounter in advertising production. It is a crucial area of research for advertising production. Therefore future studies may extend these two areas to further enrich our understanding of advertising communication.

References

admanGo (2015), "Advertising expenditures by media", available at: http://www.admango.com (accessed on September 13, 2015).

Andersen, L.P., Tufte, B., Rasmussen, J. and Chan, K. (2008), "The tweens market and responses to advertising in Denmark and Hong Kong", *Young Consumers*, Vol. 9 No. 3, pp. 189–200.

Arens, W.F., Weigold, M.F. and Arens, C. (2013), *Contemporary Advertising and Integrated Marketing Communications*, 14th edn., McGraw-Hill, New York.

Au, K.M. (2000), "Attitudes toward church advertising in Hong Kong", *Marketing Intelligence & Planning*, Vol. 18 No. 1, pp. 39–44.

Chan, F.F.Y. (2011a), "The use of humor in television advertising in Hong Kong", *Humor: International Journal of Humor*, Vol. 24 No. 1, pp. 43–61.

Chan, F.F.Y. (2011b), "Selling through entertaining: The effect of humour in television advertising in Hong Kong", *Journal of Marketing Communications*, Vol. 17 No. 5, pp. 319–336.

Chan, F.F.Y. (2012), "Product placement and its effectiveness: A systematic review and propositions for future research", *The Marketing Review*, Vol. 22 No. 1, pp. 39–60.

Chan, J.M., and Lee, P.S.N. (1992), "Communication indicators in Hong Kong: Conceptual issues, findings and implications", in Lau, S., Wan, P., Lee, M. and Wong, S. (Eds.), *The Development of Social Indicators Research in Chinese Societies*, Hong Kong Institute of Asia-Pacific Studies, The Chinese University of Hong Kong, Hong Kong, pp. 175–205.

Chan, K. (1986), "Lack of information in TV commercials", *Media & Marketing*, Vol. 25, pp. 15–16.

Chan, K. (1995a), "Hong Kong television advertising: The good, the bad and the ugly", *Hong Kong: Department of Communication Studies*. Hong Kong Baptist University.

Chan, K. (1995b), "Information content of television advertising in Hong Kong and China", *Journal of Asian Pacific Communication*, Vol. 6 No. 4, pp. 231–244.

Chan, K. (1999), "Cultural values in Hong Kong newspaper advertising, 1946-96", *International Journal of Advertising*, Vol. 18 No. 4, pp. 537–554.

Chan, K. (2000), "Hong Kong children's understanding of television advertising", *Journal of Marketing Communications*, Vol. 6 No. 1, pp. 37–52.

Chan, K. (2001), "Children's perceived truthfulness of television advertising and parental influence: A Hong Kong study", *Advances in Consumer Research*, Vol. 28, pp. 207–212.

Chan, K. and Chang, H.C. (2013), "Advertising to Chinese youth: a study of public service ads in Hong Kong", *Qualitative Market Research: An International Journal*, Vol. 16 No. 4, pp. 421–435.

Chan, K. and Cheng, H. (2003), "One country, two systems: Cultural values reflected in Chinese and Hong Kong television commercials", *Gazette: The International Journal for Communication Studies*, Vol. 64 No. 4, pp. 383–398.

Chan, K. and Cheng, Y. (2012), "Portrayal of females in magazine advertisements in Hong Kong", *Journal of Asian Pacific Communication*, Vol. 22 No. 1, pp. 78–96.

Chan, K., Ng, Y.L. and Luk, E. (2013), "Impact of celebrity endorsement in advertising on brand image among Chinese adolescents", *Young Consumers*, Vol. 14 No. 2, pp. 167–179.

Cheung, R.C.T. (2006), "Case study of a successful internet advertising strategy in Hong Kong: a portal for teenagers", *Marketing Intelligence & Planning*, Vol. 24 No. 4, pp. 393–405.

Communications Authority (2015a), "Complaints handled by the Communications Authority", available at: http://www.coms-auth.hk/en/complaints/handle/broadcasting_services/complaints_ca/index.html (accessed on September 13, 2015).

Communications Authority (2015b), "Sound broadcasting licenses", available at: http://www.coms-auth.hk/en/licensing/broadcasting/sound/overview/index.html (accessed on September 25, 2015).

Cuklanz, L. and Wong, W.S. (1999), "Ideological themes in Hong Kong public service announcements: Implications for China's future", in Kluver, R. and Powers, J. (Eds.), *Civic Discourse, Civil Society and the Chinese Communities*, Ablex, Stamford, CT, pp. 93–107.

Frith, K.T. (1997), "Undressing the ad: Reading culture in advertising", in Frith, K.T. (Ed.) *Undressing the ad: Reading culture in advertising*, Peter Lang, New York, NY, pp. 1–17.

Fung, A. (2006), "Gender and advertising: The promotional culture of whitening and slimming", in Chan, K. (Ed.), *Advertising and Hong Kong Society*, The Chinese University Press, Hong Kong, pp. 171–182.

Furnham, A. and Li, J. (2008), "Gender portrayal in food and beverage advertisements in Hong Kong: a content analytic study", *Young Consumers*, Vol. 9 No. 4, pp. 297–307.

Gao, Z. (2005), "Harmonious regional advertising regulation? A comparative examination of government advertising regulation in China, Hong Kong, and Taiwan", *Journal of Advertising*, Vol. 34 No. 3, pp. 75–87.

Gerbner, G. and Gross, L. (1976), "Living with television: The violence profile", *Journal of Communication*, Vol. 26 No. 2, pp. 173–189.

Ha, L. (1998), "Advertising appeals used by services marketers: A comparison between Hong Kong and the United States", *Journal of Services Marketing*, Vol. 12 No. 2, pp. 98–112.

Information Services Department (2014), "The media", *In Hong Kong: The Facts, Information Services Department*, HKSAR, pp. 1–2.

Jozsa, L., Insch, A., Krisjanous, J. and Fam, K.S. (2010), "Beliefs about advertising in China: Empirical evidence from Hong Kong and Shanghai consumers", *Journal of Consumer Marketing*, Vol. 27 No. 7, pp. 594–603.

Kwok, W.Y. (1994), "Corporate advertising in Hong Kong: An information analysis", Unpublished MPhil dissertation, The Chinese University of Hong Kong, Hong Kong.

Lewis, S.W. (2003), "The media of new public spaces in global cities: Subway advertising in Beijing, Hong Kong, Shanghai and Taipei", *Journal of Media & Cultural Studies*, Vol. 17 No. 3, pp. 261–272.

Ma, K.W. (2001), "Re-advertising Hong Kong: Nostalgia industry and popular history", *Positions: East Asia Cultures Critique*, Vol. 9 No. 1, pp. 131–159.

Martin, E.F., Cheng, Y.M., Wilson, G.B. and Tsu, Y.W. (1994), "Advertising images among Hong Kong Chinese: Use of individual modernity and Western orientation clusters in determining market segmentation", *Asian Journal of Communication*, Vol. 4 No. 1, pp. 12–32.

MDR Technology Limited (1994), "Survey on television broadcasting 1993/94", MDR Technology Ltd, Hong Kong.

Moon, Y.S. and Chan, K. (2002), "Cross-cultural study of gender portrayal in children's television commercials: Korea and Hong Kong", *Asian Journal of Communication*, Vol. 12 No. 2, pp. 100–119.

Moon, Y.S. and Chan, K. (2005), "Advertising appeals and cultural values in television commercials: A comparison of Hong Kong and Korea", *International Marketing Review*, Vol. 22 No. 1, pp. 48–66.

Ng, Y.L. and Chan, K. (2015), "Interpretation of female images in advertising among Chinese adolescents", *Young Consumers*, Vol. 16 No. 2, pp. 222–234.

Nielsen (2015), "Advertising expenditures by sector", available at: http://www.nielsen.com/hk/en.html (accessed on November 30, 2015).

Perez, B. (2015), "Digital campaigns boost HK advertising market", available at: http://www.scmp.com/news/article/1689458/digital-campaigns-boost-hk-advertising-market (accessed on August 18, 2015).

Peter, J.P and Olsen, J.C. (1994), *Understanding Consumer Behavior*, 3rd edn., Irwin, Burr Ridge, IL.

Prendergast, G. and Chan, C.H. (1999), "The effectiveness of exterior bus advertising in Hong Kong", *Journal of International Consumer Marketing*, Vol. 11 No. 3, pp. 33–50.

Prendergast, G., Ho, B. and Phau, I. (2002), "A Hong Kong view of offensive advertising", *Journal of Marketing Communications*, Vol. 8 No. 1, pp. 165–177.

Prendergast, G. and Chan, L.W. (2005), "The effectiveness of cinema advertising in Hong Kong", *International Journal of Advertising*, Vol. 24 No. 1, pp. 79–93.

Prendergast, G., Liu, P.Y. and Poon, T.Y. (2009), "A Hong Kong study of advertising credibility", *Journal of Consumer Marketing*, Vol. 26 No. 5, pp. 320–329.

Prieler, M., Ivanov, A. and Hagiwara, S. (2015), "Gender representations in East Asian advertising: Hong Kong, Japan, and South Korea", *Communication & Society*, Vol. 28 No. 1, pp. 27–41.

Resnik, A. and Stern, B.L. (1977), "An analysis of information content in television advertising", *Journal of Marketing*, Vol. 41 No. 1, pp. 50–53.

Sin, Y.M. and Cheng, W.L. (1984), "Advertising in Hong Kong: The consumer view", *Research Committee*, Faculty of Business Administration, The Chinese University of Hong Kong, Hong Kong.

Siu, W.S. (1996), "Gender portrayal in Hong Kong and Singapore television advertisements", *Journal of Asian Business*, Vol. 12 No. 3, pp. 47–63.

So, S.L.M. (2004), "A comparative content analysis of women's magazine advertisements from Hong Kong and Australia on advertising expressions", *Journal of Current Issues & Research in Advertising*, Vol. 26 No. 1, pp. 47–58.

So, S.L.M. (2005), "What matters most in advertising agency performance to clients: Implications and issues on their relationship in Hong Kong", *Journal of Current Issues & Research in Advertising*, Vol. 27 No. 2, pp. 83–98.

Television Broadcasts Limited (2015), Product Sponsorship, Marketing and Sales Division, Television Broadcasts Limited, Hong Kong.

Tse, W.M. (2004), "An information content analysis of Hong Kong corporate advertising: A comparison between public utilities sector and private sector", Unpublished MPhil dissertation, Hong Kong Baptist University, Hong Kong.

Wong, W.S. (1997), "Construction of ideal childhood: Reading and decoding TV advertisements directed at children in Hong Kong", *Hong Kong Cultural Studies Bulletin*, Spring, pp. 75–84.

Wong, W.S. (2000), "The rise of consumer culture in a Chinese society: A reading of banking television commercials in the 1970s of Hong Kong", *Mass Communication and Society*, Vol. 3 No. 4, pp. 393–413.

Wu, D.D. and Chan, K. (2007), "Multilingual mix in Hong Kong advertising, pre- and post-1997", *Asian Journal of Communication*, Vol. 17 No. 3, pp. 301–317.

Yau, O.H.M. and Wong, T. (1990), "How do CPA firms perceive marketing and advertising? A Hong Kong experience", *European Journal of Marketing*, Vol. 24 No. 2, pp. 43–54.

Yau, O.H.M., Wong T.C.H., Shaikh, A.L., Al-Murisi, M. and Latif, A.A.A. (1995), "Comparing accountants' perceptions toward marketing and advertising in Hong Kong and Malaysia", *Journal of Professional Services Marketing*, Vol. 11 No. 2, pp. 111–125.

Yik, H. (1999), "A content analysis of children's television advertising in Hong Kong", Unpublished MPhil dissertation, Hong Kong Baptist University, Hong Kong.

Chapter 2

The Hong Kong Advertising Scene

Lennon Tsang and Jason Wong

Introduction

Advertising is an indispensable element of all modern capitalistic societies. To truly understand the advertising industry, we must grasp the interplay between politics and economics. Hong Kong is a very special city. Since the return of sovereignty to China in 1997, Hong Kong has been governed by the "one country, two systems" formula. This was supposed to maintain the status quo of Hong Kong, including its capitalist economic system, however, with the increasing soft power exerted by mainland China in recent decades, the integrity of this system has been affected. Business interests in Hong Kong are sometimes overshadowed by political stances (Wong, 2015). This, in turn, affects the ecology of Hong Kong's advertising industry. Thus, it is instrumental to understand the political economy of Hong Kong before examining its advertising industry.

Political Economy: Increasing Reliance on Mainland China

The return of sovereignty to China in 1997 imposed a significant change on the political economy of the former colonial city. Such a change was inevitable. Although the Chinese Government had established some measure of cross-border control over Hong Kong long before the handover (Cheung, 2014), the influence on Hong Kong's social, political and economic environment had never been as substantial as it was in 2015, eighteen years after the handover. Hong Kong people (for whom an independent national identity has been devised and solidified in the term "Hongkongers") are increasingly uncomfortable with the growing inequality of wealth, the inexorable climb of property prices, the accompanying rise in consumer prices and the social pressure attributed to growing ties with mainland China ("Losing hearts and minds", 2014).

These anti-China sentiments are brought about by the increasing reliance of Hong Kong's economy on mainland China. The turning point for this relationship was not the handover in 1997, but rather the Severe Adverse Respiratory Syndrome (SARS) outbreak in 2003, which intensified mainland China's influence on the political and economic environments of Hong Kong. By the end of the SARS outbreak, Hong Kong's economic sentiments toward almost all industries had dropped to a historic low. However, with the support of the Beijing Government, Hong Kong's economy revived very quickly. Two major policies that had significant effects were the Individual Visit Scheme (IVS) and the Closer Economic Partnership Arrangement (CEPA), both launched soon after the end of the SARS outbreak.

According to a press release issued by the Hong Kong Government on September 2, 2013, entitled "Happy economic returns after 10 years of CEPA", at its inception in 2003, the IVS allowed residents of ten major Chinese cities (Beijing, Shanghai, Dongguan, Foshan, Guangzhou, Huizhou, Jiangmen, Shenzhen, Zhongshan and Zhuhai) to apply for visas to visit Hong Kong individually for a period of seven days. This policy provided swift relief to Hong Kong's tourism industry, and the economic benefits were enormous. Over the years, the IVS has been refined and modified to cover more cities, leading to increasing numbers of mainland Chinese visiting Hong Kong for sightseeing and shopping, in particular for luxury goods and grocery products, and even some illegal activities. By the end of June 2013, over 14 million mainland Chinese residents had visited Hong Kong under the IVS.

Mainland China's second effort to rescue Hong Kong's economy, the Closer Economic Partnership Arrangement (CEPA), was implemented to offer Hong Kong businesses preferential access to mainland markets. Initially, CEPA opened up eighteen service areas and eliminated tariffs on 374 products. According to "Happy economic returns after 10 years of CEPA", the expansion since 2003 has been profound. CEPA has allowed for:

- 403 liberalization measures for trade in services;

- the issuing of over 2,700 Hong Kong Service Supplier certificates;

- as of June 2012, over 4,400 Hong Kong residents had set up privately owned stores in the mainland under CEPA; and

- export value of goods enjoying zero tariff treatment under CEPA in excess of HK$52.4 billion (U.S.$6.7 billion).

CEPA, IVS and other policies of the Chinese Government undoubtedly saved Hong Kong from the devastating consequences of the SARS outbreak. However, while the economic benefits from closer ties with the mainland have been enormous, the growing anti-China sentiment is equally overwhelming.

Hongkongers-Mainlanders Conflict — Anti-China Sentiments

A poll by The Chinese University of Hong Kong in October 2014 found that the percentage of Hong Kong residents who identified as Chinese had dropped to a record low of 8.9% compared to 32.1% in 1997. In the same study, it was found that more than 25% of Hong Kong residents identified themselves as Hongkongers. Not only does this result indicate that there is very little concept of a national identity among Hong Kong people, it also shows signs of an anti-China sentiment in Hong Kong.

Since the handover, Hong Kong people have been struggling to accommodate the China factor. The "one country, two systems" formula was supposed to separate, if not people's national identities, then at least the political and economic systems of Hong Kong and China. However, the economic and social integration of Hong Kong with southern China in recent decades has rendered such separation impractical. In an article in *The China Review*, Professor Ngok Ma (Ma, 2015) of the Department of Government and Public Administration of The Chinese University of Hong Kong claimed that such social and economic integration also brought resistance against and hostility toward the mainland Chinese Government and people. Ma remarked that such sentiments rose significantly during the 2010 electoral reform of the Legislative Council. Sentiments climbed still further to reach unprecedented levels during the so-called "Umbrella Movement" protest against the electoral reform of the Chief Executive in 2014. Following the Umbrella Movement came more protests against mainland parallel traders (people who buy their stock tax-free in Hong Kong and sell it at a profit in the mainland). These radical movements demonstrate the high level of animosity Hong Kong people hold toward mainland Chinese.

Some Hong Kong people believe that the stronger social and economic ties with mainland China have increased Beijing's intervention in Hong Kong. The polarization of the democratic and pro-establishment camps has become more prominent. The pro-establishment camp criticizes the democratic camp for causing disturbances to Hong Kong and damaging Hong Kong's economy. There have been rumors that some businessmen initiated a boycott of a local newspaper which had a strong democratic background after the Umbrella Movement. Whether or not the rumor is true, the fact is that the newspaper restructured their print media business in 2015 to avoid undesirable losses.

Education Reform — Rise of Putonghua Chinese as An Official Language

Even during its colonial period, Hong Kong was always a linguistically complex and diverse society. Since the handover in 1997, it has been the aim of the HKSAR Government and educators to develop Hong Kong society to be truly biliterate in written English and Chinese and trilingual in spoken English, Cantonese and Putonghua.

In 1997, Putonghua became one of the official languages of Hong Kong. By that time, not only had many people learned to speak Putonghua, a lot of primary schools had also implemented trilingual education to promote Putonghua (Wang and Kirkpatrick, 2015). The increasing importance of Putonghua is unquestionable. However, concerns exist that its rise may harm the existence of Cantonese and in turn affect the local culture of Hong Kong.

Putonghua is undoubtedly becoming more and more important, as is the simplified version of written Chinese. Although there have long been criticisms about Hong Kong organizations solely relying on Putonghua and/or simplified characters for communication, it is not surprising that television and radio commercials are increasingly using Putonghua, or that simplified characters crop up more and more frequently in printed advertisements. The demand for Putonghua-dubbing artists and copywriters skilled in simplified characters has also increased, and this trend will only continue.

Regulatory Changes Concerning the Advertising Industry

While the political economy of Hong Kong has changed dramatically over the years, there has also been new legislation affecting the advertising industry. One example is the new labelling law. According to the Food and Drugs (Composition and Labelling) (Amendment: Requirements for Nutrition Labelling and Nutrition Claim) Regulation 2008 (Amendment Regulation), otherwise known as the new labelling law, enacted on July 1, 2010, all prepackaged food sold in Hong Kong must bear a label with a nutrition information panel (NIP) indicating the values of energy and seven core nutrients (protein, fat, saturated fat, trans fat, carbohydrates, sugars and sodium). The nutrition claims that accompany the NIP must also follow much stricter regulations. The new regulations in labelling have served to curb the claims made in advertisements, as advertisers must be more careful when they make nutritional claims about their products.

In addition to the new labelling law, the latest amendments to the Trade Descriptions Ordinance (TDO) have had an immense effect on the advertising industry. These changes came into effect on July 19, 2013, extending the scope of its coverage of false trade description of goods and services (Tanner De Witt Solicitors, n.d.). An advertisement or a below-the-line promotion event may be considered to have made a false description if it has any of the following features:

- misleading omission—hiding or showing important information unclearly;

- aggressive commercial practices—impairing consumers' freedom of choice through the use of harassment, coercion or undue influence;

- bait advertising—promoting a product or service at a price that is unavailable in a reasonable quantity and/or a reasonable period of time.

This is one example of new legislation affecting the advertising industry. Chapter 6 will give a more detailed account of the legal framework governing the advertising industry.

Media Profiles

Before looking at the trends in total market advertising expenditure (adspend) in Hong Kong, we have to take a look at the composition of the advertising media in Hong Kong. According to Nielsen Media Index, the coverage of any TV channel was 87.5% of the total population in Hong Kong in 2014. Newspapers and magazines had a coverage of 78.3% of the total advertising population (base: age 12–64) in 2014. Radio coverage dropped to 28.4% in 2014. Among all media, TV remains the most effective for advertising in terms of reach. One more phenomenon worth noting is the rise of digital TV, the coverage of which grew to 70% in 2014 and is still on the rise.

Table 2.1 shows the breakdown of different traditional media in Hong Kong in December 2014, excluding out-of-home (OOH) media. As shown, there are thirteen TV channels operated by three domestic free TV operators. Among the three domestic free TV operators, two are commercial and rely on advertising income, and the other is government-owned and does not have advertising airtime to sell. In April 2015, a new commercial domestic free TV operator was established after completion of its free-to-air TV license application. The new licensee, HKTVE, officially launched its free TV channel named Viu TV on April 6, 2016; by this time one of the original commercial domestic free TV operators had ceased operation. In other words, the domestic free TV market will continue with three players. The HKSAR Government agreed to issue two new free-to-air TV licenses in October 2014, although one of the successful applicants still has not completed the whole application process.

Regarding domestic pay TV, there were four operators operating 461 channels at the end of 2014. The domestic pay TV market is more competitive while the viewership is much smaller than the domestic free TV market. Thus, the advertising rates of pay TV are far cheaper than that of free TV.

Table 2.1

Media at a Glance

Domestic free TV		Newspapers	
Operators	3	Chinese	28
Channels	13	English	12
		Others	15
Domestic pay TV*		Subtotal	55
Operators	4		
Channels	461	**Magazines**	
		Chinese	474
Radio		English	99
Operators	5	Others	142
Channels	29	Subtotal	715

Source: Hong Kong Government and *Pay TV stations. ·

The radio market has been shrinking quite quickly in recent years. Among the four operators, three are commercial and one is government-owned. The coverage of the most popular radio channel accounted for about 15% of the population only. Also, because of the limits of the advertising format of this medium, the importance of radio in advertising media has declined greatly in the past decade.

There are fifty-five local newspapers, some fee-charging, some free. Regarding magazines, there are 715 local titles, but only less than 20% of these are of advertising value. The print media altogether had a coverage of 78.3% in 2014 which was second only to TV. However, the print media has been affected by the new media, and recent trends show there will be some consolidation of the print media industry soon.

Out-of-home (OOH) media is another important advertising media in Hong Kong. Figure 2.1 shows the rankings for out-of-home ads seen in the

Figure 2.1

Out-of-Home Ads Seen by Respondents in the Previous Month

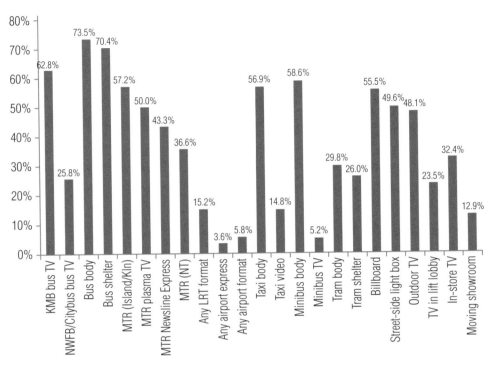

Source: 2014 Nielsen Media Index.

previous month. Buses and the Mass Transit Railway (MTR) system were the most important sites for OOH media. As shown in the chart, "bus body" had the highest viewed out-of-home ads in 2014 (73.5%). The second highest was "bus shelter" (70.4%), and the third and fourth were "KMB bus TV" (62.8%) and "minibus" (excluding TV) (58.6%) respectively. One thing worth noting is that OOH media are less affected by the emergence of the new media.

Figure 2.2 shows the advertising expenditure (adspend) of 2005–2014 and Figure 2.3 shows the adspend breakdown by media of the same period. In Figures 2.2 and 2.3, the research methodology used by admanGo is based on published rate cards of each media and no discount assumption is taken into account for the adspend figures reported. Actual adspend can be significantly lower after discount.

Figure 2.2
Total Market Advertising Expenditure

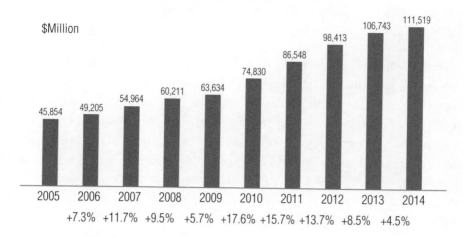

Source: admanGo (without regional publications).

Figure 2.3
Advertising Expenditure by Media

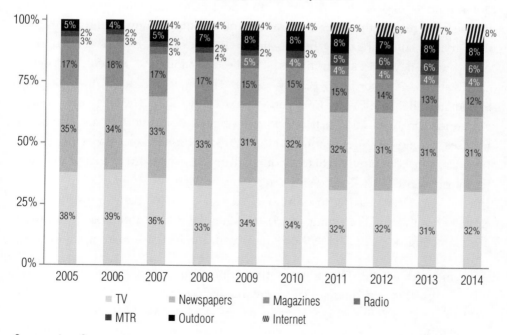

Source: admanGo.

In Figure 2.2, it can be seen that the rate of increase of the total market adspend was slowing down during this period. The total market adspend in 2014 was HK$111.5 million, which made for the smallest year-on-year increase (4.47%) in the period.

Traditional media has been the worst affected by the slowdown in the increase in total market adspend. As shown in Figure 2.3, adspend on TV dropped from 38% of all media in 2005 to 32% in 2014. Other traditional media experienced similar downsizing, with the exception of OOH media. OOH media accounted for 4% of adspend among all media in 2005, and this number increased to 8% in 2014. The probable reason is that the new media does not have much effect on how people commute and travel yet. Therefore the reach of OOH media and its advertising effectiveness remain unchanged with the emergence of the new media.

Facing the growing influence of the new media, it is very difficult for most traditional media to maintain their prevalence. For instance, TVB Jade, the most popular TV channel, had a coverage of more than 90% in 2005, but it dropped to 64.4% in 2014 according to the Nielsen Media Index. This downtrend is expected to continue. In addition to the competition imposed by the new media, the HKSAR Government is setting a new scene for the TV industry by launching new free-to-air TV licenses. The HKSAR Government issued two new free-to-air licenses while rejecting one widely supported candidate in October 2013 (Chow, 2013). The rejected candidate continued to pursue the free-to-air TV license, especially after HKSAR Government announced in April 2015 that one of the original domestic free TV operator's licenses would not be renewed (Ng, 2015). Furthermore, the U.S. online broadcasting company Netflix announced in September 2015 that it planned to introduce its movie and TV streaming service in Hong Kong. Chinese Internet broadcaster LeTV also announced its aggressive plan to invade Hong Kong's pay-TV market (Yeung, 2015). The general public and most TV viewers are expecting better quality TV programs with the increase in competition.

Compared to the TV industry, the print media may be more seriously affected by the new media. The print media coverage changed from 87.8% in 2008 to 78.3% in 2014 according to the Nielsen Media Index. The print media industry was seriously damaged in the summer of 2015, first with the permanent closure of the fifty-six-year old newspaper, *Hong Kong Daily News* in July (Lo, 2015), then *Sing Pao Daily* suspended its operations and Next Media announced the cessation of the print edition of one of its flagship magazines. While this is troubling, new print media has continued to emerge. For instance, the new magazine, *100Most*, has succeeded in capturing the young adult market. One special feature of this magazine is its use of social media.

Traditional media has been seriously affected by new media; the adspend on new media rose from 4% when it was first recorded in 2007, to 8% in 2014 (Figure 2.4). The increase in absolute value may not be too much but in terms of percentage it is a 150% increase. As such, the future of new media is very promising. An exponential increase in the adspend on new media, in particular social media, is expected. In the short run, new media is expected to develop in the following ways:

- social media will still take the lead among the new media;

- videos will become more prevalent in social media; and

- more commercial activities (purchases) will occur through social media.

Media and Advertising Trends

Big Data Era

With the emergence of the new media and their rapid growth, we can foresee a massive redirection in the advertising industry in the near future. Audience experience and marketing strategy will change enormously as Hong Kong, as well as the whole world, steps into the era of big data. It is not simply about audiences changing their behavior to consume new media, but on a deeper level, it also means an evolution from traditional non-trackable mass messaging to a customized advertising experience in which almost everything is trackable. Every single click on the Internet will be recorded and saved as big data for further mining and analysis of users' behavior. This will provide a data management platform (DMP) empowering advertisers to target their customers and tailor-make promotions and other programs for them.

With the development of DMP, including identity management platforms, buying platforms, first-party cookie platforms and cookie-based vertical stacks, the technology for the new media is becoming more mature. Advertisers are now able to collect big data across first-hand, second-hand and third-hand sources. This allows advertisers to create their own audience segments, buy digital advertising space targeting a specific audience more precisely and show them a customized ad. Ad wastage from buying digital advertising in a specific portal covering more than the target audience group is now history. Furthermore, advertisers can make use of the big data to track and target audiences through different channels. With information regarding cross-channel behavior, advertisers are now able to accurately show the appropriate ad message to the appropriate audience at the appropriate time at a lower cost.

The potential threat to the usage of big data and DMP is the privacy issue. The global community is becoming increasingly wary about Internet monitoring. What benefits consumers gain from Internet advertisements, in terms of product information, are offset by concerns about privacy infringement. The fact that every one of us is so exposed on the Internet is alarming, and governments all over the world are working toward tighter measures, in the form of legislation and ordinances, to protect individual privacy on the Internet. The use of big data will experience a major setback when such ordinances are passed.

In addition to the genesis of big data, there are other major trends for the development of the advertising industry regarding media evolution. According to a presentation by MEC, a renowned 4A media agency in Hong Kong, the key media trends are:

- digitalization of traditional media;

- transformation of media to maintain competitiveness;

- increasing importance of mobile media;

- advertisers leverage social exposure; and

- greater accuracy in targeting markets.

These trends will affect the advertising media industry in Hong Kong.

Digitalization of Traditional Media

Traditional media faces fierce competition from new media. The best way to combat such competition is to merge with new media. As the rise of new media was predicted some time ago, many traditional media companies have long since started their own websites and social media pages. The number of viewers of TV online and readers of news online continue to increase at an accelerated pace.

As traditional media producers move into the digital arena, they can further expand into social media. For instance, the most powerful free TV operators and paid newspapers have Facebook pages to redirect traffic to their webpages.

Transformation of Media to Maintain Competitiveness

According to a survey by Google, 77% of people use apps on mobile devices while commuting; even in the washroom, 30% of people are using apps. It is not an exaggeration to say that new mobile media is now a necessity and cannot be ignored by media producers. Mobile is a more convenient medium, which makes it more effective. Thus it is expected that more resources will be put into advertising tailored for mobile devices.

Advertisers Leverage Social Exposure

Internet advertising expanded from portals to search engines, and now it has reached social media. According to Facebook, there are 3.1 million people using Facebook daily in Hong Kong. Instagram usage is on the rise too. The penetration rate and coverage of social media is so high that it has become the most powerful medium. As mentioned, even the largest TV operators and newspapers in Hong Kong have set up Facebook pages to redirect traffic back to their home pages. It is not surprising that advertisers will leverage the power of social media.

Greater Accuracy in Targeting Audiences

With the personalized features of new media, people can be more easily identified and segmented by big data. Big data can also help to analyze a person's online habits. With big data, Internet advertising can be more effectively shown to target segments and people of interest. This will greatly improve the efficiency of displaying Internet advertising.

Conclusion

Technological advancements of new media will continue to be the driving force of Hong Kong's advertising and media industries. However, the unknown in the formula is the effect on Hong Kong's economy due to the political tension between the democratic camp and the pro-establishment camp in Hong Kong. Practitioners in the industries must pay attention to the technological developments and the political and economic situation in Hong Kong in order to embrace future challenges.

References

Cheung, S. (2014), "Reunification through water and food: The other battle for lives and bodies in China's Hong Kong policy", *The China Quarterly*, Vol. 220, pp. 1012–1032.

Chow, V. (2013), "Public outcry over rejection of Ricky Wong's free-to-air TV licence bid", *South China Morning Post*, October 16, 2013, available at: http://www.scmp.com/news/hong-kong/article/1332855/hktv-chief-says-free-air-tv-licence-defeated-dark-government (accessed on November 30, 2015).

Lo, A. (2015), "A dinosaur in awe of the new media wave", *South China Morning Post*, July 20, 2015, available at: http://www.scmp.com/comment/insight-opinion/article/1841337/dinosaur-awe-new-media-wave (accessed on November 30, 2015).

"Losing hearts and minds; Hong Kong and Taiwan" (2014), *The Economist*, Vol. 413, December 6, 2014 pp. 46–47.

Ma, N. (2015), "The rise of 'anti-China' sentiments in Hong Kong and the 2012 legislative council elections", *China Review*, Vol. 15 No. 1, pp. 39–66.

Ng, J. (2015), "Decision not to renew ATV licence wins government rare praise", *South China Morning Post*, April 2, 2015, available at: http://www.scmp.com/news/hong-kong/article/1753798/decision-not-renew-atv-licence-wins-government-rare-praise (accessed on November 30, 2015).

Tanner De Witt Solicitors (n.d.), "What you need to know about the latest changes to the Trade Descriptions Ordinance", available at: http://www.tannerdewitt.com/what-you-need-to-know-about-the-latest-changes-to-the-trade-descriptions-ordinance/ (accessed on November 30, 2015).

Wang, L. and Kirkpatrick, A. (2015), "Trilingual education in Hong Kong primary schools: An overview", *Multilingual Education*, Vol. 5 No. 1, pp. 1–26.

Wong, S.H. (2015), "Real estate elite, economic development, and political conflicts in postcolonial Hong Kong", *China Review*, Vol. 15 No. 1, pp. 1–38.

Yeung, S.C. (2015), "Will Netflix and LeTV have a smooth ride into HK?", *EJInsight*, September 10, 2015, available at: http://www.ejinsight.com/20150910-will-netflix-and-letv-have-a-smooth-ride-into-hk/ (accessed on January 20, 2016).

Chapter 3

Meanings of Creativity among Advertising Practitioners

Hei Ting Wong

Introduction

In the television drama *Every Step You Take* (Television Broadcasts Limited, 2015), Moses Chan plays the part of an award-winning executive creative director. He creates a new concept for a television commercial from his colleague's notes, and presents it to his client, who also happens to be his ex-girlfriend. The client initially rejects his idea, but Chan eventually convinces her to change her mind. However, his peers make the criticism that his "creation" is really just a business proposal, and is not artistically creative. Does this reflect reality? Is advertising an art or a business? What aspects of creativity are found in advertisements? How do industry insiders view their work and how do they work together to produce creative and effective advertisements? In this chapter, I will explain the advertising production process and the understanding of advertising creativity through the perspective of a person working in the advertising industry.

Is Advertising an Art or a Business?

The advertising creative process involves three parties: an advertiser who invests in advertising; a team of advertising agency personnel to decide on and design the communication objectives and translate an idea into words and visuals; and media personnel to place the advertisement into appropriate media at the appropriate time to reach the target audience. Given the briefs of these three roles, some industry insiders believe that advertising is a business, due to the emphasis on financial gain for the customer. Ng and Wu (2011) state that a successful advertising campaign enables audiences from different backgrounds to focus on one single message prescribed by the creative team. According to West (1993), there are two stages in producing an advertising campaign: in the first stage, the key message to be communicated is decided. This is referred to as the advertising strategy. In the second stage, the way the message will be communicated (i.e. the execution) is decided. Ki (1984) believes that effective advertisements will bring profit to clients because they are at the forefront of reaching target customers. Ng and Wu (2011) further argue that advertising practitioners need to create impressive advertisements that can improve the sales of the product. It is clear therefore that advertising has a direct impact upon the bottom line of businesses.

However, advertising also has certain artistic elements; Smith and Yang (2004) explicitly refer to advertising as a "commercial art". In a study targeting advertising insiders, West (1993) argued that "[i]n contrast to artistic work… sold to or performed for the public, advertisements are targeted through selected media with the intention of modifying consumer or business behavior in some way". Thus, the presentation format can vary, often drawing on "[t]he same forms of communication as art…such as photography, film, drawing and music" (West, 1993).

Creativity in Advertisements

Creativity plays a central role in advertising. Kyme and Cheng (2014) state that in advertising, creativity is "the quest for originality, the challenge of solving old problems in new ways". Reid et al. (1998) argue that advertising creativity consists of four elements: originality, imagination, goal direction and problem-solving:

> Originality is indicated by a novel approach that is regarded as new, improved, and highly distinctive; imagination is indicated by how images and concepts are formed and associated. Advertising, as a special form of creativity, differs from artistic expression and other forms of creativity-for-the-sake-of-creativity in that

originality and imagination must operate within a goal-directed and problem-solving context. In advertising, goal direction is indicated by the fact that ads are created to accomplish specific marketing communication objectives, which are usually determined and prescribed by marketing specialists; problem-solving is indicated by how well ad creations communicate brand-related problem solutions to targeted consumers.

Advertising is designed to achieve specific communication goals. Smith and Yang (2004) link effectiveness in advertising to creativity. They identify two "primary determinants of creativity": first, it "must be something new, imaginative, different, or unique—this component is generally referred to as 'divergence'"; secondly, "[t]he divergent thing produced must solve a problem or have some type of 'relevance'". Smith and Yang (2004) argue that "once a divergent idea is produced, it must be shaped in a manner to make it relevant" in order to reach the goal of the advertising campaign. As "an ad[vertisement] has a specific goal, the level of creativity is to some extent based on its ability to achieve that goal" (Smith and Yang, 2004). Therefore in advertising, creativity is linked to efficacy in achieving a communication goal. In their definitions, divergence and relevance are related to the social and/or cultural factors of the society in which the advertising campaign takes place. They claim that "ad creativity is divergence—the ad must contain elements that are novel, different, or unusual in some way", and the "ad also must be relevant—it must be meaningful, appropriate or valuable to the audience". They conclude that the function of advertising creativity is to create a sense of correspondence, as if building up an "ad resonance" between the advertisement and the audience.

Smith et al. (2007) developed quantitative scales to measure divergence and relevance. Divergence can be measured by seven aspects: originality, whether an advertisement's ideas are rare, surprising or unusual; flexibility, whether an advertisement has different ideas embedded within it and is capable of moving from one subject matter to another; synthesis, whether an advertisement combines or connects unrelated objects; elaboration, whether an advertisement provides numerous details; artistic value, whether an advertisement offers striking visual and/or verbal elements; fluency, whether an advertisement contains a large number of ideas; and imagination, whether an advertisement leads you to form vivid images in the mind. Furthermore, relevance can be measured by three aspects, namely relevance of the advertisement to the receiver, relevance of the brand to the receiver, and relevance of the ad to the product or brand (Smith et al., 2007).

Another way of measuring advertising creativity is to collect audience feedback after viewing the advertisements. Chan (1996) conducted a study by sampling sixty television commercials of a variety of products and services. Thirty of these commercials contained factual information about the products while the remaining thirty commercials did not. These commercials were categorized as informative and emotional advertisements respectively. After showing the commercials to 160 respondents, the viewers selected adjectives from a list of twenty given choices to describe the commercials. Using factor analysis, viewers' perception of the advertisements can be grouped into five dimensions: creative, hard-selling, energetic, irritating and relevant. The factor of "creative" comprised five adjectives: well made, worth remembering, clever, original and imaginative, while "relevant" included three adjectives: informative, convincing and effective. These two dimensions were similar to divergence and relevance as suggested by Smith and Yang (2004).

Creativity can be found in different aspects of advertising. Ki (1984) postulates thirteen presentation formats or attributes of advertisements that advertising practitioners can use to enhance their creativity. These are:

- storytelling;

- problem-solving;

- documentary-like chronology;

- testimonial of a product/service;

- celebrity endorsement;

- a spokesman (for a product or a service);

- a demonstration;

- suspense;

- an everyday situation;

- an analogy;

- humor;

- special effects in sound/filming technique and/or animated images; and

- a jingle.

She also commented that a good jingle should be simple with repeated lyrics—easy to sing and understand. If children learn how to sing the jingle and keep singing it, then you have free advertising.

To sum up, advertising creativity is often referred to as the ability of the advertising contents to present a product or a brand in an innovative and imaginative way, and its ability to make the product or the brand relative to the audience.

Localization and Globalization of Advertising

In the era of globalization and free-flowing information, there is a debate among advertising practitioners about whether the content of advertisements should be localized, Westernized, glocalized (thinking globally but acting locally) or globalized. This is especially relevant for foreign brands attempting to enter the Asian market. West (1993) states that "[c]ultural factors play an important role" in the approach one takes to advertising, and refers to Pollay, who is of the opinion that "advertisements tended to reflect a society's cultural values, albeit in a distorted manner". West suggests a way to achieve this: "Agency creatives need to keep up-to-date with a wide range of trends and tastes in society, particularly in the arts". They should also ensure their knowledge of sports stars and celebrities is current. For example, when Oreo first entered the China (and Hong Kong) market, Houston Rockets center Yao Ming appeared in television advertisements as their spokesman. His Chinese heritage and status as an NBA star made him a suitable person to promote the American snack in China (Bud, 2011).

It is an enduring struggle for Hong Kong's advertising industry to decide whether to glocalize or globalize advertisements or entire campaigns. Such decisions vary and may be subject to current events and local culture. Ki (1984) stated that in the 1980s, the locals preferred the "closer-to-the-root" style rather than the "high-class" style, since they did not value the aesthetics of the latter. Ki (1984) also stresses the importance of having a good Cantonese translation of foreign brand names in order to fit in with local customs and increase sales. During the late 1980s and early 1990s, with the employment of local entertainment stars such as Anita Mui and Aaron Kwok, "Hong Kong commercials were more about grand storylines beautifully told than simple ideas well executed" (Kyme and Cheng, 2014). In the early 1990s, many expatriates were also members of the local advertising industry:

> Expats and locals alike were waking up to discover new ways to apply ideas in a unique Hong Kong way, mixing local metaphors with western candidness. Sourcing references from new and inspired corners of heritage and local life. (Kyme and Cheng, 2014)

After 1997, Iris Lo, creative director of Bates, was involved in a movement that created advertisements with a local Hong Kong theme, such as her "real women" campaign for the local jewelry shop, Just Gold, in 1998 (cited in Kyme and Cheng, 2014). Lo claimed "It was a shift toward localization, we embraced Hong Kong values and treasured who we were" (Kyme and Cheng, 2014). However, in recent years, many foreign products in Hong Kong have decided to promote their brand in the original language, such as English or French. For example, McDonald's slogan "I'm lovin' it"®. This may be a sign that locals are more educated and understand simple terms in foreign languages better than in the 1980s and the early 1990s, and/or that there is more of a preference for Western culture now than there was in those years. Thus, creatives need to pay attention to changes in audience preference, and adapt to these changes.

When adapting to local cultures, copywriters must produce effective promotional messages that are intelligible to audiences. Ng and Wu (2011) state that the guiding principle of advertising is to find the uniqueness of a product and to beautify it, that is, to re-package it and to rely on the power of copy. Copy is not only a descriptive statement, it also attempts to create "noises" or talking points in society. It attracts target customers by showing an understanding of their needs, which can influence their opinion of the product or the whole brand (Ng and Wu, 2011). For example, in the fight for market share between distilled water and mineral water, distilled water used copy to successfully build up a product image of purity and thus enjoyed better sales for years. Recently, advertising campaigns for mineral water have promoted the product as "mineralized drink", which has proven to be very effective in gaining market share (Ng and Wu, 2011). The power of words can make the product appear special and attract attention, with the end goal of increasing sales (Ng and Wu, 2011). Copy is also applied to create an attractive sound bite that suits current trends; use of idioms or popular colloquialisms can help with this. For example, "blowing the whistle (吹雞)" was a term used by triad society members and was prohibited by traditional media, but is now a common term for calling out a large group of friends (Ng and Wu, 2011). Steven Chan's "the real cannot be falsified (真的假不了)" is another example; it was used in a medicine advertisement in 2010 to promote the recognition of the genuine product (Yuen, 2010). Aligning the product/brand image with local culture, copy is a tool with which to express creativity and make an advertisement more effective.

Technology has offered other factors which can help enhance creativity. Reid et al. (1998) brought attention to the "new technologies, new media types, consumer changes, and management developments". With technological advancements, advertisements can be linked to the Internet; for example, using quick response (QR) codes, more product information can be provided by connecting printed advertisements to a website. For instance, Calvin Klein released a prohibited advertising video by placing a QR code on an outdoor billboard; this link to banned material gives the audience a feeling of voyeurism (Bud, 2011). Additionally, Coca-Cola Hong Kong coordinated its recent campaign "Share a Coke, Share a Song"® with a local online music platform MOOV. Customers can listen to seventy-two popular Cantonese songs (lyrics from these songs are printed on Coca-Cola cans or bottles) by scanning QR codes. Likewise, traditional media, such as newspapers, magazines and television channels now also develop online platforms; printed advertisements can become viral videos online, and local television programs can be re-watched legally and officially online, the majority of which have inserted advertisements (Ng and Wu, 2011). Ng and Wu (2011) deemed this cross-medium advertising a breakthrough.

The handover of sovereignty of Hong Kong from Britain back to China brought both challenges and opportunities to many local industries and businesses, including advertising. For some multinational brands, Hong Kong had been the stepping stone to enter the mainland China market long before the handover. Now, as a member of the greater China region, Hong Kong inevitably faces competition from mainland Chinese businesses. The Hong Kong advertising industry developed long before the industry in the mainland, and therefore has more trained and experienced practitioners, but it lost its leading status when it was absorbed into the China market. Retired advertising practitioner Eddie Booth commented that:

> ...the Hong Kong industry needs to stand for something in its role within the China scheme of things. Hong Kong needs to reinvent itself as a creative think tank. It should be a quality center for China to look up to. (cited in Kyme and Cheng, 2014)

Carol Lam claims that "if Hong Kong still has an edge to offer within the China landscape, it should be creativity. We should be the creative hub of China" (cited in Kyme and Cheng, 2014). To achieve this, advertising practitioners suggested that the ideal trend should be the development of independent agencies by capable, experienced individuals who have previously worked in multinational agencies (Kyme and Cheng, 2014). It seems that the flexibility provided by escaping the rigid management framework of large multinational agencies can enhance creativity. By doing so, many advertising practitioners believe that Hong Kong could still lead China's advertising industry in terms of creativity.

Selling Advertising Concepts

New ideas are often unproven. Therefore it is often difficult to sell new ideas to clients. The work relationship between clients and agents can often be difficult. Kyme and Cheng (2014) declared that "[d]oing good work is one thing, selling it [to] your clients is really the hard part, and requires great skill and good management of client relationships". Willde Ng, a veteran creative director, states that achieving this is based on in-house training and goal-setting among the creatives in the agency:

> First of all, I believe you have to understand what a client needs, and look at it from the point of view of their business perspective. We trained creative people to solve business problems. Secondly, it was important to avoid the time wasted

doing round after round of ideas. We set ourselves the target of 'one shot' presentations whereby the first idea presented is what gets approved. In order to get anywhere achieving this[,] you need to nail the brief right from the start. (cited in Kyme and Cheng, 2014)

Clients have the final decision on advertising production in terms of both creative concepts and execution. Bud (2011) states that an advertisement reflects the taste of the client more than the taste of the creatives who design it. If the client sets a high standard for creativity, s/he pushes up the quality of the advertisement (Bud, 2011). However, Eddie Booth claims that:

> In our day, clients were definitely of a better quality. Nowadays, many people in marketing role…are disrespectful of quality, and pride themselves on how much money they can save. (cited in Kyme and Cheng, 2014)

Kyme and Cheng (2014) conclude that the reason for this decline in client quality is that some people in marketing have little training in strategic thinking and often fail to recognize good creativity.

Advertising practitioners rely on marketing and consumer research to define specific marketing communication problems that advertising needs to solve. Ogilvy and Mather point out that market research helps to reveal perceptions of the product among customers (cited in Ki, 1984). Market research also helps to measure the effectiveness of an advertising campaign after its launch. Clients often use market research to examine the effectiveness of an advertisement in achieving specific advertising objectives, such as delivering a key message, generating a specific feeling or emotion, enhancing the product's credibility, enhancing consumer engagement or increasing consumers' intent to purchase. Presenting creative ideas to clients may not be an easy job, but catering to clients' business targets may minimize the divide between clients and creatives, thus increasing the chances of the creation being sold.

Social Responsibility of Advertising

The copy and concept of advertisements are created based on the cultural values of the target society so that the message will be transmitted effectively.

While messages delivered in advertisements should meet certain levels of social expectations, advertising also carries social responsibility. Creatives usually attempt to make an advertisement special and different from similar products in order to catch the audience's attention. However, certain social norms need to be met and taboos should be avoided. Controversial advertising content, such as the campaign of the telecommunication company, Sunday, which featured a scary ghost and led to thousands of complaints, are commonly used to attract attention, but may lead to the audience forming a negative impression of the brand (Kyme and Cheng, 2014). Further discussion on this topic can be found in Chapter 5.

In Hong Kong, all cigarette advertisements must indicate clearly the health issues of smoking with the phrase "Hong Kong SAR Government warning" (see Chapter 6). Advertisements targeting a specific group of the population, especially children and youth, should match ethical standards and the society's ideology (Ki, 1984). Advertisements can be linked to good causes as a form of responsibility. For example, in the United States Starbucks initiated the "bring your own mug" campaign in order to reduce the use of paper cups (Bud, 2011). In this case, advertising itself makes use of the public's concern for specific causes, such as environmental concerns, and builds up a better corporate image.

Advertisements, as primary representations of the brand, need to show responsibility toward society. Ki (1984) states that she has only worked for reliable, trustworthy products. She further explains by referring to Bill Bernbach's quote, "A great ad[vertising] campaign will make bad products fail faster. It will get more people knowing it's bad" (Ki, 1984). Kitty Lun also stated in an interview (by K. Chan and K.C. Tsang, May 17, 2012) that "to pollute children just for achieving the goal is wrong". I would further argue that it is wrong if the advertisement carries a negative message and brings physical, mental and/or cultural harm to society at large. It is a matter of balance between fulfilling social responsibilities and producing an outstanding advertising campaign, and this should be a matter of conscience for advertising practitioners.

Advertising Creativity in the Digital Era

In today's digital world, marketers and advertising practitioners need to develop meaningful links with consumers through a variety of advertising and communication platforms in real time. Traditional media advertising has been supplemented or replaced by social media campaigns that often involve co-creation with consumers. Many advertisers are beginning to build corporate cultures that promote innovation, risk-taking, curiosity and disruptive change (The Internationalist, 2015). The new tactics driving brand awareness, interest and loyalty include motivating and training employees as brand ambassadors, working with start-ups for product innovation and reorganizing company structure to focus on delivering a total consumer experience, as well as integrating IT, finance and human resources departments in corporations to "mak[e] a broad impact across all company touch points" (The Internationalist, 2015). Time is also an essential element. Creatives working with social media need to respond instantly. The brand management team and the agency team must work together to maintain consistency in brand image. The role of advertising has been expanded to cover the design of an integrated branding experience. Learning fast, making constant improvements, evaluating strategies and sharing winning ideas are all important in fuelling growth and excellence (The Internationalist, 2015).

With changes in the concept of response time, the preferences of audience and clients, as well as technologies, the advertising industry needs to adapt and redefine its position. Kyme and Cheng (2014) commented on the changes to existing and the invention of new advertising media:

> The media landscape has undergone a series of mini revolutions, from the ever-evolving rise of the [I]nternet replacing television as a way of reaching people in or out of home, to the breakthrough creative ideas which have destroyed traditional media boundaries. Nowadays you don't necessarily need that billboard site or bus side, when you can place messages and ideas across everything from aircraft bodies to whole buildings.

In the virtual world of the Internet, anyone can put forward ideas in formats like photographs, drawings or videos on social media or platforms like YouTube and online blogs, so the Internet is not only a location for viral advertising, but also one for discovering new talents in the industry.

Conclusion

Advertising is a commercial art, the frontline representation of brands and products, and acts as a medium for effective communication between clients and audiences. Creativity is central in advertising: while creativity should be linked to the audience's or target market's culture to create a sense of relevance, a sense of divergence should be added to make the advertisement, the campaign or the brand outstanding in the market. Hong Kong's advertising industry developed decades ago, led by expatriates with the training and experience of working with people of different nationalities, who imbued local creatives with international perspectives and ideas. Both East and West contributed to building the concepts, executions and copy of advertising campaigns. Now a part of the Chinese advertising industry, local creatives should seek to contribute their multicultural creativity and rich experience to the greater China market of 1.4 billion consumers.

References

Bud, M. 畢明 (2011), 《廣告早晨 (原汁版)》[Director's Cut]. 紅投資有限公司Red Publish, Hong Kong.

Chan, K. (2010), *Youth and Consumption*. City University of Hong Kong Press, Hong Kong.

Ki, M.F. 紀文鳳 (1984),《點只廣告咁簡單》[Not Simply Advertising]. 博益出版集團有限公司 Publications (Holdings) Ltd. Hong Kong.

Kyme, C. and Cheng, T. (2014), *Made in Hong Kong: How Hong Kong Advertising Found Its True Creative Voice*. WE Press, Hong Kong.

Ng, P.L. and Wu, Y.L. 吳博林、胡若藍 (2011),《廣告公義》[Advertising Justice]. 經濟日報出版社 ET Press. Hong Kong.

Reid, L.N., King, K.W. and DeLorme, D.E. (1998), "Top-level agency creatives look at advertising creativity then and now", *Journal of Advertising*, Vol. 27 No. 2, pp. 1–16.

Smith, R.E. and Yang, X. (2004), "Toward a general theory of creativity in advertising: Examining the role of divergence", *Marketing Theory*, Vol. 4 No. 1/2, pp. 31–58.

The Internationalist (2015), "Organizing for growth in a digital age", *The Internationalist*, Vol. 75, pp. 8–10.

West, D. (1993), "Restricted creativity: Advertising agency work practices in the US, Canada and the UK", *Journal of Creative Behavior,* Vol. 27 No. 3, pp. 200–213.

Yuen, C. 袁靜 (2010),〈陳志雲提供的廣告語〉[An advertising slogan supplied by Stephen Chan], 《經濟日報》網上版 Hong Kong Economic Times (online edition), March 31, 2010, available at: http://lifestyle.etnet.com.hk/column/index.php/management/notadvertisment/796 (accessed on November 1, 2015).

Chapter 4

Branded Contents: Public Attitudes and Regulation

Fanny Fong Yee Chan

Introduction

In Hong Kong people are bombarded by excessive advertisements in all aspects of their daily lives. Unfavorable attitudes toward advertising together with the improvement in advertisement-skipping techniques (e.g. TiVo, IPTV, DVR devices, downloading commercial-free programs online) makes it difficult for traditional advertising to reach audiences. Product placement, blending advertising messages into media content, provides advertisers with an unobtrusive way to communicate with audiences. Product placement has been allowed in Hong Kong television programs since 2005. The surge of product placement has led to discussions about the effect of this implicit promotion and the need for further regulation. Specifically, the issue lies in whether audiences should be notified beforehand of any brand integration in media content. This chapter first reviews previous studies on placement effectiveness in Hong Kong and reports on a recent study which examines the effect of disclosing brand integration in movies shown in Hong Kong and the United Kingdom.

Product Placement as an Implicit Promotional Tool

Advertisement blocking happens in both traditional as well as new digital media. PageFair and Adobe (2015) reported that worldwide advertisement blocking increased 41% in 2015, which caused advertising media to lose nearly U.S.$22 billion in revenue. This implies that about 14% of global advertising expenditure was wasted. Over the years marketers have tried to search for surreptitious ways to promote their products.

Product placement is a method of implicit promotion which has become increasingly popular among advertisers. Balasubramanian (1994, p. 31) defined product placement as "a paid product message aimed at influencing movie (or television) audiences via the planned and unobtrusive entry of a branded product into a movie (or television program)". In other words, product placement involves embedding branded products in media content. Different scholars have classified the practice in different ways (Chan, 2012). Among them, Smith's (1985) classification is considered to be the most exhaustive and exclusive. Smith identifies three types of product placements: visual, audio and combined audio-visual. In visual placements, a product, logo, billboard or other visual brand identifier is displayed on-screen without any accompanying description. Audio placement involves mentioning brands in the dialogue instead of showing them on the screen. Combined audio-visual placement refers to a combination of the two techniques. Visual placement is the type of brand integration which is most commonly found in media content (Chan, 2016).

The Hong Kong Broadcasting Authority (now the Communications Authority) relaxed the restrictions governing product placement in 2005. Soon after this, a surge of product placements in television programs produced in Hong Kong was recorded, for example, Cathay Pacific in *Triumph in the Skies*, Geely automobiles in *The Drive of Life*, Kee Wah mooncakes in *Moonlight Resonance* and MaBelle diamonds in *The Gem of Life*. As we can see, product placement has grown rapidly over the past decade. This has led to several important public policy issues.

One recent incident involved a fine of HK$100,000 imposed on Television Broadcast Limited (TVB) by the Communications Authority. Although Cathay Pacific did not appear in the sequel to *Triumph in the Skies*, many other products were placed in the drama series (e.g. Mont Blanc, Luk Fook Jewelry, Sony, Glacéau). One episode featured a male character who used bottles of Glacéau Vitaminwater with different colors to build a heart shape on a beach in order to convey his love to his girlfriend. Another episode portrayed a female character kissing a bottle of Glacéau Vitaminwater when she thought of a man she was fond of. The brand name on the bottle was prominently displayed in both scenes. The undue prominence of the product and its obtrusiveness to viewing pleasure aroused serious concern from the Communications Authority and the general public, which led to the fine. Excessive product placements in the television programs *Season of Love* and *Come Home Love* have also resulted in the television broadcaster being warned by the Authority (Lau, 2013).

Research on Product Placement

Previous studies of product placement generally fall into five main streams (Chan, 2012):

- content analyses of brand appearances in media content;

- single-country empirical studies of placement effectiveness;

- general discussions on the research trends and framework of product placement;

- examinations of practitioners' views toward brand integration; and

- cross-cultural comparisons of the acceptability of the practice.

Most of these studies have been conducted in a Western context although calls to extend research to other racial and ethnic groups have frequently been made. A few studies have examined the practice in Asian markets over the past decade. Four published studies have focused on the Chinese context (Chen and Haley, 2014; Hang and Auty, 2008; McKechnie and Zhou, 2003; Shi 2010). Another three studies investigated Korean audiences' views on product placement (Chae and Sun, 2013; Lee et al., 2011; Lee et al., 2012). Three explored the perception of product placement in Malaysia (Balakrishnan et al., 2012), Singapore (Karrh et al., 2001) and Taiwan (Su et al., 2011).

The recent surge of product placement in programs has drawn a handful of studies to examine the practice in the Hong Kong context. Multiple methodologies were adopted in these studies as suggested by Chan (2015).

Chan (2016) conducted a content analysis of top grossing movies in 2010. The prevalence and characteristics of brand appearances in these movies were documented. The study recorded an average of thirteen brand appearances per movie and that most of the top-grossing movies were U.S. productions. In other words, Hong Kong audiences were exposed to brand integration not only in local productions but also in American movies.

Hong Kong people's views toward this implicit promotion were also explored. Chan et al. (2015) interviewed thirty-two young adults from Hong Kong and the United Kingdom (UK) about their perceptions and interpretations of product placement. In general, the young audience from Hong Kong found it acceptable to integrate brands in media content and they actually preferred the practice to traditional advertising. Kong and Hung (2012) conducted an experimental study to explore the effect of information-overload and different character attributes on the recall of and attitudes toward placed brands. It was found that college students recalled placements loaded with product information better, although they displayed negative attitudes toward those placements. This negative effect was further strengthened when the audience had a high level of involvement with the character associated with the placed brand. In another experimental study, Chan et al. (2016a) investigated the role of prominence and brand awareness on placement effectiveness among young consumers in Hong Kong and the UK. The results show that young consumers disliked prominent placements or placements of less well-known brands and were less likely to be persuaded by these placements. The effects of interaction between prominence, brand awareness and cultural dimensions were also evidenced in the study.

The most recent experimental study explored the effect of placement processing on brand persuasiveness among young audiences (Chan et al., (2016b). It was found that prominent placements elicited more extensive processing, which led to more negative attitudes toward the brand. In summary, systematic scholarly work on product placement spans just two to three decades and there is a need for more research in Asian contexts (Chan, 2012; 2015).

Regulation of Product Placement

Product placement is often accused of taking advantage of audiences who are unaware of it and trying to influence them in a subconscious way (Chan, 2012). It is generally agreed that product placement can be regulated through two forces: external and internal control. External control refers to laws and regulations enforced by governments or codes of practice laid down by established bodies such as professional associations. Internal control is the regulatory power exercised within media organizations. It is common for broadcasting media to set up their own regulatory systems in order to avoid being fined or losing viewers.

In Hong Kong, a Generic Code of Practice on Television Advertising Standards has been developed to guide the integration of branded content in television programs (Communications Authority, 2015a). Product placements in television programs are acceptable as long as they meet certain ground rules. First, the product/service placed should be justified editorially and should not cause any obtrusion to the viewing experience. Second, product/service sponsorship is not allowed in children's programs. This is to protect young viewers who may not be able to exercise sound judgment and hence are more susceptible to the influence of the embedded products/services.

The Communications Authority undertake investigations when they receive complaints concerning a particular instance of brand integration. For example, a complaint was received some time ago regarding the travelogue *Chimelong Resort Special: Fun at Panyu* broadcast on Asia Television Limited (ATV) at prime time (Communications Authority, 2015b). A viewer complained that the program had been filmed entirely within a theme park with strong promotional intent. In line with established practices, members of the Authority then viewed the program. It featured a male character guiding a group of artists around a theme park. The name and logo of the hotel and facilities in the theme park were clearly and prominently shown. Positive remarks and recommendations about the facilities were frequently made in the program. The case was then discussed and investigated by a committee set up by the Authority. It concluded that the extensive exposure and detailed descriptions of the sponsor's products and services in the program were unlikely to be incidental. It was evident that advertising materials had been embedded in the program and had a promotional effect. The Authority finally imposed a financial penalty of HK$60,000 on ATV, taking into account similar precedents and ATV's track record in compliance with relevant rules and regulations.

There are, however, virtually no regulations regarding product placements in movies and print media. Films are the most traditional and popular avenue for product placement across cultures (Chan, 2012). Under the current Film Censorship Ordinance, a movie intended for public exhibit must be submitted to the Film Censorship Authority for scrutiny of its content, but no inspection on brand appearances will be made (Office for Film, Newspaper and Article Administration, 2015). For print media, branded products are embedded in newspaper or magazine articles in the form of advertorials. Similar to the situation with movies, the Newspaper and Article Administration Division monitors mainly obscene and indecent material in print media but not editorial content with commercial intent. The composition and dissemination of advertorials are at the discretion of publishers. As we can see, product placements in television programs are subjected to more regulations and scrutiny, probably because the broadcasting service is delivered directly to our homes, free of charge.

Opinions about Further Regulating Product Placement

The subliminal effects of product placement are considered to be unethical. In view of this, consumer protection groups advocate that the promotional intent of product placement should be made explicitly and openly. Audiences are entitled to know who is trying to persuade them. Therefore consumer activists suggest that brands placed in a movie should be disclosed at the beginning or even that the embedded brands/products should be labelled whenever they appear (Avery and Ferraro, 2000). Practitioners and researchers on product placement had a round-table discussion about further regulating the practice (Galician, 2004). They generally agreed that the industry could be self-regulated although with some acknowledgements in the credits and in all promotional materials. Practitioners in a survey also expressed the view that the regulatory process may become more stringent and may be subjected to more social pressure in the future (Craig-Lees et al., 2008). Milne et al. (2008)

discussed the benefits and damages related to covert marketing practices and proposed disclosure mechanisms to protect vulnerable consumers. Likewise, Ta and Forsch (2008) reviewed the placement of pharmaceutical products and suggested disclosing sponsorship at the beginning of a broadcast instead of at the end.

There is increased social pressure on governments to regulate the use of branded products in media content. A proposal suggesting prior disclosure of all brands placed in movies was proposed in Europe (Eisend, 2009). Similarly, advocate groups such as Commercial Alert and the Screen Actors Guild in the U.S. have advised the FCC to impose stricter rules for the disclosure of product placements. It is hoped that prior disclosure will increase audience awareness and thus protect them from the persuasive intent of implicit promotion. Nevertheless, the presence of explicit warnings may in fact enhance the recall of placed brands and in a sense be counterproductive (McCarty, 2004). It is still unclear whether prior disclosure empowers audiences against subliminal persuasion or actually aids the promotion of the product. The consultation about and implementation of the prior disclosure directive is a lengthy process. Regulation of product placement remains a crucial issue and its effect on brand persuasiveness has yet to be examined. A study about the effect of prior disclosure of placed brands was therefore conducted in Hong Kong and the UK.

An Experimental Study

Effects of Prior Disclosure of Product Placement

The effects of prior disclosure perhaps could be seen as bilateral: it is believed to aid brand recall but its effect on brand persuasiveness is uncertain. Disclosing brand integration may increase awareness of the placed brands which the audience may not otherwise have noticed. Bennett et al. (1999) believe that including explicit warnings at the beginning of a movie provides additional memory cues for audiences which enhance their brand recall. For example, companies which had promotional campaigns to announce their presence in movies actually recorded increased sales (e.g. Reese's Pieces in *ET: The Extra-Terrestrial*, Ray Ban sunglasses in *Risky Business*).

However, disclosing commercial intent at the beginning of a movie may also irritate some audiences. In addition, concerns are frequently raised that product placement works best when consumers are not aware of it (Russell, 2002). Prior disclosure explicitly alerts viewers to the promotional nature of the placed brand. Audiences may then recognize that the brand appearance is purposeful and may associate it with selling intent and argue against it. In this case, the promotional effort may be wasted. Those who support further regulations on product placement tend to agree with this view. Therefore it is hypothesized that a prior disclosed product placement will be subjected to more scrutiny, and thus will be less persuasive, specifically:

H1: Participants will report (a) a less positive attitude and (b) a lower level of purchase intention toward a placed brand which has been previously disclosed.

Culture and Prior Disclosure of Product Placement

A few studies have investigated the views of audiences from different countries about further regulation of product placement and these have revealed substantial differences. For example, respondents from less assertive cultures (e.g. Korea) were more likely to find product placement unethical and misleading (Lee et al., 2011). Audiences in the United States (an assertive culture) generally do not think that product placement should be banned or regulated by the government (Sung et al., 2009). On the contrary, respondents from a less assertive culture (Singapore) were more likely to agree that the government should regulate the use of branded products in movies (Karrh et al., 2001). This may be attributed to the unique governance of Singapore. However, it may also indicate cultural differences with regard to regulating product placement, though more empirical support is needed. The interaction between culture and prior disclosure of product placement has not been empirically tested.

Cultural orientation has been mapped as the antecedent to various types of consumer behavior (Rokeach, 1973). Previous studies indicate that the cultural dimension of assertiveness shapes consumers' responses toward different advertising campaigns (Okazaki et al., 2010). Assertiveness is a cultural dimension identified in the Global Leadership and Organizational Effectiveness

(GLOBE) study by House et al., (2004). It is defined as "the degree to which individuals are assertive, confrontational, and aggressive in their relationships with others" (House et al., 2004). It is anticipated that societies with higher levels of assertiveness may find prior disclosure of placed brands unnecessary. Individuals in such cultures are generally more assertive and confrontational, and thus may not appreciate explicit warnings. Alternatively, individuals from less assertive cultures may favor explicit rules and regulations to protect them from covert selling. Therefore it is hypothesized that the assertiveness of a culture has an impact on the persuasiveness of a prior disclosed brand:

H2: Participants from assertive cultures will report (a) a less positive attitude and (b) a lower level of purchase intention toward a placed brand which has been previously disclosed than participants from less assertive cultures.

Research Design

A web-based experiment, which combined aspects of a lab-controlled experiment with a real-life situation, was used to test this. This method of experiment allowed students to watch a video online in the comfort of their own space, and yet the fact that it was online allowed the researchers to manipulate it and trigger different stimuli. Thus, a high degree of control over the experiment was maintained while at the same time using a real-life viewing environment.

Sample Profile

The sample contained 572 consumers between 18–34, with 283 from the UK and 289 from Hong Kong. The UK and Hong Kong were chosen for comparison because of the resemblance of the two social units in terms of political, economic and social infrastructure (Chan et al., 2016). Despite the similarities, the two cultures differ remarkably in assertiveness, the key cultural dimension of concern in this study (House et al., 2004). This makes them extremely desirable for a comparative experimental study. The group of 18–34-year-olds was targeted because they are the primary consumers of movies. Thus it is appropriate to examine placement effectiveness using this group.

Research Stimulus and Procedures

A content analysis study helped researchers to decide to use the placement of a branded camcorder as the research stimulus (Chan, 2016). A pretest with twenty young consumers showed that a camcorder was the most appropriate product among a wide array of products offered. The selected scenes were extracted from a science fiction movie which featured a female character using a branded camcorder to record her days after a virus outbreak on earth. The edited video clip lasted for about five minutes. Participants were randomly assigned to watch the video clip either with or without prior disclosure and were invited to respond to a list of questions afterwards.

The two independent variables were prior disclosure (with versus without) and cultural orientation (low versus high assertiveness). Prior disclosure was administered by placing a statement at the beginning of the video clip to inform participants about the placed brand. House et al.'s (2004) scale was adapted to assess individuals' levels of assertiveness. In view of acculturation, the study only considered those who had stayed in their home countries for the majority of their lives. The two dependent variables were attitude toward the brand and purchase intention (Gupta and Gould, 1997; Matthes et al., 2007).

Results and Discussion

A high correlation was noted between the appearance of a prior disclosure notice and participants registering that they had seen a prior disclosure message at the beginning of the video (see Table 4.1). Among participants who were not exposed to a prior disclosure statement, 89% reported correctly that they had not seen a prior disclosure statement. Among participants who had been shown a prior disclosure notice, 86% reported accurately that they had seen a prior disclosure statement. Participants exposed to a placed brand which had been disclosed to them prior to viewing had a slightly less positive attitude toward the brand but the difference was not significant (see Table 4.2). In other words, the results are not opposed to H1(a) but do not provide statistically significant support for it. Similarly, exposing participants to placements with or without prior disclosure did not affect their purchase intention toward the placed brand. Therefore H1(b) is not supported.

Table 4.1

Differences in Reporting Seeing a Prior Disclosure Message

Manipulations		Prior disclosure	
		Without (n = 317)	With (n = 255)
Report seeing a prior disclosure message	No	282 (89%)	37 (14.5%)
	Yes	35 (11%)	218 (85.5%)
			$r^* = 0.75, p^* < 0.001$

* r = Pearson's r correlation. p = significance level.

Table 4.2

The Effect of Prior Disclosure on Brand Attitude and Purchase Intention

Independent variables	Attitude toward brand		Purchase intention	
	M	SE	M	SE
Without prior disclosure	4.45	0.05	4.19	0.07
With prior disclosure	4.37	0.05	4.22	0.07

Results indicate that Hong Kong people were perceived to be significantly more assertive than the UK cohort (5.11 versus 4.22). This was consistent with the findings (4.67 versus 4.15) reported in the GLOBE study (House et al., 2004) although the differences in this instance were even more pronounced. No significant interaction between prior disclosure and culture was found in this study (see Table 4.3). However, participants from the assertive culture (Hong Kong) did report a less positive attitude ($M_{HK} = 4.13$ versus $M_{UK} = 4.60$) and a lower rate of intention to purchase ($M_{HK} = 4.21$ versus $M_{UK} = 4.24$) toward a placed brand which had been previously disclosed than participants from the less assertive culture (UK). In other words, the results tallied with the direction predicted by H2 but did not provide statistically significant support for it.

Table 4.3

The Interaction Effect between Prior Disclosure and Culture on Brand Attitude and Purchase Intention

Independent variables	Culture	Brand attitude		Purchase intention	
		M	SE	M	SE
Without prior disclosure	UK	4.63	0.08	4.25	0.10
	HK	4.28	0.08	4.12	0.10
With prior disclosure	UK	4.60	0.08	4.24	0.10
	HK	4.13	0.08	4.21	0.09

Cowley and Barron (2008) found that informing participants of the persuasive intent of product placement lowered their preference for that brand. However, the current study did not detect any significant effect of prior disclosure on the evaluation of placed brands. Similarly, no correlation between culture and prior disclosure was found. Both UK and Hong Kong participants exhibited similar attitudes and levels of intention to purchase toward a placed brand which had been previously disclosed.

A possible explanation is that consumers nowadays have a high exposure to various marketing practices and hence are more skeptical of different promotional tactics. Participants from both cultures may be predisposed to assume commercial elements are prevalent in movies. This is supported by the fact that moviegoers, on average, were exposed to thirteen brands per movie as revealed in a recent content analysis study (Chan, 2016). In addition, the research specifically focuses on a group of 18–34-year-olds who have grown up with new media and are believed to be more familiar with different marketing practices. They may be desensitized to different promotional tactics and thus are harder to persuade. In other words, the participants may have already assumed there will be some kind of commercial intent in movies. Therefore acknowledging them or not does not cause any significant difference to their evaluation of a placed brand.

Another implication is that although prior disclosure alerts audiences that the movie is being employed as a vehicle for promotion, it may also make audiences feel that the movie producers/brand owners are honest enough to disclose their intention explicitly. Consequently, the brand evaluation may not be as negative as anticipated. Therefore participants who were exposed to a previously disclosed brand only displayed slightly less positive attitudes than the group who had not been given prior disclosure. However, the difference was not significant enough to support the research hypothesis. It suggests that warnings related to commercial intent may not be sufficient to insulate consumers from persuasion while non-disclosure does not make audiences fall prey to promotion.

Some consumer advocate groups have lobbied for blanket legislation of product placement, but the findings here suggest this may be an overreaction. Practitioners generally believe that product placement can benefit many different parties if it is well integrated and that nobody will watch the show if the brand integration is badly designed. The industry inclines to consider product placement as an intrinsically self-regulated marketing communication activity, which means that the movie and the placed brand will automatically be penalized if the placement is overdone or too prominent.

Results from the current study appear to suggest that mandatory disclosure may not be necessary for young adults because it does not safeguard young audiences from the persuasiveness of product placements. With technological advancements and the force of globalization, regulating product placement geographically/regionally may soon become impractical. Perhaps self-censorship by the industry and scrutiny by the public are more feasible. It is believed that brand owners and movie producers are the ones to suffer if a movie or program becomes saturated with product placement and consequently annoying to audiences. Therefore practitioners have to make sure that they uphold their autonomy and credibility if they want to be free from formal regulations and close scrutiny by authorities.

Conclusion

The crossover between editorial content and promotional material is becoming more and more common and it is increasingly difficult to separate (Baerns, 2003). Products sometimes appear as an integral part of characters' experiences, perhaps to mask the original promotional intent. Although product placement is perceived to be less intrusive compared to traditional advertising messages, this promotional practice may actually be more penetrative. The effectiveness and ethical acceptability of product placement calls for subsequent media and research attention.

The directive on prior disclosure of product placement deals in movies has yet to be implemented. This chapter reports the first study to explore the role of prior disclosure on product placement effectiveness in the Asian context. However, no significant effects have been detected. Although the result does not conform to our expectations, it is still important because it sheds light on issues affecting the further regulation of product placement in movies across two cultures. It is suggested that future studies may extend to a wider international sample of consumers. In particular, the increasing use of product placements in children's entertainment media should receive more research attention (Hudson et al., 2008). Children are more vulnerable and the way they process product information may be different. Therefore the role of prior disclosure of product placement may have different effects on them. The advancement in communication technologies together with the fact that audiences are more skeptical nowadays suggests that implicit promotion is a fruitful research area which warrants further exploration.

Acknowledgements

The experimental study reported in this chapter was supported by the University of Kent and David C. Lam Institute for East-West Studies (LEWI), Hong Kong Baptist University.

References

Avery, R.J. and Ferraro, R. (2000), "Verisimilitude or advertising? Brand appearances on prime-time television", *Journal of Consumer Affairs,* Vol. 34 No. 2, pp. 217–244.

Baerns, B. (2003), "Separating advertising from programme content: The principle and its relevance in communications practice", *Journal of Communication Management,* Vol. 8 No. 1, pp. 101–112.

Balakrishnan, B.K.P.D., Shuaib, A.S. Md., Dousin, O. and Permarupan, P.Y. (2012), "The impact of brand placement and brand recall in movies: Empirical evidence from Malaysia", *International Journal of Management and Marketing Research*, Vol. 5 No. 2, pp. 39–52.

Balasubramanian, S.K. (1994), "Beyond advertising and publicity: Hybrid messages and public policy issues", Journal of Advertising, Vol. 23 No. 4, pp. 29–46.

Bennett, M., Pecotich, A. and Putrevu, S. (1999), "The influence of warnings on product placement", in Dubois, B., Lowrey, T.M., Shrum, L.J. and Vanhuele M. (Eds.), *European Advances in Consumer Research*, Vol. 4., Association for Consumer Research, Provo, UT, pp. 193–200.

Cain, R.M. (2011), "Embedded advertising on television: Disclosure, deception and free speech rights", *Journal of Public Policy and Marketing*, Vol.30 No. 2, pp. 226–238.

Chae, M.J. and Sun, H.J. (2013), "TV product placement in Korea", *Journal of Promotion Management*, Vol. 19 No. 1, pp. 54–75.

Chan, F.F.Y. (2012), "Product placement and its effectiveness: A systematic review and propositions for future research", *The Marketing Review*, Vol. 22 No. 1, pp. 39–60.

Chan, F.F.Y. (2015), "A critical realist and multimethodology framework for product placement research", *Journal of Promotion Management*, Vol. 21 No. 3, pp. 279–295.

Chan, F.F.Y. (2016), "An exploratory content analysis of product placement in top grossing films", *Journal of Promotion Management,* Vol. 22 No. 1, pp. 107–121.

Chan, F.F.Y., Lowe, B. and Petrovici, D. (2015), "Young adults' perceptions of product placement in films: An exploratory comparison between the United Kingdom and Hong Kong", *Journal of Marketing Communications,* pre-published online August 14, 2015.

Chan, F.F.Y., Lowe, B. and Petrovici, D. (2016b), "Processing of product placements and brand persuasiveness", *Marketing Intelligence and Planning*, Vol. 34 No. 3, pp.355–375.

Chan, F.F.Y., Petrovici, D. and Lowe, B. (2016a), "Antecedents of product placement effectiveness across cultures", *International Marketing Review*, Vol. 33 No. 1, pp. 5–24.

Chen, H. and Haley, E. (2014), "Product placement in social games: Consumer experiences in China", *Journal of Advertising*, Vol. 43 No. 3, pp. 286–295.

Communications Authority (2015a), "Generic code of practice on television advertising standards", available at: http://www.coms-auth.hk/filemanager/common/ policies_regulations/cop/code_tvad_e.pdf (accessed on October 18, 2015).

Communications Authority (2015b), "Television programme 'Chimelong Resort Special: Fun at Panyu'", available at: http://www.coms-auth.hk/filemanager/listarticle/en/upload/318/20130228ca_en.pdf (accessed on November 30, 2015).

Cowley, E. and Barron, C. (2008), "When product placement goes wrong: The effects of program liking and placement prominence", *Journal of Advertising*, Vol. 37 No. 1, pp. 89–98.

Craig-Lees, M., Scott, J. and Wong, R. (2008), "Perceptions of product placement practice across Australian and US practitioners", *Marketing Intelligence and Planning*, Vol. 26 No. 5, pp. 521–538.

Eisend, M. (2009), "A cross-cultural generalizability study of consumers' acceptance of product placements in movies", *Journal of Current Issues and Research in Advertising*, Vol. 31 No. 1, pp. 15–26.

Galician, M. (2004), "Product placement in the 21st century", in Galician, M. (Ed.), *Handbook of Product Placement in the Mass Media,* Best Business Books, Binghamton, NY, pp. 241–258.

Gupta, P.B. and Gould, S.J. (1997), "Consumers' perceptions of the ethics and acceptability of product placements in movies: Product category and individual differences", *Journal of Current Issues and Research in Advertising*, Vol. 19 No. 1, pp. 37–50.

Hang, H. and Auty, S. (2008), "Investigating product placement in video games: The effect of mood on children's choice", in Borghini, S., McGrath, M.A. and Otnes, C. (Eds.), *E - European Advances in Consumer Research*, Vol. 8, Association for Consumer Research, Duluth, MN, pp. 39–40.

House, R.J., Hanges, P.W., Javidan, M., Dorfman, P. and Gupta, V. (2004), *Culture, Leadership, and Organizations: The GLOBE Study of 62 Societies*. SAGE Publications, Thousand Oaks, CA.

Hudson, S., Hudson, D. and Peloza, J. (2008), "Meet the parents: A parent's perspective on product placement in children's films", *Journal of Business Ethics*, Vol. 80 No. 2, pp. 289–304.

Karrh, J.A., Frith, K.T. and Callison, C. (2001), "Audience attitudes toward brand (product) placement: Singapore and the United States", *International Journal of Advertising: The Review of Marketing Communications*, Vol. 20 No. 1, pp. 3–24.

Kong, F. and Hung, K. (2012), "Product placement in television drama: Do information overload and character attribute matter?", *International Journal of Trade, Economics and Finance*, Vol. 3 No. 2, pp. 96–102.

Lau, S. (2013), "TVB fined by watchdog and warned over 'bad taste' after host's remark", *South China Morning Post*, December 4, available at: http://www.scmp.com/news/hong-kong/article/1372377/tvb-fined-watchdog-and-warned-over-bad-taste-after-hosts-remark (accessed on December 12, 2015).

Lee, M., Kim, K. and King, K.W. (2012), "Audience responses to product placement and its regulations: Focusing on regulatory conditions in the United States and Korea", *Journal of International Consumer Marketing*, Vol. 24 No. 4, pp. 275–290.

Lee, T.D., Sung, Y. and Choi, S.M. (2011), "Young adults' responses to product placement in movies and television shows", *International Journal of Advertising*, Vol. 30 No. 3, pp. 479–507.

Matthes, J., Schemer, C. and Wirth, W. (2007), "More than meets the eye: Investigating the hidden impact of brand placements in television magazines", International Journal of Advertising, Vol. 26 No. 4, pp. 477–503.

McCarty, J.A. (2004), "Product placement: The nature of the practice and potential avenues of inquiry", in Shrum, L.J. (Ed.), *The Psychology of Entertainment Media*, Lawrence Erlbaum, Mahwah, NJ, pp. 45–61.

McKechnie, S.A. and Zhou, J. (2003), "Product placement in movies: A comparison of Chinese and American consumers' attitudes", *International Journal of Advertising*, Vol. 22 No. 3, pp. 349–374.

Milne, G.R., Bahl, S., and Rohm, A. (2008), "Toward a framework for assessing covert marketing practices", *Journal of Public Policy and Marketing*, Vol. 27 No. 1, pp. 57–62.

Office for Film, Newspaper and Article Administration (2015), Film Censorship Ordinance, available at: http://www.legislation.gov.hk/blis_ind.nsf/WebView?OpenAgent&vwpg=Cu rAllEngDoc*392*100*392.1#392.1 (accessed on October 15, 2015).

Okazaki, S., Mueller. B. and Taylor, C. (2010), "Global consumer culture positioning: Testing perceptions of soft-sell and hard-sell advertising appeals between U.S. and Japanese consumers", *Journal of International Marketing*, Vol. 18 No. 2, pp. 20–34.

PageFair and Adobe (2015), "Global ad blocking report", available at: http://blog.pagefair. com/2015/ad-blocking-report (accessed on October 8, 2015).

Rokeach, M. (1973), *The Nature of Human Values*. The Free Press, New York.

Russell, C.A. (2002), "Investigating the effectiveness of product placements in television shows: The role of modality and plot connection congruence on brand memory and attitude", *Journal of Consumer Research,* Vol. 29 No. 3, pp. 306–319.

Shi, Y. (2010), "Product placement and digital piracy: How young Chinese viewers react to the unconventional method of corporate cultural globalization", *Communication, Culture & Critique*, Vol. 3 No. 3, pp. 435–463.

Smith, B. (1985), "Casting product for special effect", *Beverage World*, Vol. 104 (March), pp. 83–91.

Su, H.J., Huang, Y.A., Brodowsky, G. and Kim, H.J. (2011), "The impact of product placement on TV-induced tourism: Korean TV dramas and Taiwanese viewers", *Tourism Management*, Vol. 32 No. 4, pp. 805–814.

Sung, Y., de Gregorio, F. and Jung, J. (2009), "Non-student consumer attitudes toward product placement: Implications for public policy and advertisers", *International Journal of Advertising*, Vol. 28 No. 2, pp. 257–285.

Ta, S. and Forsch, D.L. (2008), "Pharmaceutical product placement: Simply script or prescription for trouble?", *Journal of Public Policy & Marketing*, Vol. 27 No. 1, pp. 98–106.

Chapter 5

Controversial and Offensive Advertising

Kara Chan and Dickson Yeung

Introduction

Due to the extreme numbers of advertisements vying for viewers' attention today, advertisers have increasingly turned to controversial advertisements to set their ads apart from the masses. Controversial advertising is defined as advertising that has the potential to elicit negative emotions such as embarrassment, disgust, offense or outrage from the audience due to the product nature or its style of execution (Wilson and West, 1981). Proponents of controversial advertising believe that these methods are particularly effective in communicating with a young, educated target audience, based on the assumption that such people tend to be more open-minded and ready to challenge social norms. In this chapter, we introduce the "three Ms" concept of offensive advertising and report on several studies of consumers' attitudes toward offensive advertising. We then outline the regulatory framework for passing judgment on whether a particular advertisement is found to have breached television advertising standards. Case studies of how consumers' complaints of offensive advertisements have been dealt with demonstrate the authority's interpretation of the regulatory framework. This chapter does not deal with offensiveness of advertising due to puffery, deception or false advertising claims. These issues are covered in the next chapter on advertising regulation.

The "Three Ms" of Offensive Advertising

There are three major characteristics of advertisements, which have implications on their level of offensiveness. These are known as the three Ms: matter, media and manner (Prendergast and Ho, 2006). Matter refers to the product that is being advertised. Certain products lend a level of offensiveness to their advertisements. Advertisements involving products and services that are harmful, controversial or unacceptable in a social or cultural context may be perceived as offensive (Katsanis, 1994). Cultural taboos are important to note as certain products may be seen as culturally unacceptable, and advertisements for such products might be seen as offensive. Products related to sex are a common example of products that are often culturally unacceptable in advertisements. In many Asian or Muslim-dominated cultures, sex is seen as a highly private matter, so advertisements promoting products and services related to sex would be seen as offensive. In many Western cultures, sex is regarded more liberally, so such advertisements would be less offensive.

Katsanis (1994) suggested that the following products and services are especially controversial: products related to personal hygiene and birth control; drugs for terminal illnesses; firearms; and services related to abortion, sterilization, funerals, palliative care, treatment of mental illnesses and venereal diseases. Concepts such as political views, racial or religious prejudices and terrorism can also be controversial.

The next "M", media, refers to the medium used to propagate the advertisement. Generally speaking, the more public the medium is, the less tolerance there is for offensive advertising. For example, billboards are a very public medium and offensive advertisements there would likely elicit more complaints than similar advertisements in adult magazines, which are a less public medium. Generally, cable TV and magazines are relatively safe places for advertisers to test their advertisements for offensiveness — if advertisements in these media receive complaints, it is likely that these complaints would be multiplied if the advertisements were shown in more public media.

The third "M", manner, refers to the way the advertisement conveys information. This is the most important characteristic of advertisements, since people tend to be more offended by the manner in which advertisements are made than the products for which they are made. Advertisements that use fear, sex and silliness can be irritating to the public (Greyser, 1972). The use of fear may subject a person to harmful or offensive images (Henthorne et al., 1993).

A Study on Public Perceptions of Offensive Advertising

A survey of Hong Kong people using quota sampling was conducted to examine consumers' perceptions of offensive advertising (Prendergast and Ho, 2006). Altogether 100 male and 100 female individuals aged over 16, both with and without tertiary education, were interviewed in shopping malls. They were interviewed face-to-face and asked to rate fourteen products and services as well as seven appeals according to their offensiveness on a six-point scale (one being "inoffensive" and six being "extremely offensive"). They were also asked to rate their own tolerance of potentially offensive advertisements shown in nine media on a six-point scale (one indicating "very tolerant" and six indicating "very conservative").

Results found that the mean scores for offensiveness of products advertised ranged from 2.03 to 3.20. The top five products and services perceived to be offensive were chatline services, funeral services, gambling, condoms and dating services. The three products and services perceived to be least offensive were alcohol, pharmaceuticals and hair replacement products. Chatline services were found to be the most offensive products to advertise, because of the explicitness of such services and the poor taste with which they are often presented.

The mean scores for offensiveness regarding advertising appeals ranged from 2.73 to 4.2. These scores were much higher than those related to the nature of products and services advertised. This shows that the way advertisements are presented tends to be more offensive than the nature of the products and services advertised. The top five offensive appeals were those which involved sexism, indecent language, nudity, unnecessary fear and intimacy. The mean scores of these five appeals were 4.2, 4.0, 4.0, 3.9 and 3.5 respectively, and were all above the midpoint of the six-point scale used in the study (3.5). The two least offensive methods of appeal involved cultural insensitivity and sexual connotations.

Regarding tolerance of potentially offensive advertisements in nine media, the mean scores ranged from 3.20 to 3.92. Respondents were most intolerant of potentially offensive advertisements in direct mail, on billboards and in newspapers, while they were most tolerant of such advertisements in women's magazines, men's magazines and on cable television.

Prendergast and Ho (2006) found that respondents with a higher level of education were more tolerant of offensive advertising than respondents with a lower level of education. There was no gender difference regarding offensiveness of advertising, except regarding the use of nudity in advertising appeals. Female respondents found nudity in appeals significantly more offensive than male respondents (4.29 vs. 3.61). Prendergast and Ho (2006) found that the use of offensive advertising has a negative impact on consumers' purchase intentions. Respondents reported that when there were alternative products with similar consumer benefits available in the market, they would not buy from the brand that adopted an advertisement that they found offensive.

A Study of Young Adults' Responses to Offensive Advertising

Another way of studying offensive advertising is to measure how individuals respond to selected advertisements that are potentially offensive. One study was conducted among Chinese consumers (Li, 2006) and was extended to include German consumers (Chan et al., 2007).

Li (2009) argued that social and cultural values play an important role in influencing consumers' responses toward potentially offensive advertising. Li (2009) suggested that consumers from high-context and collective cultures are more critical of sex-related products and advertising appeals, as well as advertisements of products which may have a negative social impact, while consumers from low-context and individualistic cultures are less critical. Li (2009) constructed six controversial print advertisements. Two of them contained sexual connotations and sexism, two contained the theme that money is more important than family relationships and two attempted to degrade either Chinese products or Chinese revolutionary heroes. Participants were exposed to these advertisements and were asked to select from a batch of twelve positive and negative adjectives to describe the advertisements. The six positive adjectives were: convincing, lively, interesting, informative, creative and clever. The six negative adjectives were: offensive, uncomfortable, irritating, sickening, ridiculous and impolite. Results found that respondents were most offended by advertisements containing sexual connotations or sexism. Respondents were also offended by advertisements degrading Chinese products and Chinese heroes. Respondents were least offended by advertisements that degraded family relationships. Female respondents were more likely to find advertisements containing sexual connotations or sexism offensive than male respondents. This is consistent with previous studies, which found that female respondents were more likely to take offense at nudity in advertisements than male respondents (Prendergast and Ho, 2006).

Li's (2006) study was extended to study responses to offensive advertising among German respondents. Based on theories about information context, individualism and female consciousness, it was hypothesized that Chinese consumers would be less tolerant of offensive advertising than German consumers. A survey of 563 respondents aged 17–58 from urban China (Shanghai) and Germany (Saarbrücken) was conducted. Six print advertisements containing sexism, disrespect toward authority and other themes were constructed for the study.

Overall, as hypothesized, Chinese respondents were less tolerant of offensive advertising as they liked the advertisements less than German respondents. However, they were more likely than German respondents to find the advertisements convincing and informative. Chinese respondents and German respondents were found to have different perceptions of advertising. The two print advertisements that received the most negative reactions both contained sexually oriented images. The study also revealed that perceived offensiveness had a significant impact on respondents' intentions to reject the products and brands.

A Qualitative Study of Responses to Offensive Advertisements

In another study among Hong Kong adults, interviewees were arranged in six focus groups, two of which were all male, two of which were all female and two of which were of mixed genders (Liu, 2013). Each group was shown a series of offensive ads, four of which contained sexual connotations, four of which contained nudity and four of which contained sexism. Ads with sexual connotations were defined as ads that "involve the use of content which is interpreted as sexual at a subconscious level, including the use of nonsexual perceptible objects that can connote sexual body parts and sexual actions" (Liu, 2013, p. 226). Ads with nudity were defined as ads that "involve the revealing display of the model's body" (Liu, 2013). Ads with sexism were defined as ads that "incorporate the stereotypical and potentially derogatory portrayal of models based on their sexual identity" (Liu, 2013).

The study found that women were very emphatic in their condemnation of the ads that contained nudity, and were more vocal in all-female groups than mixed gender groups. They questioned the arbitrary link between the use of nudity and the product advertised and condemned the portrayal of women as sex objects. Female interviewees' comments about male nudity advertisements illustrated the conflict between the moral self and the libidinous self. One interviewee felt that endorsing male nudity was contradictory to her identity as a moral citizen who wished to uphold ethical societal values. However, she also stated that, identifying as a heterosexual woman, she exhibited favorable attitudes toward appealing images of the opposite sex.

Male viewers also expressed concern about the ads containing sexism. This finding denotes the third-person effect, which is when viewers are not offended by an advertisement but still find it offensive because they believe it would offend others. Men in mixed gender groups also tended to behave differently than men in all-male groups. In the company of women, men tended to be less comfortable about discussing anything sex-related. In particular, they tended to avoid saying the word "sex". Also, they tended to voice harsher opinions on homosexuality than participants in male-only groups. The study also found that viewers would sometimes refer to their cultural identities in condemning or defending advertisements; some made judgments on the offensiveness of advertisements based on cultural beliefs. For example, one viewer remarked that use of nudity was acceptable in Italy but not in China. Another interviewee commented that the Chinese are more conservative about sex, and therefore these advertisements were unacceptable.

Regulation of Television Advertisements in Hong Kong

Television advertisements in Hong Kong are governed by the Communications Authority. Like in the UK, Hong Kong's regulations on advertisements vary for different media. Television advertisements have stringent restrictions, as by law all advertisements from 4:00 PM to 8:30 PM must be suitable for children to view on their own. According to the Television Advertising Standard, advertisement or advertising material is defined as:

> Any material included in a television program service which is designed to advance the sale of any particular product or service or to promote the interests of any organization, commercial concern or individual; whether by means of words, sound effects (including music) and/or of visual presentation and whether in the form of direct announcements, slogans, descriptions or otherwise, as well as any promotional reference in the course of a program to any products or services. (Communications Authority, 2013)

Hong Kong's television advertising standards mandate that all advertisements broadcast on television should be legal, clean, honest and truthful. Advertising matter should be presented with "courtesy and good taste. Disturbing materials such as overly persistent repetition, and words and phrases implying emergency should be avoided" (Communications Authority, 2013). Furthermore, advertisements should not use fear appeals unduly. The Communications Authority update their standards for television advertising regularly.

Anyone wishing to lodge a complaint about an advertisement can contact the Communications Authority, which will launch an investigation into the offending advertisement and publicize the results of their investigation. Audiences can also raise complaints with traditional media such as newspapers, or share their views on social media. However, controversy over advertisements is rare in Hong Kong, as airtime is costly and an unfavorable investigation from the Authority could severely damage a firm's returns from their investments in advertising. In the years 2001–2015, the Communications Authority received less than 2,000 complaints a year about television advertisements. This is considered low with a television audience population of several million.

Case Studies of Controversial Advertisements

In this section, we provide a series of case studies from recent decades of how the Communications Authority evaluates controversial advertisements. The types of complaints and the decisions made by the Authority are summarized in Table 5.1. This illustrates how the regulatory authority interprets the television advertising standards.

The first area is related to fear. Our case study begins with a Sunday Telecom advertisement. The ad involves increasingly close encounters between a taxi driver driving at night and an eerie apparition of a woman, and ends with a phone plan promotion and the phrase, "So cheap it's scary". It received a record number of nearly 2,000 complaints. The regulating authority found the complaints substantiated and issued a serious warning on the grounds that the commercial contained unnecessary use of fear.

Two theme parks issued advertisements for Halloween events that also received complaints. One, by Ocean Park, involved a number of traditional Chinese demonic figures promoting a Halloween event, while the other, by Disneyland, involved three teenagers entering a haunted house and getting frightened by various occurrences such as doors moving and pianos playing by themselves. These advertisements were judged to be within the Authority's standards, and no action was taken against them. This was partly because the visual presentation of fear was more imaginary.

Another commercial, again by Sunday Telecom, included a blend of horror and violence, albeit in an ostensibly comedic fashion. Most of the ads involved the main character drilling through walls, furniture and household appliances, but also included a few shots of him drilling through unresponsive human heads. Although the interaction between the power drill and the human head was bloodless and completely unrealistic, viewers nevertheless slammed the ad as disturbing and horrific, leading to a warning being issued by the Communications Authority.

Another area of complaint involves bad taste. Two commercials by PPS, a twenty-four-hour payment service provider, involved having bushes of hair sprout from a character's body (one from the armpits, one from the chest) spelling out the word "Bill" while entangling the character to symbolize the troubles of bills. They received a number of complaints regarding their perceived bad taste. However, the Communications Authority considered these complaints unsubstantiated and took no action besides restricting one commercial from being broadcast between 4:30 PM and 8:30 PM.

A third advertisement that received many complaints for bad taste was by Itacho Japanese Restaurant. It involved a boy of around eight or nine years old responding favorably to a meal presented by a waitress in a low-cut dress. After an investigation, the advertisers were advised that their advertising content was inappropriate due to its sexual connotations.

The tissue manufacturer, Tempo, released an advertisement that involved several scenes of a young man at work and at home carrying around a piece of tissue paper with someone's lips imprinted on it. The advertisement received some complaints for its bad taste in displaying the unhygienic idea of a person carrying around the same tissue for an extended period of time. These complaints were found to be unsubstantiated.

A further area of complaint involves inappropriate content. For example, one advertisement by Jolly Shandy involved a woman screaming hysterically throughout most of the ad. Naturally, it received complaints, and the Communications Authority issued the advertiser with strong advice.

Another advertisement that offended viewers was by Prime Credit, a personal loan company. The ad involved a child running toward his father, looking over the father's disheveled appearance and then promptly running off to hug the leg of a well-dressed man in an expensive suit. Complaints condemned the ad for the way it distorted human relationships and denigrated the poor. The Communications Authority issued advice to the advertisers.

What the offending advertisements lack is context. Some ads failed to link their various eccentricities to their advertised products and services, which opened them up to criticism for gratuitousness and inappropriateness. In contrast, the Halloween commercials by Ocean Park and Disneyland were not condemned because they did have a context, and their use of fear appeal was directly linked to the matter of their advertisements. As such, their use of fear appeal was acceptable to the Communications Authority.

Conclusion

To conclude, offensive advertising in the medium of television is not prevalent in Hong Kong. Most advertisers are cautious in their marketing communications so as not to be offensive to consumers. Being a predominately Chinese society, many consumers are conservative toward sex. While use of sexual appeal may be acceptable for products related to physical attraction and fashion, its use for unrelated products can often be objectionable to both male and female audiences. Offensiveness is related to the nature of the medium. Specialized media for a target audience with a higher level of education can be venues to test out controversial advertising appeals. The Communications Authority pays much attention to the congruency between the nature of the product and the context of the advertising message in determining whether a complaint is justified.

Table 5.1

Cases of Offensive Television Advertising

Advertiser/title of commercial	Year the ad was launched	Reason for complaint	Action taken
Sunday Telecom/Taxi driver	2000	Provoking fear	Serious warning given
Sunday Telecom/Mighty drill	2002	Provoking fear, disturbing, cruel and violent	Warning given
Jolly Shandy beverage/ Scream	2004	Annoying, unnerving, bad role model for children	Strong advice given
Prime Credit/Poor dad	2005	Bad theme, distorting human relationships, denigrating the poor	Advice given
Ocean Park/Nine Chinese ghosts	2005	Horrifying, unnerving, unsuitable for children	Complaint unsubstantiated
Disneyland/Haunted house	2007	Horrifying, unnerving, unsuitable for children	Complaint unsubstantiated
Tempo/Boy kissing tissue	2008	Bad taste, unhygienic, promoting stealing and fetish behavior	Complaint unsubstantiated
Itacho Japanese Restaurant/Child's meal	2009	Sexual connotations, bad taste, not suitable for children	Advice issued concerning its inappropriate sexual connotations
PPS/Robbery	2012	Disgusting, bad taste	Complaint unsubstantiated; restricted for broadcast outside 4:30–8:30 PM
PPS/Couple dating	2012	Disgusting, bad taste	Complaint unsubstantiated

Source: Communications Authority (formerly known as Broadcasting Authority).

References

Chan, K., Li, L., Diehl, S. and Terlutter, R. (2007), "Consumers' response to offensive advertising: a cross cultural study", *International Marketing Review*, Vol. 24 No. 5, pp. 606–628.

Communications Authority (2013), "Generic code of practice on television advertising standards", available at: http://www.coms-auth.hk/filemanager/common/policies_regulations/cop/code_tvad_e.pdf (accessed on July 9, 2015).

Greyser, S. A. (1972), "Advertising-attacks and counters", *Harvard Business Review*, March, pp. 22–28.

Henthorne, T.L., LaTour, M.S. and Nataraajan, R. (1993), "Fear appeals in print advertising: An analysis of arousal and ad response", *Journal of Advertising*, Vol. 22 No. 2, pp. 59–68.

Katsanis, L.P. (1994), "Do unmentionable products still exist? An empirical investigation", *Journal of Product & Brand Management*, Vol. 3 No. 4, pp. 5–14.

Li, M. (2006), "Consumers' response to offensive advertising in China", in Cheng, H. and Chan, K. (Eds.), *Advertising and Chinese Society: Impacts and Issues*, Copenhagen Business School Press, Denmark, pp. 175–190.

Liu, Y.Y.T. (2013), "Tread along the line between edgy and offensive: A study of Chinese students' response toward offensive advertising", Unpublished Master's dissertation, HKBU Institutional Repository, Hong Kong Baptist University, Hong Kong.

Prendergast, G. and Ho, B. (2006), "Offensive advertising", in Chan, K. (Ed.), *Advertising and Hong Kong Society*, The Chinese University Press, Hong Kong, pp. 95–113.

Prendergast, G., Ho, B. and Phau, I. (2002), "A Hong Kong view of offensive advertising", *Journal of Marketing Communications*, Vol. 8 No. 3, pp. 165–177.

Wilson, A. and West, C. (1981), "The marketing of 'unmentionables'", *Harvard Business Review*, January/February, pp. 91–102.

Chapter 6

Advertising Regulations in Hong Kong

Annisa Lee

Introduction

The purpose of advertising regulation is to ensure the quality and credibility of ads in order to protect consumers from deceptive advertisements and maintain a reasonable level of consumer trust and confidence. In this chapter, we discuss five major forces in the regulation of advertising:

- natural market force;
- organized consumer forces;
- government regulation;
- industrial self-regulation; and
- media scrutiny.

Each force ebbs and flows with varying intensities in different countries, depending on the makeup of their political and economic systems. Interestingly, in Hong Kong's seemingly laissez-faire business environment, the government exerts the greatest impact on advertising regulation.

Natural Market Force

Advocates of this force believe that in any free market respecting freedom of commercial speech, the market should be entirely self-regulated by the invisible hand. Consumers can seek out the lowest prices and best quality goods and services themselves. If advertising is offensive or ineffective, consumers will move away from the product/service and no longer trust the advertisers. This is especially true when consumers exchange views through social media: the court of public opinion will judge the ads and mobilize many to boycott a brand. As a result, advertisers will then change and correct problematic advertisements to attract potential buyers. The market will therefore make adjustments by itself and reach its equilibrium in the long term. The problem with this self-adjusting mechanism is that it can take a long time to take effect while a specifically timed campaign may have already caused irreversible damage. Occasionally, with competitive brands the standards of their ads can degenerate together, especially when upward adjustment requires more conscientious effort. Cases 1 and 2 are examples of two ads reviewed in the natural market force.

Case 1: On November 14, 2015, it was reported that some Facebook users cut their MasterCards and posted them online because in an advertisement MasterCard featured the much-criticized actor Oscar Leung using MasterPass (*Apple Daily*, 2015). A lot of users followed suit and MasterCard had to pull the ad.

Case 2: A picture was posted on social media exposing the discrepancy between a real McDonald's breakfast and the ideal one presented in the ad. The photo generated a lot of media attention (*Apple Daily*, 2016) and many netizens reposted the picture. McDonald's made a public apology.

Organized Consumer Forces

Organized consumer groups are grassroots efforts with specific shared goals and interests. They usually investigate the public's complaints about ads and carry out their own research. If a complaint is justified, they will ask the advertiser to pull the ad, or appeal to the government and/or create widespread publicity, sometimes with the support of celebrities. The power of consumer groups stems from the rights of consumers, including the right to satisfy basic needs, the right to safety, information, consumer education, a healthy and sustainable environment, the right to choose, to be heard and to

Figure 6.1

An Outdoor Banner Hung by Greenpeace

redress their grievances (Consumer Council, n.d.). Many consumer groups are gaining momentum in Hong Kong. Advocacy groups like Greenpeace, WWF (The Worldwide Fund for Nature), PETA (People for the Ethical Treatment of Animals) and LGBT (lesbian, gay, bisexual and transgender), minority, disability and women's rights groups contend with advertisers to protect their interests and rights through proper media representation of their groups or their causes in ads. This force organizes consumers to fight for meaningful causes but it can become radical at times due to zealous ideology.

Case 3: Greenpeace hung a banner over an outdoor ad with the words "Behind the glamour" at Times Square, Causeway Bay, during Christmas, 2015 to ask consumers to "Buy smart, buy less" (Greenpeace East Asia, 2015).

Government Regulation

Although there is no comprehensive ordinance dedicated solely to advertising regulation in Hong Kong, the Communications Authority, Consumer Council and Trade Description Ordinance with efficient executory operations regulate problematic ads and maintain advertising standards. As a major part of business and marketing activities, advertising also involves contracts, intellectual property, privacy, medical and tort laws which enable the court to protect consumers' rights and impose sanctions on liable advertisers. The breach of some could result in being charged with a criminal offense. Due to the enormity of the field, this section highlights the more prominent regulatory bodies and rules involved.

Communications Authority and Codes of Practice

The Communications Authority (CA) is an independent statutory body created by the Communications Authority Ordinance in 2012 to regulate the broadcasting and telecommunications industries in accordance with the Broadcasting Ordinance, the Broadcasting Miscellaneous Provisions Ordinance, the Telecommunications Ordinance and the Unsolicited Electronic Message Ordinance. The CA developed elaborate codes of practice and clear standards relating to programming and advertising applicable to television, radio and telecommunications licensees.

The Generic Code of Practice on Television Advertising Standards (Communications Authority, 2013a) comprises nine chapters of detailed regulations and is updated regularly. When forming a view about the acceptability of any advertising material, the CA will give consideration to five major factors, including types of licensees (e.g. paid cable television receives more lenient treatment than terrestrial television); categories of ads (e.g. alcohol ads are subjected to stringent regulation, while some categories such as advertisements for betting and fortune telling are totally forbidden), time of day (e.g. prime time is monitored more closely than night hours), target audience (e.g. children warrant more attention than adults) and circumstances in which the ads are shown (e.g. extent of a viewer's control). Ads are expected to be in good taste, truthful and with claims adequately substantiated. If the public has any concerns about an ad on air, they can file a complaint with the CA. From 2012 to 2015, the CA investigated forty-four complaints about TV ads, seven of which were considered unjustified. Table 6.1 tabulates the nature of the thirty-seven cases that breached the law. Since five of them are listed in multiple categories the total number of cases is forty-two.

Table 6.1

Categories of Complaints Received by the Communications Authority, 2012–2015

Nature of breach	Number of cases
Unjustisfied product placement	24
Specific product categories (e.g. alcoholic beverages, real property)	6
Excessive sponsor identification	3
Unclear identification of advertisements in program	2
Misleading information	3
Unsubstantiated claims	2
Concern about the portrayal of children in advertisement or children as target audience	2
Total	42

Depending on the severity and nature of the breach, the CA can impose one of the following five sanctions on the licensees: issue advice or strong advice; warning or serious warning; issue correction and/or apology; impose a financial penalty; and suspension or revocation of license. In very serious cases, the CA may suspend a license for up to thirty days, or conduct an inquiry or make a recommendation to the Chief Executive in Hong Kong to revoke a license. (Case 4 breached paragraph 5(c) of Chapter 7 of the Code and Case 5 breached paragraph 10(a) of Chapter 9 of the Code).

Case 4: A complaint was made against TVB for broadcasting three versions of ads for ParknShop which involved the participation of child actors to promote alcoholic beverages. Since according to paragraph 5(c) of Chapter 7 of the Television Advertising Code, "children should not be permitted to participate in the presentation of advertisements for alcoholic liquor", the CA decided that TVB should be advised to observe more closely the relevant provisions of the Television Advertising Code (Communications Authority, 2014a).

Table 6.2

Sanctions on Breaches of the Generic Code of Practice on Television Advertising Standards Imposed by the CA on Licensees, 2012–2015

	Advice or strong advice	Warning or serious warning	Issue corrective ads	Apology	Financial penalty	Total
2012	3	16	0	0	1	20
2013	3	2	0	0	3	8
2014	3	3	0	0	1	7
2015	2	0	0	0	0	2

Case 5: In February 2014, the CA imposed a fine of HK$100,000 on TVB for breaching paragraph 10(a) of Chapter 9 of the Television Advertising Code, according to which "the exposure or use of the sponsor's products and/or services within a programme should be clearly justified editorially, not obtrusive to viewing pleasure and not gratuitous". The program series, *The Taste of Taipan Snowy Mooncakes Mini 2013* (大班冰皮月餅特約：大班群星添戲Fun) was considered to be designed to introduce the sponsor's snowy mooncakes gratuitously, rather than to add a festive atmosphere as claimed by TVB. Its presentation, in particular the conspicuous display of the sponsor's tin or bag with the brand name shown whenever the characters talked about snowy mooncakes, could not be considered as being editorially justified and was obtrusive to viewing pleasure (Communications Authority, 2014b).

Most media licensees comply with CA decisions because of their ultimate ability to directly appeal to the Chief Executive of Hong Kong for license revocation, which is in reality a rare punishment. Between 2012 and 2015, the CA dealt with forty-four complaints and seven were unjustified. Among the remaining thirty-seven cases, only five were penalized financially. The rest of the sanctions were light (see Table 6.2 for details).

The Radio Code of Practice on Advertising Standards (Communications Authority, 2013b) is basically an abridged version of The Generic Code of Practice on Television Advertising Standards with only thirty-four points and three appendices. Most of the content is similar to that in the television

Table 6.3

Cases in Violation of the Trade Descriptions Ordinance Enforced by the Customs and Excise Department

	2012	2013	2014
Number of cases	533	752	1,076
Persons arrested	506	663	752
Values of seizures (HK$ million)	158	146	93

version. From 2012 to 2015, a total of only three complaint cases breached the relevant provisions in this Code. Two of them communicated misleading information, and one invited the public to donate money to political parties without the CA's prior approval. In addition, another four radio programs gave undue prominence to a product or a brand name, which contravened provisions that regulate advertising in the Radio Code of Practice on Programme Standards.

The Customs and Excise Department and the Trade Descriptions Ordinance

While the Communications Authority is the author of the Trade Descriptions Ordinance (Department of Justice Bilingual Laws Information System, n.d. b), in relation to the commercial practices of licensees under the Telecommunications Ordinance and the Broadcasting Ordinance, the Customs and Excise Department is the proactive agency tasked with enforcing the TDO, sometimes by seeking an undertaking from the trader, applying to the court for an injunction or instituting criminal proceedings (Customs and Excise Department and Communications Authority, 2013). The Amended TDO extended its jurisdiction in 2013 to prohibit specified unfair trade practices deployed by traders against consumers, including false descriptions of services, misleading omissions, aggressive commercial practices, bait advertising, bait-and-switch and wrongly accepting payment (Customs and Excise Department, n.d. c). Table 6.3 summarizes the enforcement cases since the inception of the TDO (Customs and Excise Department, n.d. b).

Among these 2,361 cases, the most frequent infringements of the TDO related to advertising false descriptions of goods/services, misleading omissions, bait advertising and bait-and-switch. These areas will be examined in more detail.

False Trade Descriptions of Goods/Services

In this category, a trader commits an offence if s/he applies a false trade description to any goods/services supplied (Trade Descriptions Ordinance, Chapter 362 s 7, s 7A.).

Case 6: A vendor supplied lip balm weighing 7 g per unit through a group-buying website with an ad depicting a false net weight of 10.75 g and a false price discount of 94% off. Both the vendor and website were believed to have committed the offence of supplying goods with false descriptions. As a result of prosecution, both parties undertook not to engage in conduct of this kind for two years, and to put in place a compliance and implementation program for staff in accordance with TDO requirements (Customs and Excise Department, 2015).

Misleading Omissions

A misleading omission occurs if a trader omits or misrepresents information which causes or is likely to cause the average consumer to make a transactional decision that s/he would not have made otherwise (Customs and Excise Department, n.d. a).

Case 7: A dried seafood retailer displayed three placards advertising dried seafood products, with two different price units (catty and 500 grams) shown against each of the products. The print of "500 g" was so small that the price unit could easily be read as "catty". Furthermore, a test purchase revealed that the shop intentionally avoided clarifying the price units or any relationship between a catty and 500 grams, while purporting that 476 grams of the goods it supplied were equivalent to one catty (604 grams). The shop was convicted of engaging in misleading commercial practice through omission by providing misleading information. It was fined $20,000, and the dried seafood products concerned were confiscated (Customs and Excise Department, 2015).

Bait Advertising

Bait advertising takes place when a trader advertises goods or services at a bargain price during a specific period in order to attract consumers but does not plan to supply enough products at that price so as to persuade consumers to buy at a higher price (Customs and Excise Department, n.d. a).

Case 8: A customer saw a promotion for smartphone model A for sale at $2,000 in an electronic products company. However, there was no indication of the duration of the promotion or the quantity to be supplied on the ad. The company advertised this promotion in newspapers and on its website for two consecutive weeks, but the customer was unable to place an order with the company. In fact, the company was only prepared to offer five smartphones and they were all sold within thirty minutes after posting the ad. In this case, the company may have committed the offense of bait advertising.

Bait-and-Switch

An invitation to consumers by a trader to purchase a product at a specified price is a bait-and-switch if, having made the invitation, the trader, with the intention of promoting a different product, refuses to show or demonstrate the product to consumers; refuses to take orders for the product or deliver it within a reasonable time; or shows or demonstrates a defective sample of the product (Customs and Excise Department, n.d. a).

Case 9: A customer saw a large poster outside a shop promoting a dehumidifier for $800. He told a shop attendant that he wanted to buy it. However, instead of demonstrating how to use it, the shop attendant repeatedly pointed out its poor performance and persuaded the customer to buy another model priced at $2,000.

The Drug Office and Undesirable Medical Advertisements Ordinance

The Drug Office of the Department of Health oversees the Undesirable Medical Advertisements Ordinance (UMAO), Chapter 231 (Department of Justice Bilingual Laws Information System, n.d. c), which was first enacted in 1953. Its amendments came into force in June 2012 with a purpose to protect public health through prohibiting or restricting ads that can lead to the improper management of certain health conditions.

UMAO prohibits or restricts the publication of ads concerning medicine, surgical appliances or treatments for the purpose of treating or preventing certain specified diseases or conditions, such as benign or malignant tumors, venereal disease, heart disease, endocrine disease, cardiovascular disease and gynecological or obstetrical disease. In addition, it is forbidden to publish, or cause to be published, any ads promoting sexual virility, desire or fertility; claiming to restore lost youth; offering to correct deformity or the surgical alteration of a person's appearance; or offering services to procure a foetal miscarriage. Any person who contravenes the provisions of UMAO is guilty of an offence and shall be liable upon a first conviction to a fine at level five and imprisonment for six months, and upon a second or subsequent conviction for an offense under the same section to a fine at level six and imprisonment for one year (Department of Justice Bilingual Laws Information System, n.d. c).

Case 10: In early 2013, despite two warning letters issued by the Department of Health, the newspaper *Mingpao* continued to publish an ad for Chen Tai Moxibustion Care Centers, which claimed that their treatment could cure badly bruised faces, inflammation, blurred vision and other afflictions. Since the claims mentioned the curing of a condition affecting sight, in violation of the UMAO, *Mingpao* pleaded guilty and was fined $10,000. The advertiser was fined $20,000 (*Oriental Daily*, 2013).

Consumer Council

Sometimes regarded as a consumer organized force, most consumer councils around the world, such as the American Consumer Council, are independent non-profit organizations dedicated to empowering consumers with education and advocacy skills to choose and use the best and most reliable goods or services. The Consumer Council in Hong Kong, on the other hand, is a rare consumer statutory body initiated by the Government's Consumer Council Ordinance (Chapter 216, Department of Justice Bilingual Laws Information System, n.d. a) in 1977. The chairman, vice-chairman and members of the Council are all appointed by the Chief Executive of Hong Kong for renewable terms of two years. The Council operates like a government agency with elaborate multi-level capacities and is funded mostly (95%) by the government. The mission of the Council is to become "a trusted voice of consumers in striving to build in the market an environment of safe, fair and sustainable consumption". It gives advice on all sorts of consumer products and services including electricity, IT, food, cosmetics and telecommunications marketing. The Council has also become a powerful protector of consumers' rights with its "name and shame" policy to showcase brands with faulty products and services on news programs. Another of its functions is to promote good practices in the dissemination of consumer information so that consumers can make informed choices. The Council regularly publishes guidelines, reports or policy recommendations for the public and the government, in order to remind businesses that their promotional materials and ads need to be truthful, unbiased and sensible, without any misleading elements, and in compliance with the requirements stipulated in the related legislation. Not only does the Council have strong liaisons with the media for publicity, it also works with the Hong Kong Police and the Customs and Excise Department to ensure legal protection for consumers.

Case 11: In 2011, the Consumer Council raised concerns that some beneficial claims made by various formula milk products might be exaggerated and even misleading. For example, there is insufficient evidence to prove that ß-Glucan can improve the body's immune system, nor that PhD (phospholipid) has a beneficial effect on the mental development of infants/young children as claimed. The Council urged the government to establish a local code to regulate against advertising or promoting breast-milk substitutes (Consumer Council, 2011).

We have discussed some of the rules and laws related to advertising regulation. Many other media and business laws regulate advertising in different areas, such as the Control of Obscene and Indecent Articles Ordinance (Chapter 390) for decent ad content; the Unconscionable Contract Ordinance (Chapter 485) for unfair representation; the Public Health and Municipal Services Ordinance (Chapter 132) for food labeling and description; and the Hong Kong Trade Marks Ordinance (Chapter 559) for protection of logos and intellectual property.

Industry Self-Regulation

Advertising self-regulation is a system by which advertising agencies, advertisers, trade associations and media industries set voluntary rules and standards of practice that go beyond legal obligations to maintain consumer trust, avoid publicity crises and limit government interference. In Hong Kong, the Association of Accredited Advertising Agencies of Hong Kong (HK4As) is in charge of the formulation and implementation of self-regulation among advertising practitioners, and the Hong Kong Advertisers Association (HK2As) promotes higher professional standards and ethics among advertisers.

Established in 1957, the HK4As is conventionally run by elected senior members of member agencies who share common goals, which include planning for the future of the advertising industry, setting and enforcing business ethics and advertising standards, providing arbitration among agencies and creating a platform for engagement, awards, education, services and other activities. In December 2015, HK4As had thirty full members and twenty-five affiliated members from Hong Kong and twenty-two full members from mainland China.

HK4As issued a Code of Practice to ensure that employees of the membership agencies endorsed ethical business practices. HK4As also sets and maintains standards and business practices for the industry such as remuneration, import duties, statutory charges and taxation. The HK4As states very clearly that the purpose of their Code of Practice is "to ensure that each member will carry on his profession and business in such a manner as to protect the public interest and uphold the dignity and interests of the profession, the Association and its members generally", and "to force competition between advertising agencies into the area of upgrading the quality and extending the scope of their various services, rather than restricting such activities to meet a financial need" (The Association of Accredited Advertising Agencies of Hong Kong, n.d.). Any members found to have contravened the Code will be penalized. The Code comprises twenty-three sections of detailed requirements for ad creation, including the need to pay special attention to credible claims, comparative advertising, product categories and target audiences, particularly children (The Association of Accredited Advertising Agencies of Hong Kong, n.d.).

The Hong Kong Advertisers Association (HK2As) was founded in 1961 by a volunteer group of advertisers as a non-profit organization with the aim to promote higher professional standards and ethics, protect the interests of advertisers, provide an effective channel to voice their opinions to the media and the government and to encourage sharing through conferences, talks, tours and activities. The HK2As does not have a code of ethics and it depends on the executive committees to voice their concerns for advertising regulation.

The HK2As raised its concerns with the government about the implementation of the Trade Descriptions Ordinance which it said had a lot of grey areas, causing some advertisers to bear liability and to be charged with criminal offences. HK2As expressed the view that they could not accept the new legislation (The Hong Kong Advertisers Association, 2013).

For many years, the Hong Kong Government has not regulated advertising with much forcefulness until the initiation of the Trade Description Ordinance which imposes stronger penalties and tighter surveillance. The HK2As protested against it and asked for more leniency for advertisers. When the government and the media expose the problematic ads, the brands' reputations are affected and may subsequently suffer a decrease in sales and popularity among consumers. It is therefore advisable that the HK4As and HK2As should step up their self-regulatory system and review the public or competitors' complaints before the government intervenes.

Effective self-regulation builds trust with consumers by ensuring advertising that is honest, legal, decent and truthful and providing quick and easy redress when transgressions occur. Around the world, many countries have strong and elaborate self-regulatory systems in place. Some have self-regulatory organizations (SROs) to enforce the industry's commitment to the self-imposed standards. SROs offer consumers increased protection and a cost-effective, accessible and responsive alternative to legal avenues. SROs monitor ads, respond to complaints, initiate investigations and give advice—a more efficient way to modify problems.

For example, the European Advertising Standards Alliance (EASA) is a non-profit organization comprised of SROs representing the advertising industry in Europe. An average of 53,116 complaints was brought to the attention of

European SROs in the five-year period from 2006 to 2010—much larger than what is likely to realistically be addressed through the official legal system. In the U.S., the Advertising Self-Regulatory Council (ASRC) establishes a very elaborate system for self-regulation, including the National Advertising Division (NAD), Children's Advertising Review Unit (CARU), National Advertising Review Board (NARB), Electronic Retailing Self-Regulation Program (ERSP) and Online Interest-Based Advertising Accountability Program. The self-regulatory system is administered by the Council of Better Business Bureaus. In 2012, ASRC resolved more than 175 cases (Peeler, 2013). The National Advertising Division (NAD) conducts external monitoring, adjudicates industry compliance with broad standards and fosters voluntary industry participation. The NAD reviews an average of 100 cases per year. The NAD may refer a case to the appropriate regulatory agency, most commonly the Federal Trade Commission, if a challenged advertiser declines to participate in the process (Villafranco and Riley, 2013). On the international level, the International Chamber of Commerce (ICC) Commission on Marketing and Advertising promotes effective self-regulation that is harmonized to best practice around the world. The Consolidated ICC Code (International Chamber of Commerce, 2011) forms an integral aspect of this work and has served as the foundation for the national and sectorial codes of most self-regulatory systems existing today. Self-regulatory systems with rules based on the ICC Code are operating in over thirty-five countries, across six continents and the ICC Code is being used to develop rules and new self-regulatory systems in a half dozen other countries including China, Serbia, Croatia and Ukraine (International Chamber of Commerce, n.d.). These systems demonstrate that self-regulation can be effective and Hong Kong has a lot to learn from them. The problems of self-regulation, however, are a lack of staff, budgetary resources and legitimate power, and the fact that it can be self-serving to the industries without a balance of public involvement.

Media Scrutiny

Most media have gatekeepers. Different gatekeepers have different rules and strengths in regulating advertising. A newspaper editor or editorial committee can filter out ads that are not compatible with the style of the carrier. Broadcasting organizations maintain their own set of guidelines for deceptive advertising. The media can also monitor ads and expose misdemeanors to the public. In today's age of information, if a brand has problems and these are widely publicized by the media, the reputation of the brand will suffer and many consumers will stop purchasing their products. The company needs to activate crisis control to stop the viral dissemination and downward slide of public opinion.

Case 12: In 2012, MassMutual Asia Ltd, a financial company, launched a series of TVC and outdoor advertisements with the theme "Where dreams are made" (敢想 未來才會更精彩). In each version of the advertisement, a child made a wish, such as "I wish to retire at the age of 40", "I wish to save money to buy real estate" and "I wish to stay healthy" (Li, 2015). The series was widely criticized by the media for presenting unrealistic values for children, such as buying real estate or early retirement. In addition, children have many more ways of securing a happy future for themselves. The media attention attracted a lot of negative comments among the public and the brand had to pull the ads.

Conclusion

The purpose of advertising regulation is to ensure the quality of ads and build brand trust among consumers. For this purpose, ethical issues should also be considered. Advertising regulations and professional codes are in fact subsets of the domain of advertising ethics. As Cunningham said, advertising ethics is "what is right or good in the conduct of the advertising function. It is concerned with questions of what ought to be done, not just with what legally must be done" (Cunningham, 1999). The topic of ethics in advertising has been examined in micro, macro and meso perspectives. The micro perspective focuses on the effects of specific advertising practices on individuals, such as ads with persuasive appeals; false or misleading promises; unidentified sponsors of editorial material; ads with a controversial message (i.e. sexual appeals, appeals through fear, and political messages), the advertising of dangerous or problematic products (i.e. alcohol and cigarettes); the appropriateness of targeting vulnerable groups like children; and issues of privacy of consumers. The macro perspective focuses on the aggregate effects of advertising on society, or the unintended social consequences of advertising, such as encouraging excessive materialism; creating, or at least reinforcing problematic stereotypes for sexes, races, ages, occupations; and creating false values which result in problematic behavior, such as pollution, over-consumption of high sugar products, dieting and alcohol consumption. The meso perspective is a level between the micro and macro levels, a level of the organization or groups of organizations, agencies, clients or media, which deals with issues related to organizational climate, culture, systems, policies, self-regulatory codes and other collective actions (Drumwright, 2007).

References

Advertising Self-Regulatory Council (n.d.), "ASRC snapshot", available at: http://www. asrcreviews.org/about-us/ (accessed on January 20, 2016).

Apple Daily (2015), "搵負評王掀剪咕潮 梁烈唯MasterCard廣告被鬧爆即del" [MasterCard's advertisement backfired for using much-panned celebrity as spokesperson], November 14, available at: http://hk.apple.nextmedia.com/realti me/10890993/20151114/54427185 (accessed on January 20, 2016).

Apple Daily (2016), "老麥新早餐多士硬過人字拖" [McDonald's breakfast toast is harder than flip-flops], January 1, available at: http://hk.apple.nextmedia.com/realtime/ news/20160101/54599288?top=12h (accessed on January 20, 2016).

Communications Authority (2013a), "Generic code of practice on television advertising standards", available at: http://www.coms-auth.hk/filemanager/common/policies_ regulations/cop/code_tvad_e.pdf (accessed on January 19, 2016).

Communications Authority (2013b), "Radio code of practice on advertising standards", available at: http://www.coms-auth.hk/filemanager/common/policies_regulations/cop/ code_radioad_e.pdf (accessed on January 19, 2016).

Communications Authority (2014a), "Complaint cases — Television advertisement for 'PARKnSHOP'"(百佳超級市場), available at: http://www.coms-auth.hk/filemanager/ listarticle/en/upload/733/20140630ca_en.pdf (accessed on January 19, 2016).

Communications Authority (2014b), "Complaint cases — Television programme 'The Taste of Taipan Snowy Mooncakes Mini 2013'" (大班冰皮月餅特約：大班群星添戲Fun), available at: http://www.coms-auth.hk/filemanager/listarticle/en/upload/630/20140218ca_en.pdf (accessed on January 19, 2016).

Consumer Council (2011), "Beware of Misleading Claims of Follow-up Formula — Choice #421", available at https://www.consumer.org.hk/ws_en/news/press/20111115-0.html (accessed on October 25, 2016).

Consumer Council (n.d.), "Mission and functions", available at: https://www.consumer.org. hk/ws_en/profile/mission/mission.html (accessed on January 19, 2016).

Cunningham, P.H. (1999), "Ethics of advertising", In The Advertising Business, Jones, J.P. (Ed.), Sage, London, pp. 499–513.

Customs and Excise Department (2015), "Successful prosecutions and accepted undertakings under the Trade Descriptions Ordinance (Cap. 362)", available at: http://www.customs. gov.hk/filemanager/common/pdf/TDO_Case_Booklet_en.pdf (accessed on February 3, 2016).

Customs and Excise Department (n.d.a), "Articles", available at: http://www.customs.gov.hk/ en/consumer_protection/trade_desc/unfair/articles/index.html (accessed on January 19, 2016).

Customs and Excise Department (n.d.b), "Statistics — Enforcement results", available at: http://www.customs.gov.hk/filemanager/common/pdf/statistics/enforcement_cases_ en.pdf (accessed on January 19, 2016).

Customs and Excise Department (n.d.c), "Unfair trade practices", available at: http://www.customs.gov.hk/en/consumer_protection/trade_desc/unfair/index.html (accessed on January 19, 2016).

Customs and Excise Department and Communications Authority (2013), "Enforcement guidelines for the trade descriptions (Unfair trade practices) (Amendment) Ordinance 2012", available at: http://www.customs.gov.hk/filemanager/common/pdf/pdf_forms/Enforcement_Guidelines2_en.pdf (accessed on January 19, 2016).

Department of Justice Bilingual Laws Information System (n.d.a), "Consumer Council Ordinance (Chapter 216)", available at: http://www.legislation.gov.hk/blis_pdf.nsf/4f0db701c6c25d4a4825755c00352e35/E9CB0A1201844FDD482575EE004E364E/$FILE/CAP_216_e_b5.pdf (accessed on January 31, 2016).

Department of Justice Bilingual Laws Information System (n.d.b), "Trade Descriptions Ordinance", available at: http://www.legislation.gov.hk/blis_pdf.nsf/6799165D2FEE3FA94825755E0033E532/620C44C5887E4501482575EE0071B7D7?OpenDocument&bt=0 (accessed on January 19, 2016).

Department of Justice Bilingual Laws Information System (n.d.c), "Undesirable Medical Advertisements Ordinance", available at: http://www.legislation.gov.hk/blis_ind.nsf/WebView?OpenAgent&vwpg=CurAllEngDoc*231*100*-231.1#231.1 (accessed on January 19, 2016).

Drumwright, M.E. (2007), "Advertising ethics: A multi-level theory approach", in Tellis, G.J, and Ambler, T. (Eds.), *The Sage Handbook of Advertising*, Sage, London, pp. 398–416.

Greenpeace East Asia (2015), "Buy smart, buy less", available at: http://www.greenpeace.org/hk/news/stories/toxics/2015/12/buy-smart-buy-less/ (accessed on January 20, 2016).

International Chamber of Commerce (2011), "Advertising and marketing communication practice (Consolidated ICC Code)", available at: http://www.iccwbo.org/advocacy-codes-and-rules/document-centre/2011/advertising-and-marketing-communication-practice-(consolidated-icc-code)/ (accessed on January 20, 2016).

International Chamber of Commerce (n.d.), "Marketing and advertising", available at: http://www.iccwbo.org/advocacy-codes-and-rules/areas-of-work/marketing-and-advertising/ (accessed on January 20, 2016).

Li, B.F. 李八方 (2015), "美心妹妹廣告教細路做樓奴" [Girl in Maxim's advertisement teaches kids to become brick slaves], September 3, available at: http://hk.apple.nextmedia.com/news/art/20150903/19280756 (accessed on January 20, 2016).

Oriental Daily (2013), "刊不良醫藥廣告 《明報》罰款萬元" [Mingpao was fined ten thousand dollars for publishing undesirable medical advertisements], August 20, available at: http://orientaldaily.on.cc/cnt/news/20130820/00176_022.html (accessed on January 19, 2016).

Peeler, C.L. (2013), "Four decades in, ad industry's self-regulation is the gold standard", Advertising Age, available at: http://www.asrcreviews.org/wp-content/uploads/2014/06/2013-Lee-Peeler-Ad-Age-Four-Decades-in-Ad-Industrys-Self-Regulation-is-the-Gold-Standard.pdf (accessed on January 20, 2016).

The Association of Accredited Advertising Agencies of Hong Kong (n.d.), "Code of practice", available at: http://www.aaaa.com.hk/en/abouthk4as/pdf/Code_of_Practice.pdf (accessed on January 19, 2016).

The Hong Kong Advertisers Association (2013), "Statement by HK2A on Trade Descriptions (Unfair Trade Practices)(Amendment) Ordinance 2012", available at: http://www.hk2a.com/20130717/HK2A.html (accessed on January 20, 2016).

Villafranco, J.E. and Riley, K.E. (2013), "So you want to self-regulate? The national advertising division as standard bearer", *Antitrust*, Vol. 27 No. 2, pp. 79–84.

Chapter 7

Personal Loan Advertisements in Hong Kong: A Semiotic Study

Kara Chan, Hong Cheng, Melannie Zhan and Dickson Yeung

Introduction

One of the criticisms of advertising is that it makes people buy things they do not need (Belch et al., 2014). Commercial advertisements are particularly accused of causing dissatisfaction among consumers with what they have or encouraging them to use material goods to solve unrelated problems (Belch et al., 2014). This chapter first examines how Hong Kong people manage their money. It goes on to discuss the issue of credit card debt faced by many consumers, particularly among younger generations. Personal loans are marketed aggressively in Hong Kong as a means to solve credit card debt. This chapter introduces semiotic analysis as a research tool to explore deep social meanings nested in the advertisements. Three recent television commercials for personal loan services in Hong Kong were selected for this study. The consumption values and ideologies embedded in the advertisements are examined and discussed. Commercial-oriented advertisements were selected for analysis in this chapter. A similar approach to analyze public services advertisements will be the focus of Chapter 13.

Money Management

Money management is essential to sound financial planning. A large-scale survey found that a majority of respondents (Hong Kong people aged 18–64) were living with a surplus (76%) or a break-even (17%) financial status. Only 7% of the respondents lived with a deficit. Respondents with a monthly household income below HK$20,000 (about U.S.$2,500) were more likely to live with a deficit (Investor Education Centre, 2014). The same study employed cluster analysis to classify the respondents according to their money-management styles into five groups: money makers, conservative savers, survivors, big spenders and happy-go-lucky individuals. The big spenders group were often unable to properly manage their expenses as they had trouble controlling impulsive shopping desires and tended to seek immediate gratification through consumption. Very few respondents in this group, accounting for one-sixth of the survey sample, had savings and they did not care much to save (Investor Education Centre, 2014). The largest group was the happy-go-lucky individuals, which accounted for over one-third of the survey sample. Often affected by their peers, they tended to spend money largely in hedonistic pursuits, such as entertainment. Most of them were young (aged below 30) and from the medium income group (Investor Education Centre, 2014).

Credit Card Debt

While credit cards and personal loan products can be used to help achieve one's financial goals, excessive borrowing and poor debt management may lead to bankruptcy. A survey among young people aged 18–35 who had at least one credit card found that credit card debt problems were prevalent. On average, the respondents owned 2.5 credit cards. They spent an average of 36% of their monthly income on credit card expenses. The average respondent was in debt, and would need nineteen months to pay off all loans. The amount of debt was higher among younger respondents with low incomes than older respondents with high earnings. Altogether, 37% of the respondents had used credit card overdrafts to settle credit card bills. Furthermore, over 60% of them reported that they were unaware that they needed to pay interest rates of up to 30% upon failing to pay the credit card bills on time (Chau, 2013; *Hong Kong Economic Journal*, 2015).

Another survey found that about one in five Hong Kong people had borrowed money over the past twelve months, and that among these individuals, 20% had failed to pay their debts on time. The two most common forms of borrowing were credit card overdrafts and credit card partial repayments. The reasons reported most frequently for such behavior were entertainment and consuming favorite items (Investor Education Centre, 2014).

The aggressive marketing of credit cards to young people and college students has become controversial. Credit card companies are criticized for unethical practices that encourage young people to become overloaded with debt (Austin and Phillips, 2001). Consumers, especially young consumers, may not have the economic resources to purchase their desired products and services. As such, they may fall into debt.

High-End Consumption

The consumption environment in Hong Kong is characterized by a keen interest in high-end branded goods (Chan, 2010). Many luxury product marketers consider Hong Kong a major market in the Asia-Pacific region. Hong Kong consumers ranked among the top three luxury shoppers in the region in terms of spending power, luxury goods ownership, as well as intent to shop for luxury goods (MasterCard, 2012). There are several popular luxury brands in Hong Kong, including Hermès, Burberry, Cartier, Chanel, Dior, Louis Vuitton, Gucci and Prada.

To maintain awareness, luxury brands spend enormous sums on advertising every year. In the first six months of 2015, seven luxury brands including Hermès, Burberry, Cartier, Chanel, Christian Dior, Louis Vuitton and Prada spent a total of HK$444 million on advertising. Among them, Dior (36%) was the largest spender. The second and third largest were Chanel (24%) and Louis Vuitton (13%) (admanGo, 2015). A survey of 685 Hong Kong students aged 11–24 found that respondents endorsed materialistic values (Chan, 2010). It was found that 60% of them agreed that they would be happier if they could afford to buy more things. Nearly half of the sample agreed that their lives would be better if they owned certain things they did not then have. Yau (1988) argues that Chinese consumers are under strong pressure to meet the expectations of others or to impress others through conspicuous consumption. A content analysis of newspaper advertisements found that hedonistic ideas such as "beauty", "luxury", "prestige", "foreign", and "fun" were often portrayed in Hong Kong ads (Tse et al., 1989). Enjoyment is also the dominant value portrayed in television commercials in Hong Kong (Moon and Chan, 2005).

Advertising Personal Loans

Banks and financial institutions are keen to promote personal loans as solutions for credit card debt. For example, in the period from January to November 2015, banks and financial companies spent an average of HK$290 million per month on the promotion of personal loans. Most of these were spent on print (39%) and television (33%) (admanGo, 2015). The top three advertisers, Promise Finance, United Asia Finance and PrimeCredit (Asia), together accounted for 53% of personal loan advertising expenditure in all media. Most of these advertisements included images of adults aged 20–40, indicating that young adults were their major target.

A Semiotic Study of Personal Loan Advertisements

Originating from linguistics and literary and cultural analysis, semiotics is a qualitative research method for examining textual material by focusing on signs—more accurately, on the system of signs. Studies of signs can be traced back to such thinkers from early antiquity as Plato, Socrates and Aristotle, and were later furthered by British philosopher John Locke, whose employment of the Greek word *semeiotiké* led to the modern usage of the term semiotics, and Swiss linguist, Ferdinand de Saussure, who contributed significantly to "the science of signs" (Barnouw, 1989). French theorist, Roland Barthes, was one of the first to study advertising from a semiotic perspective (Leiss et al., 2005). Barthes (1972) is particularly well known for his examination of the ideologies that go into the process of "fixing" meaning.

Judith Williamson (1978) made great strides in "oppositional decoding" advertising. She simply defines a sign as "a thing—whether object, word, or picture—which has a particular meaning to a person or group of people". A sign within a system of meaning may be divided into two components: the

Figure 7.1

Williamson's Semiotic Analysis Formula

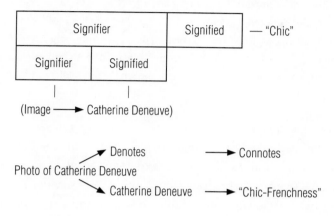

Source: Williamson (1978, p. 100).

signifier and the signified. The signifier is the material vehicle of meaning; the signified is its meaning. The signifier is its concrete dimension; the signified is its abstract side. While we can separate the two for analytical purposes, in reality they are inseparable.

The most enlightening part in Williamson's (1978) writing is her discussion of the notions of denotation and connotation. According to her, denotation is "the work of signification performed within a sign as it were: it is the process whereby a signifier 'means'—denotes—a specific signified". By connotation, she refers to "a similar process but one where the signifier is itself the denoting sign: the sign in its totality points to something else". She termed that something else a "referent system".

To illustrate her notions, Williamson (1978) took Catherine Deneuve, a French actress and fashion model as an example. As she put it, "Catherine Deneuve is signified by a photograph but 'she' in turn becomes a signifier: for wealthy—chic-Frenchness". This process of analysis can be diagramed as in Figure 7.1.

In her explanation of the above diagram, Williamson (1978) wrote,

> The signifiers of connotation . . . are made up of signs (signifiers and signifieds united) of the denoted system . . . As for the signified of connotation, its character is at once global and diffuse; it is . . . a fragment of ideology . . . These signifieds have a very close communication with culture, knowledge, history, and it is through them . . . that the environmental world invades the system. (p. 101)

It is apparent that the major strength of semiotic analysis lies in its sensitivity to the layered levels of meaning in advertisements designed for people in specific historical and cultural contexts (Leiss et al., 2005). However, "the meaning of an advertisement does not flow on the surface just waiting to be internalized by the viewer, but is built up out of the ways the different signs are organized and related to each other, both within the advertisement and through external references to wider belief systems" (Leiss et al., 2005). Leaving room for individual and impressionistic interpretations, semiotic analysis may enable researchers to "dissect and closely examine a cultural code, and its sensitivity to the nuances and oblique references in cultural systems" (Leiss et al., 2005).

A previous semiotic study of personal loan television commercials (Chan and Cheng, 2009) found that the advertisers advocated personal loans as quick, care-free solutions to solve credit card debts. These commercials tend to trivialize credit card debt, portraying it as a common phenomenon of everyday life. The advertisements also suggested that getting help from financial institutions was a more effective method than soliciting help from family members or friends.

In this chapter, Williamson's formula will be applied in our semiotic analysis of personal loan television commercials. A semiotic analysis was conducted on three selected television commercials for personal loans aired in Hong Kong. All three advertisements encouraged audiences to borrow money from the advertiser to pay off credit card debts. All three advertisements were broadcast on prime-time evening programs on free-to-air Chinese television channels in 2014 and 2015. These commercials were chosen as they have different target markets. As mentioned earlier in this chapter, the major strength of semiotic analysis lies in its sensitivity "to the different, layered levels of meaning in advertising—considered as a text designed to be read by people in specific historical and cultural contexts" (Leiss et al., 2005). This strength allows us to pursue in-depth examinations of these advertisements.

Television Commercial A (Couple Relaxing at a Seaside Resort)

The first television commercial chosen for our study was a thirty-second spot launched by UA Finance in March 2015 (UA Finance, 2015b). The commercial opened with a shot of a young couple lying down, wearing face masks in a seaside resort with no other guests in sight. Over the background music mixed with birdsong, and the sounds of the wind and waves, a resort employee could be heard asking the couple if they were interested in subscribing to the VIP program. The female customer appeared interested, but forlornly told her husband that they'd already exhausted their resources on their wedding. "Don't worry", replied the husband, "we just need to make a call". This was followed by a close-up of the hotline number. A woman in UA uniform then appeared and outlined the benefits of the UA No Show personal loan hotline, mainly its streamlined loan application process; animated subtitles popped up in sync with her sales pitch. In the next scene the happy couple was now walking away from the resort, as the husband said: "What a shame there was no chance to show them your pretty face". The advertisement closed with UA's logo, the No Show loan hotline number, the moneylender's web address, its license number, and the slogan, "Yes, UA".

In this commercial, the resort facilities serve as signifiers, and the hefty expenses of the resort are the signified. The calm opulence of the leisure resort environment and the friendliness of the resort employee imply the luxury, exclusivity and professionalism of the service. The wife's words, tone and expression all denote the couple's dismay at their lack of resources in the wake of their wedding and honeymoon. To mitigate this scarcity, the couple's response is to borrow money to satisfy their immediate want. Since most loan applications are complicated and time-consuming, and given the immediate nature of the couple's monetary want, an especially quick and convenient way to borrow money is required. This is also implied by the location of the resort, which appears secluded and removed from any bank or financial service company. The commercial then provides the solution of calling the

UA No Show hotline. The signifier is the action of dialing the hotline, and the signified is UA's professional and prompt service. The next scene shows the satisfied couple leaving the resort. Their smiling faces signify the effectiveness of the hotline in solving their problem. Additionally, the name "No Show" also counts as a signifier, indicating the convenience of the advertised loan application procedure.

In Hong Kong, young couples often spend lavishly on weddings and honeymoons. Thus the couple's financial situation in the commercial is one that people can easily relate to. A second feature of the commercial is that it uses VIP status to coax the couple into spending more money than they have currently available. Many services classify customers according to their cumulative spending; those reaching certain thresholds are granted VIP status with special privileges or benefits. Such status signifies superior social standing beyond the walls of the facility providing the status, increasing the desirability of attaining the necessary level of expenditure.

Television Commercial B (Two Men Playing Videogames)

The second television advertisement was a thirty-second commercial launched by UA Finance in April 2015 (UA Finance, 2015c). In the sitting room of a house in a private housing estate, two young men were playing video games. One of them said: "You play a stingy game".

"Yes, I've got to be stingy these days", answered the other.

"If you need money, go get a loan", the first man urged.

"It would be great if we could apply for a loan at home", his friend replied. The entire conversation was underscored by tense background music and the sound effects from the video game. Just as their conversation ended, an airship with the UA logo appeared and flew into the estate, stopping at the two men's balcony. The airship used a giant mobile phone as a gondola for passengers, and two young ladies in UA uniforms appeared on it in a flash of light. At this moment, the men looked at each other with shocked expressions. The commercial proceeded to show a close-up of the two young ladies walking down the steps of the airship, approaching the two young men. One UA employee said sweetly: "No problem. You can make a call to the UA No Show

Personal Loan Hotline anytime, anywhere". One young man smiled, picked up his phone, and dialled the hotline number right away. A close-up shot showed the hotline number on his phone. The other UA employee explained the details of the loan application—that it did not require customers to show up in person or provide any documentation. "You can borrow money easily by making a call. It doesn't interrupt what you're doing and it saves you a lot of time", the first added. The frame returned to the young men exchanging excited looks, implying the success of the hotline in meeting their needs. This implication was reinforced by the television screen on which the young men were gaming displaying the word "win". The next shot showed the young men standing on the balcony and watching the UA airship leave, with smiles on their faces. The advertisement closed as in the previous commercial.

In this commercial, the signifier is the portrayal of the young men playing video games, and the signified is that they are playing a game at home rather than going out because either they cannot afford to, or because they prefer to stay at home. The UA airship is also a signifier, indicating the sophisticated and quick response offered by the loan service. The appearance of the airship stopping outside the balcony indicates that customers can take advantage of UA's offer without leaving their homes. The professional outfits of the UA personnel are signifiers of professionalism and credibility. Their friendly presentation about loan applications shows that their service is consumer-oriented. Also, the use of a mobile phone as the airship's gondola underlines the need for nothing more than a mobile phone to apply for UA's No Show loans.

The word "win" displayed on the television is another signifier, this one of the effectiveness of UA's loan in dealing with financial troubles. It indicates that people win when they take advantage of the offer. The setting of the advertisement emphasizes the convenience of the No Show offer, it implies that people can take advantage of the offer from the comfort of their homes.

Television Commercial C (Young Lady Shopping)

The third commercial advertisement was a thirty-second spot, which was launched by UA Finance in April 2015 (UA Finance, 2015a). The advertisement opened with a shot of the Arc de Triomphe in France, with relaxing music playing in the background. A fashionable young lady walked along a street with a happy face, arms laden with shopping bags. Spotting a silver purse in a shop window, her expression became downcast and she voiced aloud her regret that she could not buy the purse because of all her credit card debt. An airship with the UA logo appeared then, with a massive shopping bag as a gondola, and landed in a square in front of the shopper. Two young ladies in UA uniforms welcomed the shopper aboard, inviting her to borrow from UA. The customer boarded without hesitation, and seated herself on a luxurious sofa as the airship passed by the Eiffel Tower. One employee said "Pay for the principal, save lots of interest and enjoy flexible repayment terms. Without credit card debts, you could go shopping around the world!" As she spoke, billboards visible from the airship displayed her messages, and at one point the customer swept a pile of credit card receipts off a table. The scene changed to show the customer making luxury purchases in different shopping venues. "I can buy all goods I like", she said in a cheerful tone as she tried on shoes, jewelry and dresses, accompanied by upbeat background music. Finally, she watched the UA airship pass by overhead in a shopping street in Japan. The airship flew over this contemporary city night scene with the narration, "Enjoy an even more wonderful life!" The commercial had the same closing as the others.

In this commercial, shopping areas in different countries serve as signifiers, and a luxurious lifestyle as the signified. The items purchased also signify a luxurious lifestyle. The many shopping bags carried by the main character and the spacious retail setting indicate that the woman enjoys shopping in high-end shopping centers. The appearance of a UA airship landing in front of the young lady is another signifier, which signifies the possibility of a timely solution to debt. Again, the professional outfits of the UA personnel signify professional, competent and credible services. The positioning of the UA personnel sitting beside the young woman communicates their friendly service, implying that the woman is more than just a customer to them. The pile of credit card payment slips signify the unpaid credit card debt. Moreover, the act of sweeping away these receipts is also a signifier, indicating the simple solution provided by UA. The closing shots of Tokyo and Paris at night signify that the woman continues her shopping day and night. The foreign places shown—Paris, London, Milan and Tokyo—are themselves signifiers for fashion centers in general: the message is that if UA can help this woman fulfill her shopping desires abroad, they can help you fulfill yours here in Hong Kong, too.

Although Hong Kong is renowned as a shopper's haven, some people are not satisfied to shop locally, aspiring instead to sate their demands in such global fashion centers as western Europe and Japan. One study found that Hong Kong consumers ranked top in international leisure travel among consumers in seventeen surveyed countries in Asia Pacific, with 85% of respondents having traveled abroad for leisure in the previous twelve months. The same study found that Hong Kong consumers had a keen interest in luxury shopping, with intentions to buy designer clothes, leather goods, jewelry, designer accessories and shoes (MasterCard, 2015). A study among young female consumers found that consumption of luxury fashion brands was motivated by such brands' ability to communicate social status. The experience of guilt from overspending on such purchases was alleviated by the rationalization of high quality and long usage (Wu et al., 2015).

Why do Hong Kong consumers want to shop overseas? One reason is the strength of the Hong Kong dollar when compared with the Japanese yen and the Euro in recent years. Another reason is that incoming Chinese consumers seeking luxury products in Hong Kong have created a less comfortable shopping environment for Hong Kong consumers. Furthermore, luxurious brands are less likely to cut their prices because of the increased demand for their products. So, Hong Kong consumers seek better deals overseas. Furthermore, Hong Kong consumers are often attracted by newly released luxury products which tend to be available only in certain areas outside Hong Kong. Nowadays, nearly all major Hong Kong-issued credit cards are accepted globally, making it possible for Hong Kong consumers to shop in more countries.

Conclusion

The three television advertisements selected for the study shared three features. First, each of them highlighted the accessibility of the advertised service. In the first two commercials, the advertising copy and the product name "No Show" emphasized that customers do not need to be physically present at the financial services provider's premises to take advantage of their services, nor do they need to present documentation or fill in any application forms. Loans were depicted as being just one call away. The commercials also show that the hotline operates seven days a week, nine hours a day. Even though the third commercial did not mention the ease of applying for a loan, it was clearly implied by the proactive role of the sales representatives. In Hong Kong, the personal identity card is the official document for all major civic and consumption activities such as voting and subscription to utilities and phone services. Banking services often require a personal identity card as well as filled-in forms for credit card applications or opening a bank account. By removing the need for ID cards and application forms, the advertisements demonstrate that getting a personal loan is extremely easy.

Second, all three commercials implied that debt problems are trivial and universal. Unlike the credit loan advertisements analyzed in a previous study (Chan and Cheng, 2009) which portrayed debts as dangerous, troublesome and burdensome, the commercials examined in the current chapter suggested that debt problems are merely a nuisance in one's daily life. None of these three commercials portrayed debts as serious or urgent. In the first commercial, the young wife briefly mentioned that they had spent a lot on their wedding, possibly implying that they were already in debt. However, instead of trying to repay the debt, the husband shrugged off the problem. His only concern was how to get more money for immediate consumption. In the second commercial, the indebted circumstances of the characters were implied by the need to be "stingy". In the third commercial, the debt problem was illustrated by the pile of credit card payment slips that the female shopper swept away. The only reason debt was considered a problem was because it prevented her from buying her desired accessories immediately. The deliberate downplaying of the seriousness of the debt problem was demonstrated in the commercials through the lack of verbal or visual emphasis.

Third, the three commercials were highly targeted in terms of demographics, psychographics as well as behavioral profiles. The first commercial targeted newly married couples. The second commercial employed videogames as a platform to connect with young male consumers. The third commercial targeted young female shoppers with a keen interest in high fashion and jewelry. The reasons for acquiring a personal loan in the first and the third commercials were for enjoying a spa at a luxurious venue and purchasing accessories. It was consistent with the survey findings that buying preferred items and paying for entertainment were the top two reasons for borrowing among Hong Kong consumers (Investor Education Centre, 2014). Marriage is a life-changing event and often celebrated with high levels of expenditure on things like banquets, photography and videography, honeymoons and jewelry. A survey found that on average a Hong Kong couple spends U.S.$40,000 (about HK$311,850) on a wedding, about one third more than the average wedding expenses of American couples (Yuan, 2015).

The second commercial featured two young men, who expressed a wish to get a loan from the comfort of their home rather than physically going to a financial institution. The third commercial featured a young female who was interested in shopping around the globe. With improvements in education and job opportunities, women in Hong Kong are more financially confident than women in many other countries, as a global study revealed (Chiu, 2014). Due to the strong U.S. currency, which the Hong Kong dollar is tied to, in recent years, Hong Kong dollars are worth more than before when converted to Japanese yen and euro. As a result, Hong Kong consumers are attracted to the low prices of the products sold in Japan and Europe. Shoppers visit these countries in order to take advantage of the strong Hong Kong currency, and in the hope of purchasing the latest luxury brand products. These three highly targeted commercials reflect that the personal loan market is divided into narrowly defined consumer groups.

To conclude, this study illustrates that semiotic analysis enables researchers to investigate the deep meanings in advertising messages. This study also demonstrates that advertising messages are constructed based on a thorough understanding of the social and psychological needs of different target markets. Characters and settings are carefully designed to resonate with specific target groups in order to create a bond and exert influence

References

admanGo (2015), "Advertising expenditure by product category and by brand", available at: www.admanGo.com (accessed October 28, 2015).

Austin, M.J. and Phillips, M.R. (2001). "Educating students: An ethics responsibility of credit card companies", *Journal of Services Marketing*, Vol. 15 No. 7, pp. 516–528.

Barnouw, E. (1989), *International Encyclopedia of Communications*. Oxford University Press, New York.

Barthes, R. (1972), *Mythologies*, trans. A. Lavers. Noonday Press, New York.

Belch, G.E., Belch, M.A., Kerr, G. and Powell, I. (2014), *Advertising: An Integrated Marketing Communication Perspective*. 3rd edn. McGraw-Hill Education, New South Wales.

Chan, K. (2010), *Youth and Consumption*. City University of Hong Kong Press, Hong Kong.

Chan, K. and Cheng, H. (2009). "Materialism and consumer socialization: A semiotic analysis of personal loan advertisements", *Communicative Business*, No. 1, pp. 60–79.

Chau, G. (2013), "Cash advances going toward credit card bills", *Hong Kong Standard*, October 9, available at: http://www.thestandard.com.hk/section-news. php?id=138336&story_id=40580243&d_str=20131009 (accessed on December 25, 2015).

Chiu, K. (2014), "Women come on strong about handling money", *Hong Kong Standard*, March 6, available at: http://www.thestandard.com.hk/section-news. php?id=143189&story_id=41739701&d_str=20140306 (accessed on December 24, 2015).

Hong Kong Economic Journal (2015), "Young Hongkongers under a pile of credit card debt, says survey", October 14, available at: http://www.ejinsight.com/20151014-young-hongkongers-under-a-pile-of-credit-card-debt-says-survey/ (accessed on December 24, 2015).

Investor Education Centre (2014), "IEC research: Knowledge, attitude and behaviour toward money and debt management", available at: http://www.hkiec.hk/web/en/tools-and-resources/research/money-management-2014.html (accessed on December 25, 2015).

Leiss, W., Kline, S., Jhally, S. and Botterill, J. (2005), *Social Communication in Advertising: Consumption in the Mediated Marketplace*. 3rd edn. Routledge, New York.

MasterCard (2012), "Hongkongers most optimistic about luxury spending in Asia/Pacific region", November 14, available at: https://www.mastercard.com/hk/consumer/_assets/press-center/HK_CPP_Luxury_Shopping_E_Final_wshk.pdf (accessed on December 29, 2015).

MasterCard (2015), "Going global: Hongkongers remain Asia Pacific's top international tourists, MasterCard survey reveals", September 24, available at: https://www.mastercard.com/hk/consumer/_assets/press-center/HK-MasterCard%20Survey%20on%20Consumer%20Purchasing%20Priorities_H1%202015_Eng_wshk_....pdf (accessed on January 20, 2016).

Moon, Y.S. and Chan, K. (2005), "Advertising appeals and cultural values in television commercials: A comparison of Hong Kong and Korea", *International Marketing Review*, Vol. 22 No. 1, pp. 48–66.

Tse, D.K., Belk, R.W. and Zhou, N. (1989), "Becoming a consumer society: A longitudinal and cross-cultural content analysis of print ads from Hong Kong, the People's Republic of China, and Taiwan", *Journal of Consumer Research*, Vol. 15 No. 4, pp. 457–472.

UA Finance (2015a), "UA Finance 亞洲聯合財務「咭數一筆清」貸款 [UA Finance Debts Consolidation Loans], online video, available at: https://www.youtube.com/watch?v=bry5Re_3_NI (accessed on January 20, 2016).

UA Finance (2015b), "UA Finance 亞洲聯合財務「No Show」私人貸款 - O2O「悠閒度假」篇" [UA Finance "No Show" Personal Loans — an O2O leisurely holiday], online video, available at: https://www.youtube.com/watch?v=gh4f8lPAT4U (accessed on January 20, 2016).

UA Finance (2015c), "UA Finance 亞洲聯合財務「No Show」私人貸款 - 「年青人」篇" [UA Finance "No Show" Personal Loans — young people], online video, available at: https://www.youtube.com/watch?v=9oaZSlA1f4I (accessed on January 20, 2016).

Williamson, J. (1978), *Decoding Advertisements: Ideology and Meaning in Advertising*. Marion Boyars, London.

Wu, M.S., Chaney, I., Chen, C.S. , Nguyen, B., Melewar, T.C. (2015) "Luxury fashion brands: Factors influencing young female consumers' luxury fashion purchasing in Taiwan", *Qualitative Market Research*, Vol. 18 No. 3, pp. 298–319.

Yau, O.H.M. (1988), "Chinese cultural values: Their dimensions and marketing implications", *European Journal of Marketing*, Vol. 22 No. 5, pp. 44–57.

Yuan, M. (2015), "Spending on weddings reach record high in Hong Kong", *Forbes*, March 30, available at: http://www.forbes.com/sites/myuan/2015/03/30/spending-on-weddings-reach-record-high-in-hong-kong/ (accessed on December 27, 2015).

Chapter 8

Gender Portrayal in Advertising

Kara Chan and Yolanda Cheng

Introduction

As reported in Chapter 5, Hong Kong people often find advertisements with sexual content and sexual connotations offensive. That women are portrayed as sex objects is one of the frequent complaints made against advertisements in Hong Kong. A Japanese restaurant using sexual appeal to sell its children's menu received many complaints. The Communications Authority issued a warning for its inappropriate sexual connotations (Chan et al, 2012). The public and especially parents are concerned about the use of sexual images in advertising and its impact on children.

Advertising contains a range of images of women taking on different roles and shown in different settings. These images, regardless of their commercial nature, can be seen as representative of existing social values. This chapter explores the concept of gender stereotyping and how it can be measured. It discusses how the political, social and economic circumstances of a society influence gender roles as depicted in advertisements. It also reports on a recent study of female images in a popular magazine in Hong Kong, and discusses the potential impact of media on gender roles in a society.

Ways of Measuring Gender Stereotypes

The term "gender stereotypes" refers to the "relatively fixed and overgeneralized attitudes and behavior that are considered normal and appropriate for a person in a particular culture based on his or her biological sex" (Psychology Dictionary, n.d.).

Gender stereotypes have often been used by advertisers as a communication strategy to establish a shared experience of identification with consumers (Hovland et al., 2005). These stereotypes often include the portrayal of young and physically appealing women, as well as the portrayal of women in decorative roles or as sex objects.

In measuring gender stereotypes, the research focus has been on the roles, activities, settings, benefits and the types of products related to a particular gender. Another feature of interest is whether a member of a particular gender is present or absent in the advertisements. For example, alcohol advertisements are found to often show men only.

The following questions are often asked about advertising:

- presence
    - how often do females or males appear in the ad?
    - how often do females or males speak about the product as a narrator, or as a voice-over?

- roles
    - do the females or males engage in economic activities?
    - are the females or males depicted as authoritative?
    - are the females or males depicted in domestic or non-domestic settings?
    - what are the products that females or males endorse?

- benefits
    - how does the consumer benefit from using the product?

- demographic profile
    - what are the ages of the females or males?
    - are they physically attractive?

One of the ways to measure gender stereotyping is through a systematic analysis of advertisement contents. This technique is called content analysis. In conducting content analysis, a researcher will select an appropriate sample of advertisements from a selected medium (e.g. television commercials or newspaper advertisements), construct the categories of content, establish a coding system, code the content according to the established definitions, analyze the data and draw conclusions (Wimmer and Dominick, 2006).

Research Findings in the Past

Over the past decades, content analyses of television programs, television commercials and print advertisements have found that women are under-represented and portrayed in stereotyped roles (Cheng, 1997; Courtney and Whipple, 1983; Furnham et al., 2000; Furnham and Paltzer, 2010). In a review of fourteen studies in eleven countries over twenty-five years (1975-1999) regarding gender stereotyping in television commercials, Furnham and Mak (1999) found that certain stereotypes remained consistent across different cultures:

- women are frequently shown as product users, whereas men are frequently shown as authoritative central figures;

- women are often shown in dependent roles, whereas men often play the autonomous roles such as narrators and professionals;

- when commercials include end comments, they are more often offered by men;

- women are more often portrayed at home while men are more often portrayed in outdoor settings;

- women are frequently associated with home and personal care products, while men are frequently associated with automobiles and sports products;

- women are more likely to be associated with social approval and self-enhancement, while men are shown to be associated with pleasurable rewards; and

- consistently the women shown are younger than the men.

Furnham and Paltzer (2010) reviewed thirty content analysis studies in over twenty countries since 2000 and found similar patterns of gender stereotypes.

Research on advertising and women's beauty focuses on the overall beauty and body image of the female characters in the advertisements (Frith et al., 2004). Regarding portrayals of beauty, Englis et al. (1994) found that classic feminine, sex kitten and trendy were the three most prevalent beauty types in U.S. magazine advertisements. A study of female images in magazine advertisements in Singapore, Taiwan and the United States found that Western models are more often depicted as the sex kitten, while Asian models are more often shown as the classic beauty type (Frith et al., 2004). Scholars argue that female roles and beauty types are created by social norms and cultural perspectives. They are also integral to the audience's formation of their self-image (Fung, 2002; Solomon et al., 1992).

Gender Stereotyping in Advertising in Hong Kong

In the 1990s, many feminist groups and scholars initiated studies of women and the media. Wu (1995) found that nearly half of the television commercials sampled contained contents promoting gender inequality or gender stereotypes. Siu (1996) found that men were more likely to be portrayed as product authorities and women were more likely to be portrayed as product users in television commercials. Chau (1997) found that female characters in youth magazines were more likely to be featured in a domestic setting, as wives or mothers, and featured in passive roles. Female characters also appeared as professionals less frequently than male characters.

Similarly, men are more frequently depicted as central figures and authoritative endorsers and more often they provide voice-overs in television commercials (Furham et al., 2000). A qualitative study of toy commercials found that boys expressed aggressiveness through adventures and challenges while girls expressed femininity through housework and a concern with beauty (Wong, 1997).

Culture and Gender Portrayal

Williams and Best (1990) proposed the model of traditional versus egalitarian gender role ideologies to differentiate cultures according to their degree of endorsement of traditional gender norms. Traditional role ideology views men as superior to women, and egalitarian role ideology considers men and women as equals (Williams and Best, 1990). Because men and women are seen as equals, egalitarian role ideology prescribes that males and females will have less role differentiation in society. On the other hand, traditional role ideology expects males and females to take on different roles in society. The dominant gender role ideology in a society will affect how men and women are portrayed in that society's media, including in advertising messages.

While advertising is affected by the dominant gender role ideology, it is not completely determined by it. On the one hand, advertising provides images and language that are relevant to target audiences while keeping pace with cultural, economic and social changes (Zhang et al., 2009). On the other hand, advertising is often a "distorted mirror" (Pollay, 1986) that neglects the cultural values upheld by society at the discretion of advertisers. For example, even though traditional Confucian values endorse virtues such as humility, patience and thrift, these values seldom occur in Chinese television advertisements (Zhang et al., 2008). Williams and Best (1990) conclude that egalitarian gender ideologies are preferred in countries with relatively high social economical development, a high proportion of Protestant Christians, a low proportion of Muslims, a high proportion of working women, a high proportion of women enrolled in universities and a greater degree of individualism. It was also found that male respondents showed a stronger preference for traditional gender roles, while female respondents displayed a stronger preference for egalitarian gender roles (Williams and Best, 1990).

Gender Situation in Hong Kong

Because of improvements in education, economic development and the influence of the Western feminist movement, the status of women in Hong Kong has achieved significant improvements in the last two decades (Lee and Collins, 2008). In terms of socioeconomic development and availability of education for women, Hong Kong is on a par with many Western societies. The proportion of Christians (including Catholics) are higher than the proportion of Muslims in Hong Kong society (12% and 4% respectively) (Information Services Department, 2014). These facts imply that egalitarian roles are more likely to be embraced. As a former British colony, Hong Kong has laws protecting women from gender bias in terms of education, employment and pay packages (Chan, 2000). As of 2008, Hong Kong provides twelve years of free education to all children, both males and females. (Previously, nine years of free education was provided.) The proportion of females with post-secondary education is 26%, which is slightly lower than the 32% among males (Census and Statistics Department, 2014). The female labor participation rate for Hong Kong is 51% (Census and Statistics Department, 2014), which is lower than the female labor participation rate of 56% in the United States (U.S. Bureau of Labor Statistics, 2009). A higher female labor participation rate is usually associated with more gender equality, as more females are able to support themselves financially. The Hong Kong government takes an active role in promoting gender equality. The Equal Opportunities Commission was established in 1996 and introduced the Sex Discrimination Ordinance, and the Women's Commission was set up in 2001 to promote the well-being and interests of women in Hong Kong (Lee and Collins, 2008).

Despite economic development and improvements in the social status of women, many argue that there is still gender inequality in society. This is seen in the discouragement of meaningful deconstruction of media ideologies as well as discussion of gender from a feminist point of view (Lee and Fung, 2009). Hong Kong is influenced by the Chinese patriarchal culture that discourages gender equality. The traditional Chinese female ideal is obedient and respects and maintains the patriarchal hierarchy within the kinship system (Croll, 1995). Chinese tradition favors males, as they are responsible for passing down family names, and Chinese culture accords greater esteem, privileges and status to males while restraining the roles of women. Chinese women are expected to submit their individuality to their families, obeying their fathers when young, their husbands when married, and their sons when widowed. The virtues of a Chinese woman are defined by her role as wife and mother (Cheung, 1996). Leadership was a problem for women in Hong Kong as women made up only 16% of the 2012–16 members of the Legislative

Council and women are under-represented at senior levels in corporations across many professions and industries. (The Women's Foundation, 2006). A survey of 1,530 Hong Kong people found that gender stereotyping was prevalent (Women's Commission, 2009). About half of the respondents answered that women should focus more on families than on careers, while about a third believed that men know more about politics than women. About 17% reported that women were less able to make major decisions than men. Regarding community participation, about 8% answered that Hong Kong society does not need more women to serve as organization or community leaders. Altogether 25% said women should not work in jobs traditionally handled by men. The findings indicated that the concept of women working at home while men work outside is deeply rooted in society (Women's Commission, 2009). Fung and Ma (2000) argued that this deep-seated notion has been cultivated through families, the education system and society.

A Study of Female Images in Magazines

A quantitative content analysis study of advertisements in a popular lifestyle magazine in Hong Kong was conducted. Its objectives were:

- to examine beauty types and occupational roles of female figures portrayed in magazine advertisements;

- to compare and contrast portrayals of Chinese and Caucasian females in magazine advertisements; and

- to explore differences in portrayals of beauty and occupational roles of advertisements targeting females and advertisements targeting both genders.

Next Magazine, the second most popular lifestyle magazine in Hong Kong based on readership, was selected for the study. *Next Magazine* has been published weekly since 1990, and its readership in 2011 was 736,000 (The Nielsen Company, 2011). Altogether six issues of *Next Magazine* from July 2008 to May 2009 were selected by a systematic process.

Each individual advertisement that took up at least one full page and contained at least one dominant female image was treated as one unit of

Table 8.1

Breakdown of Advertisements by Product Category

Product category	Sample profile (N=215)	
	Freq.	%
Cosmetics, skincare and personal care	65	30.2
Beauty slimming treatment/service	39	18.1
Women's clothing and accessories	37	17.2
Retail, services and others	31	14.4
Food and medicine	26	12.1
Furniture, home appliances and electronics	17	7.9
Products targeting women	141	65.6
Products targeting men and women	74	34.4

analysis. Advertisements without a dominant female figure were excluded from the sample. The most prominent female figure visually in the advertisement was selected for coding. The beauty type, occupational role and race of the female figures were coded according to the operational definitions shown in Appendix 1. The coding frame of Frith et al.'s (2004) study was adopted.

The sample consisted of 215 advertisements. Table 8.1 shows the sample profile. Cosmetics, skincare, perfume, contact lenses and personal care advertisements made up 30% of the sample; beauty and slimming treatment services composed 18%; and women's clothing and accessories contributed 17%. These three product categories accounted for about two-thirds of the advertisements, and were classified as product categories targeting women. The remaining one-third of the advertisements involved retail, services, food, medicine, furniture, home appliances and electronic products. We classified them as product categories targeting both genders.

Altogether 141 of the advertisements (65%) depicted Chinese women, while sixty-six advertisements (31%) depicted Caucasian women. The remaining eight advertisements (4%) depicted central female figures from other races;

Table 8.2

Portrayal of Beauty Type by Race of Female Figure

Beauty type	Chinese		Caucasian		Total	
	Freq.	%	Freq.	%	Freq.	%
Classic feminine	98	69.5	37	56.1	135	65.2
Sex kitten	19	13.5	7	10.6	26	12.6
Casual	16	11.3	3	4.5	19	9.2
Cute	6	4.3	4	6.1	10	4.8
Trendy	1	0.7	13	19.7	14	6.8
Others	1	0.7	2	3.0	3	1.4

Chi-square=29.7 ($p<0.001$); expected frequencies for four cells were less than 5.

Note: The eight ads featuring non-Chinese and non-Caucasian female figures were excluded from Tables 8.2, 8.3 and 8.4.

these advertisements were excluded in the subsequent analysis because they were too few.

Portrayals of Beauty among Chinese and Caucasian Females

Table 8.2 shows the portrayal of beauty by race for the 207 advertisements featuring either Chinese or Caucasian women. The beauty type most frequently used was classic feminine. Of the 207 advertisements, 135 (65%) used the classic feminine beauty type. The sex kitten and casual beauty types contributed another 13% and 9% respectively. The remaining advertisements used trendy, cute or other beauty types. The races of women in the advertisements were associated with certain beauty types. Chinese models were more often portrayed as a classic feminine beauty, while Caucasian models were more often portrayed as the trendy beauty type. The proportion of Chinese models in the casual beauty type (11.3%) was more than twice that of Caucasian models (4.3%). Nearly equal proportions of Chinese and Caucasian figures were portrayed as the sex kitten (13.5% vs. 10.6%) and cute types (4.3% vs. 6.1%).

The prevalence of the classic feminine beauty type in the advertisements demonstrates the advertisers' intentions to adopt a conservative approach to appeal to their adult audience. Readers of *Next Magazine* are predominantly females aged between 25 and 54 (The Nielsen Company, 2009). The dominance of the classic feminine beauty type (rather than the dominance of the casual beauty type) may suggest to the audience that a woman's physical appearance is more important than her ability or talents. The dominance of the classic beauty type resembled findings from a study of female figures from magazine advertisements in Singapore, Taiwan and the U.S. (Frith et al., 2004; Lin and Yeh, 2009). The tendency to portray women across cultures in the classic beauty type supports the theory that certain aspects of beauty are universal and shared by Eastern and Western cultures.

Caucasian female models were more often featured in the trendy beauty type than Chinese female models (19.7% vs. 0.7%). This finding supports the theory that Western concepts of beauty are linked with trendiness and modernity (Frith et al., 2004). Also, Caucasian female models and Chinese female models were equally likely to be featured as a sex kitten. This finding contradicts the theory that advertisers across cultures present Caucasian female models as more sexually liberal than Asian female models (Frith et al, 2004). This suggests that the portrayal of Chinese female figures as sex kittens is considered acceptable in Hong Kong. The occurrence of the cute beauty type in Hong Kong was lower than that in Singapore, Taiwan and the U.S. It was proposed that depicting women in a childish manner diminishes their standing in society as fully-fledged adults who may be threatening to men (Frith et al., 2004). The lower use of the cute beauty type in the advertisements may again be attributed to the mature readership profile of the magazine.

Occupational Roles of Chinese and Caucasian Females

Table 8.3 shows the portrayal of occupational roles by race of female figures. Female figures were most often featured in a decorative role (56%) and as celebrities (31%). Only two females were featured as housewives. Female figures were seldom featured in professional roles or in recreational roles. Also, the race of female figures was associated with the portrayal of occupational roles. Caucasian models were more likely to be featured in

Table 8.3
Portrayal of Occupational Role by Race of Female Figure

Occupational role	Chinese		Caucasian		Total	
	Freq.	%	Freq.	%	Freq.	%
Decorative	68	48.2	47	71.2	115	55.6
Celebrity	56	39.7	9	13.6	65	31.4
Recreational	7	5.0	9	13.6	16	7.7
Professional	8	5.7	1	1.5	9	4.3
Housewife	2	1.4	0	0.0	2	1.0

Chi-square=21.1 (p<0.001); expected frequencies for three cells were less than 5.

decorative roles, while Chinese models were more likely to be featured in celebrity as well as recreational roles. None of the sampled advertisements showed Caucasian models as housewives.

The two dominant female roles in magazine advertisements were decorative and as celebrities. Almost 90% of the advertisements sampled used these roles. Women were seldom shown in recreational roles, professional roles or as housewives. Despite the fact that over half of Hong Kong's female population participates in the workforce, less than 5% of female figures in magazine advertisements were shown in professional roles. The lack of female figures depicted in professional roles shows that most advertisers neglected opportunities of relating to female consumers.

Despite the fact that only 5% of the Hong Kong population is non-Chinese, the sample revealed an over-representation of Caucasian female models. This result resembled a study of magazine advertisements in mainland China that indicated that nearly 60% of the female models were non-Asian. Non-Asian models were most frequently portrayed in sophisticated urban images and were used predominantly by global brands (Hung et al., 2007). Caucasian female models are employed to represent a modern lifestyle, Western taste and high living. This indicates that Hong Kong society tends to think highly of foreign models and Western beauty trends.

Table 8.4

Product Categories by Race of Female Figure

Product category	Chinese		Caucasian		Total	
	Freq.	%	Freq.	%	Freq.	%
Cosmetics, skincare and personal care	41	29.1	22	33.3	63	30.4
Beauty slimming treatment/service	35	24.8	4	6.1	39	18.4
Clothing and accessories	13	9.2	23	34.8	36	17.4
Retail and services	18	12.8	9	13.6	27	13.0
Food and medicine	24	17.0	2	3.0	26	12.6
Furniture, home appliances and electronics	10	7.1	6	9.1	16	7.7

Chi-square=32.9 (p<0.001).

The use of Caucasian female models in Chinese Hong Kong culture can also be linked to the cultural interpretation of color (Fung, 2006). Traditional Chinese women believe the Chinese axiom that "fairness is able to cover up a lot of ugliness" (Fung, 2006). Hong Kong females believe that a white skin color is an important goal which will have a positive effect on their lives. Interviewees expressed their desire to stay competitive when compared in terms of beauty to other women in beauty (Mak, 2007). The adoration of a modern Western lifestyle and a cultural belief in whiteness as beauty contribute to the dominance of Caucasian female models in Hong Kong.

Table 8.4 shows the product categories by race of female figures. According to the table, correlations exist between race and product categories. Chinese models were more likely to be used to advertise beauty and slimming services as well as food and medicine, and Caucasian models were more likely to feature in clothing and accessories advertisements.

It appears that advertisements for slimming services tend to employ local celebrities with whom the target audience is familiar. Previous findings suggested that Western female models are more likely to be linked to body

Table 8.5

Portrayal of Beauty Types by Product Target

Beauty type	Products for F		Products for M/F		Total	
	Freq.	%	Freq.	%	Freq.	%
Classic feminine	91	64.5	50	67.6	141	65.6
Sex kitten	24	17.0	2	2.7	26	12.1
Casual	4	2.8	15	20.3	19	8.8
Cute	6	4.3	4	5.4	10	4.7
Trendy	13	9.2	3	4.1	16	7.4
Others	3	2.1	0	0.0	3	1.4

Chi-square=28.4 (p<0.001); expected frequencies for three cells were less than 5.

Table 8.6

Portrayal of Occupational Roles by Product Target

Occupational role	Products for F		Products for M/F		Total	
	Freq.	%	Freq.	%	Freq.	%
Decorative	94	66.7	24	32.4	118	54.9
Celebrity	40	28.4	26	35.1	66	30.7
Recreational	2	1.4	14	18.9	16	7.4
Professional	5	3.5	8	10.8	13	6.0
Housewife	0	0.0	2	2.7	2	0.9

Chi-square=39.1 (p<0.001); expected frequencies for three cells were less than 5.

beauty while Asian models are more likely to be linked to facial beauty (Frith et al., 2004). The current study provides a different pattern. In the current study, Caucasian female models were found to be used to advertise facial beauty in the same numbers as Chinese female models. However, Chinese female models were more likely to be used in body-improving products such as slimming services, while Caucasian female models were more likely to be used in body-enhancing beauty products such as clothing.

Tables 8.5 and 8.6 show the beauty types and occupational roles by target group of the advertisements. Both beauty types and occupational roles were associated with target groups for certain products. Advertisements of products for women were more likely to feature the sex kitten beauty type, while advertisements of products for both genders were more likely to feature the casual beauty type. Advertisements of products for women were more likely to portray women in decorative roles, while advertisements of products for both genders were more likely to depict women in recreational and professional roles.

Impact of Images Featuring Female Stereotypes on Audiences

How does the audience respond to the different types of female images in advertisements? Many researchers have argued that these stereotyped portrayals of men and women on television and in print media can convey messages and beliefs about gender roles. Our study found that advertisements for products targeting women portray women in predominantly decorative roles and as sex kittens. The high percentage of female figures portrayed as sex kittens in these advertisements may communicate to women that they need to be sexy in order to gain admiration from males. The cultivation theory proposes that heavy television viewers are more likely to perceive media portrayals as reality (Gerbner et al., 2002). A study conducted by the Equal Opportunities Commission found that children in Hong Kong are profoundly influenced by gender stereotypes, affecting choices from selection of school subjects to career aspirations (Equal Opportunities Commission, 2000). Other studies indicated that reading women's magazines and watching television correlated with respondents' dissatisfaction with their bodies (Prendergast and Leung, 1999). Women often referred to popular magazines when forming their self-identities (Fung, 2002).

Conclusion

Several content analysis studies of advertising in Hong Kong provide evidence of gender stereotyping. Female models were found to be portrayed mainly in decorative and celebrity roles. The classic beauty type was the dominant beauty type in the study, as reported in this chapter. This suggests that many advertisers share a belief in the importance of classic beauty for Hong Kong women. There was a significant difference in the portrayal of Chinese and Caucasian models in the advertisements. Caucasian female models were more often shown as trendy than Chinese female models were, suggesting an emphasis on modernity and trendiness in Hong Kong's concepts of Western beauty. Advertisements for products targeting females were more gender stereotyped than advertisements for products targeting both genders. In the next chapter, we will examine how audiences respond to different types of female images in advertisements.

Appendix 1   Operational Definitions

Beauty Types

Classic feminine: the model is slightly older than the average fashion model, feminine, and usually wears soft and feminine apparel.

Cute: the model wears clothes more suitable for younger ages. She may have a small ponytail or pigtails, accessories with cartoon characters or a childish facial expression.

Sex kitten: the model usually wears sexy attire, lingerie or revealing or tight clothes. Her facial expression or body posture may be suggestive.

Casual: the model wears everyday clothes or clothes for physical exercise/recreational activities. She usually has light make-up.

Trendy: the model wears colorful fashionable clothes, has oversized accessories and often has wild or tousled hair.

Race

The Caucasian models are ethnically white and usually North American or European. The Chinese models are ethnically oriental.

Occupational Roles

Celebrity: the model is a famous person from the entertainment or sports world, such as popular film and television stars, sports personalities, fashion models, etc.

Decorative: the model is not depicted as having a functional role. She is shown only for her attractiveness and beauty.

Housewife: the model is represented as a housewife in a family setting, as a mother with children or carrying out household activities.

Professional: the model is featured in a career or business environment.

Recreational: the model is dressed in a way that suggests she is engaged in some recreational activity such as visiting friends, shopping or doing sports and other outdoor activities such as walking or jogging.

Source: Frith et al. (2004)

References

Census and Statistics Department (2014), *Women and men in Hong Kong: Key statistics, Census and Statistics Department*, Hong Kong.

centralxfield (2009), "板長壽司、板前壽司、和味兒童餐 [Itacho sushi and Itachae sushi— Yummy Japanese set meals for kids]", online video, available at: http://www.youtube.com/watch?v=X5A3zTVNeuA (accessed on December 4, 2015).

Chan, K., Ng, Y.L. and Williams, R.B. (2012), "Adolescent girls' interpretation of sexuality found in media image", *Intercultural Communication Studies*, Vol. 21 No. 3, pp. 63–81.

Chan, Q. (2000), "Bid to break through pay barrier for women", *South China Morning Post*, May 19, p.11.

Chau, K. C. (1997), "Gender roles portrayals in print advertisements of youth's popular magazines in Hong Kong: A content analysis", *Unpublished undergraduate project*, City University of Hong Kong, Hong Kong.

Cheng, H. (1997), "'Holding up half of the sky?' A sociocultural comparison of gender-role portrayals in Chinese and US advertising", *International Journal of Advertising*, Vol. 16, pp. 295–319.

Cheung, F.M. (1996), "Gender role development", in Lau, S. (Ed.), *Growing up the Chinese Way: Chinese Child and Adolescent Development*, Chinese University Press, Hong Kong, pp. 45–67.

Courtney, A.E. and Whipple, T.W. (1983), Sex Stereotyping in Advertising. Lexington Books, MA.

Croll, E. (1995), "Not the moon: Gendered difference and reflection: Women of reform", in Croll, E. (Ed.) *Changing Identities of Chinese Women: Rhetoric, Experience, and Self-perception in the Twentieth Century*, Hong Kong University Press, Hong Kong, pp. 136-179.

Englis, B.G., Solomon, M.R. and Ashmore, R.D. (1994), "Beauty before the eyes of beholders: The cultural encoding of beauty types in magazine advertising and music television", *Journal of Advertising*, Vol. 23 No. 2, pp. 49–64.

Equal Opportunities Commission (2000), *A Baseline Study of Students' Attitudes Toward Gender Stereotypes and Family Roles*, Equal Opportunities Commission, Hong Kong.

Frith, K.R., Cheng, H. and Shaw, P. (2004), "Race and beauty: A comparison of Asian and Western models in women's magazine advertisements", *Sex Roles*, Vol. 50 No. 1/2, pp. 53–61.

Fung, A. (2002), "Women's magazines: Construction of identities and cultural consumption in Hong Kong", *Markets and Culture*, Vol. 5 No. 4, pp. 321–336.

Fung, A. (2006), "Gender and advertising: The promotional culture of whitening and slimming", in Chan, K. (Ed.), *Advertising and Hong Kong Society*, The Chinese University Press, Hong Kong, pp. 171–181.

Fung, A. and Ma, E. (2000), "Formal vs. informal use of television and sex role stereotyping in Hong Kong", *Sex Roles*, Vol. 42 No. 1/2, pp. 57–81.

Furnham, A. and Mak, T. (1999), "Sex-role stereotyping in television commercials: A review and comparison of fourteen studies done on five continents over 25 years", *Sex Roles*, Vol. 41, pp. 413–437.

Furnham, A., Mak, T. and Tanidjojo, L. (2000), "An Asian perspective on the portrayal of men and women in television advertisements: Studies from Hong Kong and Indonesian television", *Journal of Applied Social Psychology*, Vol. 30 No. 11, pp. 2341–2364.

Furnham, A. and Paltzer, S. (2010), "The portrayal of men and women in television advertisements: An updated review of 30 studies published since 2000", *Scandinavian Journal of Psychology*, Vol. 51, pp. 216–236.

Gerbner, G., Gross, L., Morgan, M., Signorielli, N. and Shanahan, J. (2002), "Growing up with television: Cultivation processes", in Bryant, J. and Zillmann, D. (Eds.), *Media Effects: Advances in Theory and Research*, Lawrence Erlbaum Associates, Hillsdale, NJ, pp. 43–67.

Hovland, R., McMahan, C., Lee, G., Hwang, J.S. and Kim, J. (2005), "Gender role portrayals in American and Korean advertisements", *Sex Roles*, Vol. 53, pp. 887–899.

Hung, K.H., Li, S.Y. and Belk, R.W. (2007), "Global understandings: Female readers' perceptions of the new woman in Chinese advertising", *Journal of International Business Studies*, Vol. 38, pp. 1034–1051.

Information Services Department (2014), *Hong Kong the facts: Religion and custom*, Information Services Department, Hong Kong.

Lee, J.F.K. and Collins, P. (2008), "Gender voices in Hong Kong English textbooks — Some past and current practices", *Sex Roles*, Vol. 59 No. 1–2, pp. 127–137.

Lee, M. and Fung, A. (2009), "Media ideologies of gender in Hong Kong", in Cheung, F.M. and Holroyd, E. (Eds.), *Mainstreaming Gender in Hong Kong Society* , The Chinese University Press, Hong Kong, pp. 291–309.

Lin, C.L. and Yeh, J.T. (2009), "Comparing society's awareness of women: Media-portrayed idealized images and physical attractiveness", *Journal of Business Ethics*, Vol. 90 No. 1, pp. 61–79.

Mak, A.K.Y. (2007), "Advertising whiteness: An assessment of skin color preferences among urban Chinese", *Visual Communication Quarterly*, Vol. 14 No. 3, pp. 144–157.

Perreault, W.D. and Leigh, L.E. (1989), "Reliability of nominal data based on qualitative judgments", *Journal of Marketing Research*, Vol. 26, pp. 135–148.

Pollay, R.W. (1986), "The distorted mirror: Reflections on the unintended consequences of advertising", *Journal of Marketing*, Vol. 50, No. 2, pp. 18–36.

Prendergast, G. and Leung, K.Y. (1999), "The relationship between media consumption and eating disorder symptomatology: A. Hong Kong study", *Business Research Center Working Paper No. WP99024*, Hong Kong Baptist University, Hong Kong.

Psychology Dictionary (n.d.), "What is gender stereotypes?", available at: www.psychologydictionary.org/gender-stereotypes (accessed on June 22, 2015).

Siu, W.S. (1996), "Gender portrayal in Hong Kong and Singapore television advertisements", *Journal of Asian Business*, Vol. 12, pp. 47–63.

Solomon, M., Ashmore, R. and Longo, L. (1992), "The beauty match-up hypothesis: Congruence between types of beauty and product images in advertising", *Journal of Advertising*, Vol. 21 No. 4, pp. 23–34.

The Nielsen Company (2009), *2009 Nielsen Media Index: Hong Kong Yearend Report*, The Nielsen Company, Hong Kong.

The Nielsen Company (2011), *2011 Nielsen Media Index: Hong Kong Yearend Report*, The Nielsen Company, Hong Kong.

The Women's Foundation (2006), *The Status of Women and Girls in Hong Kong 2006*, The Women's Foundation, Hong Kong.

U.S. Bureau of Labor Statistics (2009), "Employment status of the civilian non-institutional population 16 years and over by sex: 1973 to date", available at http://www.bls.gov/cps/cpsaat2.pdf (accessed on October 21, 2015).

Williams, J.E. and Best, D.L. (1990), *Measuring Sex Stereotypes: A Multinational Study*. Sage, Beverly Hills, CA.

Wimmer, R.D. and Dominick, J.R. (2006), *Mass Media Research: An Introduction*. 8th edn. Wadsworth, Boston, MA.

Women's Commission (2009), *Findings of Survey on Community Perception on Gender Issues*, Women's Commission, Hong Kong.

Wong, W. (1997), "Construction of ideal childhood: Reading and decoding television advertisements directed at children in Hong Kong", *Hong Kong Cultural Studies Bulletin*, Vol. 7, Spring No., pp. 75–84.

Wu, R. (1995), "Women", in Cheung, S.Y.L. and Sze, S.M.H. (Eds.), *The Other Hong Kong Peport 1995*, The Chinese University Press, Hong Kong, pp. 121–156.

Zhang, L., Srisupandit, P.T. and Cartwright, D. (2009), "A comparison of gender role portrayals in magazine advertising", *Management Research News*, Vol. 32 No. 7, pp. 683–700.

Zhang, Y.B., Song, Y. and Carver, L.J. (2008), "Cultural values and aging in Chinese television commercials", *Journal of Asian Pacific Communication*, Vol. 18 No. 2, pp. 209–224.

Chapter 9

Responses to Gendered Advertisements

Yu Leung Ng and Kara Chan

Introduction

In the previous chapter, it was found that female models in advertisements in Hong Kong are often limited to decorative and celebrity roles. The beauty of female models is often emphasized to attract attention and is thought to enhance a brand image. How do audiences respond to different types of female images in advertisements? A study among adolescent girls in Hong Kong found that they were active in interpreting female images in the media (Chan, 2014). This chapter introduces Hirschman and Thompson's (1997) interpretative strategies as a framework to examine the types of relationships between media content and media audiences. The chapter also introduces a gender self-socialization model developed by Tobin and his associates (Tobin et al., 2010), which attempts to clarify various gender concepts. A qualitative study using focus group analysis was employed to examine if images of women in the advertisements resonate with adolescents as ideal images of women.

Gender Socialization

Sex refers to a person's "biological endowment as a male or a female", while gender refers to the "psychological/sociological construct of what it means to be a man or a woman" (Rice and Dolgin, 2005). Gender is a wider concept than sex as it includes all the expectations of a person in a particular culture based on his or her biological sex (Rice and Dolgin, 2005). Children and adolescents learn about these expectations of their cultures through a process called gender socialization. Masculinity and femininity are personality and behavioral characteristics of a male or female assigned by his or her society according to its cultural standards (Rice and Dolgin, 2005).

Arnett's (1995) self-socialization theory attempts to explain how children and adolescents process information related to gender. According to the theory, children and adolescents actively search for information and change their behavior in order to adopt the behavior of their ideal role model. These role models are often sourced from the media. Thus, the media plays a strong and potent role in the gender socialization of adolescents (Arnett, 1995; Brown, 2000).

Three Gender Concepts: Gender Identity, Gender Stereotypes and Self-Perceptions

Adolescence is a transitional stage of self-discovery between childhood and adulthood (Erikson, 1968), a period when people develop and consolidate different gender cognitions. Tobin and his associates proposed three gender concepts and three hypotheses to explain cognitive development of gender (Tobin et al., 2010). The three key concepts are gender identity (e.g., I am a girl), gender stereotypes (e.g., on the playground, boys do X and girls do Y) and self-perception of gender-type attributes (e.g., as a female, I do Y).

Gender identity is defined as the connections children and adolescents form between themselves and a gender category. An adolescent understands that he or she belongs to one sex rather than the other. It is the internalized societal pressure of gender conformity that causes an adolescent to form his or her beliefs or behavior to fit in with or be accepted by his or her religion, society or culture (Bem, 1981). For example, preadolescent girls reported that girls should be gentle and restrained in their physical movements and should not behave in a rough manner like boys (Chan et al., 2011).

Gender stereotypes are beliefs about differing attributes between males and females. Specifically, they are concerned with how females believe that they are or they should be different from males (Huston, 1983), and vice versa.

Chan et al. (2011) found that preadolescent girls combined traditional and contemporary female stereotypes in their perception of what girls or women should be or should do. On the one hand, interviewees commented that girls or women should be presentable and have good manners. On the other hand, they believed that girls and women should pursue their dreams and be true to themselves. In other studies, however, adolescent girls agreed that the maxim "Men are breadwinners; women are homemakers" was appropriate (Chan and Ng, 2012; 2013b).

Self-perceptions of gender-type attributes are self-perceptions of attributes that characterize males and females as groups (Tobin et al., 2010). Interests (e.g. girls should have fun and enjoy life; Chan et al., 2012), abilities (e.g. girls can pursue studies and work; Chan and Ng, 2013a), intentions (I want to pursue my dream; Chan, 2014) and visions for future selves (I want to be a successful woman in the future; Chan et al., 2012) can characterize the self (Tobin et al., 2010). When preadolescent and adolescent girls were asked about their gender perceptions, areas they gave as defining included skillsets, work type, activities, interests and lifestyle (Chan et al., 2011; Chan et al., 2012; Chan and Ng, 2013a).

Gender Self-Socialization Model and the Three Hypotheses

Tobin et al. (2010) developed a gender self-socialization model (GSSM) to integrate the three gender concepts coherently. The GSSM proposes that the interaction of each possible pair of gender concepts is able to shed light on how an individual develops his or her sense of gender (Tobin et al., 2010). Altogether three such hypotheses were developed. The stereotype emulation hypothesis states that the more a child or an adolescent identifies with a gender stereotype, the more he or she aspires to take on the attributes typical of that stereotype. This represents the interactive influences of gender identity and gender stereotypes on self-perception (e.g. I am a typical girl and girls are skinny, so I should be skinny).

The stereotype construction hypothesis states that the more a child or adolescent identifies with a set of attributes associated with a particular gender, the more he or she projects the attributes onto the gender stereotype

(Tobin et al., 2010). This represents the interaction of gender identity and self-perception on gender stereotype (e.g. I am a girl and I am skinny, so girls are skinny).

The identity construction hypothesis states that the more a child or adolescent's self-perceived attributes fit the gender stereotypes of his or her culture or society, the more he or she develops a gender identity based on those stereotypes (e.g. I am skinny and girls are skinny, so I am a girl).

How children and adolescents process gendered information in the media is an area of terminological confusion. Tobin et al.'s (2010) GSSM of gender concepts attempts to integrate main gender theories into a single theoretical framework and provide a clear explanation of gender. The clarity of gender concepts can serve as a heuristic blueprint for marketers and advertisers to generate marketing insights for targeting adolescents.

Adolescents' Responses to Gendered Advertisements

Hirschman and Thompson's (1997) interpretive strategies attempt to explain how adolescents respond to media images. The three strategies for interpreting are viewing the image as inspiring and aspiring (i.e. media users aspire to media images which are perceived as ideal self-images or ideal self-concepts); deconstructing and rejecting the image (i.e. media users separate undesirable media images and self-images or self-concepts); and identifying with images (i.e. media users connect self-images or concepts of self to ideal media images). Empirical evidence for the three interpretative strategies was found in measuring female audiences' responses to advertisements with different female images. It was found that female media-users tended to reject the strong woman image (i.e. a woman portrayed as talented, ambitious and independent of spirit) while aspiring to be a woman concerned with luxury, leisure and adornments. They identified with the woman concerned with physical appearances and rejected the woman reliant on a man (Hung et al., 2007). Another study found that adolescents aspired to be like the elegant woman, rejected the strong woman and identified with the urban sophisticated female portrayed in television advertisements (Ng and Chan, 2014).

A Study of Adolescents' Responses to Advertising Using Different Female Images

A focus group study was conducted to examine how adolescent girls and boys interpret and respond to images of women in television advertising. Forty-eight interviewees (twenty-four males, twenty-four females) aged 15–18 were recruited through social networks. Verbal consent from parents was obtained for those under 18. The interviewees were divided into eight focus groups (six interviewees each) according to school grade and sex. Interviewees of the same sex and grade were grouped together to encourage free expression of their perceptions. They were students in forms 3 to 6 of school or year one of university (equivalent to the American grades 9 to 12 and college freshman year) in institutions in Hong Kong. Two senior students of Hong Kong Baptist University served as moderators.

The two moderators showed four selected television commercials to the interviewees and asked a series of questions (see the Appendix). The interviews were conducted in Cantonese in January and February, 2014.

The four commercials were found on YouTube. They offered four different images of women: an urban sophisticate, a strong woman, a "flower vase" (a Chinese term that refers to a woman considered only for her physical beauty and not her character or intelligence) and a nurturer. The first commercial, by Canon (aacafe, 2009), featured a young female Asian tourist in a city in Europe asking local people in their language to take photos for her. The woman was classified as an urban sophisticate. The second commercial, by Chanel (Chanel, 2011), featured a Caucasian female model outpacing a group of men in a motorcycle race. She was classified as a strong woman. The third commercial was for Kellogg's. We used a clip that was on YouTube, but it is no longer available; see Jin Huang (2013) for a version of the same commercial. It featured a young Asian woman exhibiting her slim body to female peers, and she was classified as a flower vase. The final commercial was for Kinder Joy. Again, the clip that we used was on YouTube but is no longer available; see hktvcclips (2012) for a version of the same commercial. It featured a mother taking care of her children; she was classified as a nurturer. These classifications came from a previous content analysis study (Hung et al., 2007).

Altogether 110 transcribed pages were analyzed in total. We used the constant comparative method to analyze and generate meaningful categories in order to explore and investigate the interpretation strategies systematically (Glaser and Strauss, 1967; Strauss, 1987). Based on the process of data analysis, the coders constructed, discussed and refined the notes (Glaser and Strauss, 1967). Trends were identified and representative quotes were selected.

Hirschman and Thompson's (1997) interpretive strategies were adopted in data analysis. Specifically, interviewees who perceived the images in a commercial as ideal self-images were interpreted as having an aspirational relationship; interviewees who perceived the images as undesirable self-images were interpreted as having a deconstructive and rejectionist relationship, and those who connected self-images to ideal media images were interpreted as having an identificational relationship. The interpretive strategies provide us with ways to categorize responses to images. The final codes were discussed and agreed on by the two authors, who selected representative quotes and translated them into English.

Interviewees' Interpretations of the Female Characters' Appearances, Personalities and Work/Family Lives

In terms of appearance, the interviewees said that the urban sophisticate in the first ad looked young, cute and active in her casual clothing and light make-up. One interviewee (female, form 5) said: "She is a young girl dressing her age. Her hairstyle and her casual dress-up make me feel comfortable".

The strong woman in the second ad was perceived to be cool and elegant, as well as having a model figure. Interviewees commented that she wore heavy makeup and fashionable clothing. One interviewee said she looked a bit masculine.

Interviewees highlighted the fact that the flower vase in the third ad was tall and thin. Two male interviewees stated that she looked sweet. A female interviewee remarked that she looked as though she wanted to attract attention. Another female interviewee (female, form 3) said: "She is thin. And many girls may want to look like her".

The nurturer in the fourth ad was judged to have a motherly image. Six interviewees perceived her to be old but three thought she was young. One interviewee (male, form 3) said: "She ties her hair in a bun, maybe because she needs to do housework. A bun can make housework easier. She has a simple outfit. It may facilitate doing housework and taking care of children. So she cannot wear beautiful clothing. She loves her children very much. Looks like a typical full-time housewife".

In terms of personality, interviewees perceived that the urban sophisticate in the first ad was outgoing, active and kind. She was also seen as being enthusiastic and curious to learn new things. Said one interviewee (female, form 3): "I think she is a warm-hearted and active girl. If she faces any difficulties, she will solve the problem actively, such as asking people to take a photo for her. And she is a cheerful person, because she always smiles. She smiles when she talks to people". Six of them thought she was independent as she was travelling alone. Six interviewees commented that she was polite and kind. An interviewee (male, form 3) put it this way: "She is kind toward others. She takes the trouble to learn the local language".

Interviewees commented that the strong woman in the second ad was wild and confident and had a unique personality. They felt she persisted in doing whatever she wanted and did not care about what others thought. Interviewees also remarked that she was strong and independent. In their words: "She is an independent woman who doesn't need to depend on men. And she is confident. She has a cool smile", (female, form 4). "I think she is a confident person. When she rides a motorcycle, she barely gives the men on motorcycles a glance. She may think that she is as good as them", (male, form 5).

The flower vase in the third ad was also perceived to be confident. Interviewees emphasized that her confidence was based on her physical beauty. As one form 6 female said: "She is kind of a show-off. It is like she tells others that she is slim and wears tight clothes after losing weight".

Interviewees said that the nurturer in the fourth ad was kind-hearted and caring. She indulged her children with toys. One interviewee (male, form 3) described her as follows: "I think she cares a lot about her children. She buys snacks and toys for them, and she takes the time to play and eat with them".

Regarding work and family life, interviewees thought that the urban sophisticate in the first ad came from a rich family because her family supported her travel. They guessed that she did not have a boyfriend, perceiving that she was single and probably had an easy job. She might be working in the arts or the creative industries. One interviewee (male, year 1) said: "She has a good relationship with her family. [Interviewer: Why?] She travels alone and she is cheerful. She is willing to share her happiness with others. I think she shares her happiness in life with her family".

The strong woman in the second ad was also perceived as being independent, single and career-minded. She was also judged to be a model. According to an interviewee (female, form 3): "I think a lot of men date her, but she despises them. It is because she is strong and good at work. She has enough money to live alone. And she is probably very good at work and has a very high salary so that she doesn't need to depend on anyone".

Interviewees felt the flower vase in the third ad had an easy life and did not need to work. She spends time chatting with friends and going shopping. Three interviewees thought that she was single, and she was keeping fit to stay attractive. An interviewee (male, form 5) put it this way: "I think she lives alone. She may not live with her boyfriend, because she shares her dietary method of keep fit with her friends. Her social life is quite happy. I think her family and work life is colorful".

Interviewees noted that the nurturer in the fourth ad was a housewife. None of the interviewees thought she had a job. They also noted that she concentrated only on taking care of her children. One interviewee (male, year 1) said: "It is a typical family. The husband is the breadwinner and the wife is the homemaker. They enjoy family life."

Do the Female Characters in the Advertisements Represent Interviewees' Ideal Image of Women?

The interviewees were then asked which of the four female characters in the ads best represented their ideal image of women. Twenty-nine interviewees selected the urban sophisticate. Five chose the strong woman and five chose the nurturer. Only three selected the flower vase. Six interviewees did not select any ads.

Of the interviewees who chose the urban sophisticate as their ideal image, thirteen were female and sixteen were male. They emphasized that she was active and passionate. Her passion to pursue dreams won their admiration. Two interviewees put it this way: "It seems that she lives a free life. She can do whatever she wants and go to different places to experience more and learn more" (female, form 5). "She is doing what young people nowadays want to do. And only young people can travel alone, because they have the passion to explore new things. It is like we will regret not doing these things when we are young" (female, form 6).

Male interviewees mentioned that the girl in the ad was friendly and outgoing. They said they did not like girls who were passive. "I don't think girls should just stay at home reading books. My ideal girl needs to travel to many places and have different experiences. Experience makes a person sophisticated and mature" (male, form 3). "I think girls don't need to be gentle and quiet. A bit adventurous, like boys, is better" (male, form 5).

Three female and two male interviewees selected the strong woman as their ideal image. The two male interviewees thought she was attractive and sexy. A female interviewee expressed the belief that she looked like a character in the American teen drama *Gossip Girl* who dresses beautifully and attracts many men. Another female interviewee (female, form 3) said: "She has a stable job and her job is special. She is cool when she is riding her motorcycle. I like her because she has a mind of her own and her own unique personality".

Five interviewees, all female, admired the nurturer. They said that family meant a lot to them. Here is an illustrative quote of an interviewee (female, form 3): "I think the final goal of being a woman is to have children and be a good mother. When we get old, we have children to stay with us. So I think this is the most ideal one".

Only three interviewees selected the flower vase image. Again, all three were female. They appreciated her healthy and beautiful appearance. An interviewee (female, form 6) remarked: "Maybe she cares too much about her appearance, but she gives me a feeling of generosity. She is sociable. Nowadays, having good social skills is important".

Using Hirschman and Thompson's (1997) three interpretive strategies, the findings demonstrate that only a few female interviewees aspired to be like the nurturer. Most of the female interviewees rejected the strong woman and the flower vase. Most female interviewees identified with the urban sophisticate. They noted parallels between their own interests and characteristics and hers. Pursuing one's dreams and having the courage to express views were valued. This echoes findings in previous surveys that showed adolescent girls agree strongly that females should pursue their dreams and appreciate their own strengths (Chan and Ng, 2012; 2013b).

Most of the female interviewees separated their self-concept from the strong woman and the flower vase. Regarding the strong woman, only a few female interviewees valued financial independence. They preferred personality traits such as independence and confidence to gentleness and kindness (Chan and Ng, 2013a). However, the majority of them said they would not choose to stay single (Chan and Ng, 2012). Regarding the flower vase, most interviewees rejected her because she was only concerned with her appearance. This supports an earlier finding that adolescent girls criticize skinny female images in ads (Chan et al., 2012).

An analysis of the interviews revealed that interviewees held stereotypical gender role views about being single or married. Single females were allowed to be adventurous but married females with children were restricted to domestic roles. Interviewees tended to believe there was no space for self-actualization and individualization after getting married.

This study also investigated adolescent boys' ideal images of women in the ads. Male interviewees' responses to the ads were not made with reference to their self-images, but to the images of their significant other or their future partner. Almost all male interviewees selected the urban sophisticate and the remaining two of them chose the strong woman. Girls who were friendly and cheerful attracted them. Traditional girls who were gentle and quiet did not draw their attention. Adolescent boys were more likely to be interested in youthful and active girls. The two male interviewees who selected the strong woman only did so because of her appearance. None of the male interviewees chose the flower vase, indicating that adolescent boys do not like females who are concerned only with looking prettier and slimmer; neither did male interviewees prefer the nurturer, perhaps showing that they were not yet concerned with ideas of family life. This echoes a previous experimental study showing that an advertisement using an image of a woman alone has a more favorable advertising effect among adolescent girls than adolescent boys (Chan et al., 2014).

The present study shares similarities with a previous study of adolescents in mainland China (Ng and Chan, 2014). Adolescents in both mainland China and Hong Kong selected the urban sophisticated female as their ideal female image in response to gendered ads. This indicates that marketers and advertisers should adopt similar strategies in these markets when targeting adolescents. In fact, most female characters in ads are of the urban sophisticate type (Hung et al., 2007). This preference among adolescents may be due to the high frequency with which this category occurs in media.

Do Interviewees' Gender Concepts Follow the Framework of GSSM?

There is evidence that Tobin et al.'s (2010) GSSM framework was adopted in the selection of the ideal female image. The stereotype emulation hypothesis was reflected in the interviewees' selection of the urban sophisticate, the strong woman and the flower vase. Thirteen female interviewees identified with the urban sophisticate's passion for travel and curiosity to explore new things. As a result, they expressed the desire to be like her. Here is an illustrative quote of an interviewee (female, form 5): "She went travelling, taking photos and stayed with other people. She went to different places. I think enriching experiences are a good thing. I want to be her".

Three female interviewees admired the strong woman for her independent personality. They identified with this independence and perceived that if they had that kind of personality they could be attractive to many men. A female interviewee (female, form 4) said: "She looks like an actress in a U.S. drama. She dresses nicely and guys are attracted to her. So I want to be like her".

Three female interviewees selected the flower vase as their ideal female image, as they identified with the gender stereotype that girls should be fit, and so perceived that they themselves should be fit. As a result, they admired her for her appearance. An interviewee (female, form 4) put it this way: "For me, she is close to my ideal female image. She has a great body. This is my goal".

The stereotype construction hypothesis is illustrated by interviewees' selection of the nurturer. Female interviewees chose the nurturer as their ideal female image because they valued highly the concept of family. As represented by this particular gender identity, they thought that marriage and motherhood were important for women. Here are two illustrative quotes: "She stays at home and doesn't need to work. She doesn't have to worry about anything, so she can concentrate on taking care of her children" (female, form 3). "She values her family. Taking care of children and housework etc." (female, form 3).

Finally, the identity construction hypothesis was reflected in the choice of the urban sophisticate. Some interviewees perceived that the characteristics of the urban sophisticate matched their own interests, such as travelling and taking photos. As a result, they selected this female character as their ideal female image because she appealed to their gender identities. In one female interviewee's (female, form 3) words: "Few people travel alone. She explores somewhere new . . . I think her personality matches mine. I like the arts and I also want to travel alone, drawing pictures, taking photos and pursuing freedom".

Marketing Implications

Adolescence is an important life stage for the formation of concepts of self and gender identity. Marketers should have a clear understanding of the self-concepts of their target audience in a changing social and economic environment in order to communicate effectively with them. This study enlightens marketers on the profiles of female characters in advertisements that can resonate with adolescent boys and girls. First, the current study finds that contemporary and active young female images are mostly likely to trigger aspiration from female adolescents and admiration from male adolescents. This ideal female image is expressed through an active lifestyle, participation in out-of-home activities, interaction with other members of society and freedom to travel. This image is also best portrayed as being of a higher socio-economic status with more than sufficient economic means to pursue one's dreams. Contrary to the dominant use of classical and mature females in Hong Kong advertising (Chan and Cheng, 2012), the ideal female images among adolescents are not females who put great effort into attaining a beautiful face or a perfect body, as seen from the unpopularity of the flower vase image. Marketers should therefore pay more attention to constructing a female character with a unique personality that goes beyond mere physical appearance.

The image of a housewife in the current study did not garner as much appreciation as it did among interviewees in mainland China (Ng and Chan, 2014). The reason most likely lies in the difference between a full-time housewife and a married woman who is portrayed as successful in both work and family. Marketers should therefore consider using the image of a nurturer who is able to achieve work-family balance to gain greater appreciation from the adolescent audience.

The study presented here displayed the potential threats to a brand in the employment of a strong woman in its advertising. Marketers should use this concept with caution or use it only for a niche market. One possible strategy is to downplay the competitiveness of the female character and the inclusion of positive social relations with significant others. Success of a female should be portrayed as an end product rather than a process.

This study supports Tobin et al.'s (2010) GSSM that the integration and assimilation of gender identity, gender stereotypes and self-perception affects interviewees' perceptions of gender. The three hypotheses in the GSSM propose that a gender concept is the product of the cognitive interaction of the other two gender concepts. The interviewees' responses illustrate the hypothesized thinking process, even though the strength of such interaction was not manifested. The results provide marketers with different ways of leveraging on gender concepts. For example, in constructing an urban sophisticate as an ideal female image, an SLR camera marketer might adopt the stereotype emulation hypothesis: "Girls nowadays are independent and pursuing dreams. So, go explore the world with an SLR camera". Or the same marketer could leverage the stereotype construction hypothesis: "I am a girl and I am exploring the world with an SLR camera. So, girls are adventurous." In this way, the marketer can help establish a normative environment that facilitates the marketing of SLR cameras to female consumers. Lastly, the marketer can leverage on the identity construction hypothesis: "I am exploring the world with an SLR camera and girls are adventurous, so I am a girl". In this way, the marketing communication will establish a strong gender statement and be able to better resonate with a market segment.

Conclusion

Based on Tobin et al.'s (2010) gender self-socialization model, we examined how Hong Kong adolescents interpret images of women from gendered advertisements. The results show that adolescents develop their ideal female images from the ads that best suit their ideal appearance, personality, work life and family life. The limitations of the results beyond its forty-eight interviewees should be noted.

Acknowledgements

Part of this chapter has been published in Ng, Y.L, and Chan, K. (2015), "Interpretation of Female Images in Advertising Among Chinese Adolescents", *Young Consumers*, Vol. 16 No. 2, pp. 222–234.

Appendix

List of questions for focus group study:

1. Please describe the appearance of the woman in each advertisement (if necessary, I can show you the advertisement again).

2. Please describe the personality of the woman in each advertisement (if necessary, I can show you the advertisement again).

3. Please describe the work and family life of the woman in each advertisement (if necessary, I can show you the advertisement again).

4. Of the four women featured in the advertisements, which is your ideal female image? Why?

5. Apart from the women in the four advertisements, what is your ideal female image?*

Note: * Answers to Question 5 are not reported in the present study.

References

aacafe (2009), "CANON EOS 500D TVC", online video, September 15, available at: https://www.youtube.com/watch?v=1nR76LqOm1Y (accessed on November 15, 2014).

Arnett, J.J. (1995), "Adolescents' uses of media for self-socialization", *Journal of Youth and Adolescence*, Vol. 24 No. 5, pp. 519–533.

Bem, S.L. (1981), "Gender schema theory: A cognitive account of sex typing", *Psychological Review*, Vol. 88 No. 4, pp. 354–364.

Brown, J.D. (2000), "Adolescents' sexual media diets", *Journal of Adolescent Health*, Vol. 27 No. 2, pp. 35–40.

Chan, K. (2014), *Girls and Media: Dreams and Realities*. City University of Hong Kong Press. Hong Kong.

Chan, K. and Cheng, Y. (2012), "Portrayal of females in magazine advertisements in Hong Kong", *Journal of Asian Pacific Communication*, Vol. 22 No. 1, pp. 78–96.

Chan, K. and Ng, Y.L. (2012), "Segmentation of Chinese adolescent girls using gender roles and ideal female images", *Journal of Consumer Marketing*, Vol. 29 No. 7, pp. 521–531.

Chan, K. and Ng, Y.L. (2013a), "Canadian Chinese adolescent girls' gender roles and identities", *Intercultural Communication Studies*, Vol. 22 No. 2, pp. 19–39.

Chan, K. and Ng, Y.L. (2013b), "How Chinese adolescent girls perceive gender roles: A psychographic study", *Journal of Consumer Marketing*, Vol. 30 No. 1, pp. 50–60.

Chan, K., Ng, Y.L. and Liu, J. (2014), "How Chinese young consumers respond to gendered advertisements", *Young Consumers*, Vol. 15 No. 4, pp. 353–364.

Chan, K., Ng, Y.L. and Williams, R.B. (2012), "What do adolescent girls learn about gender roles from advertising images?", *Young Consumers*, Vol. 13 No. 4, pp. 357–366.

Chan, K., Tufte, B., Cappello, G. and Williams, R.B. (2011), "Tween girls' perception of gender roles and gender identities: A qualitative study", *Young Consumers*, Vol. 12 No. 1, pp. 66–81.

Chanel (2011), "Coco Mademoiselle: The film — Chanel", online video, March 8, available at: https://www.youtube.com/watch?v=aRV-2_Un-kk (accessed on November 15, 2014).

Erikson, E.H. (1968), *Identity, Youth and Crisis*. Norton, New York.

Glaser, B.G. and Strauss, A.L. (1967), *The Discovery of Grounded Theory: Strategies for Qualitative Research*. Aldine, Chicago.

Hirschman, E.C. and Thompson, C.J. (1997), "Why media matter: Toward a richer understanding of consumers' relationships with advertising and mass media", *Journal of Advertising*, Vol. 26 No. 1, pp. 43–60.

hktvcclips (2012), "2012 Kinder", online video, available at: https://www.youtube.com/watch?v=uXnyAAoU9hs (accessed on November 15, 2014).

Hung, K.H., Li, S.Y. and Belk, R.W. (2007), "Glocal understandings: Female readers' perceptions of the new woman in Chinese advertising", *Journal of International Business Studies*, Vol. 38 No. 6, pp. 1034–1051.

Huston, A.C. (1983), "Sex-typing", in Hetherington, E.M. (Ed), *Handbook of Child Psychology: Socialization, Personality, and Social Development* Vol. 4, Wiley, New York, pp. 388–467.

Jin Huang (2013), "2013 Kellogg's Special K TVC", online video, available at: https://www.youtube.com/watch?v=TeEcrW-H8pE (accessed on November 15, 2014).

Ng, Y.L. and Chan, K. (2014), "Do females in advertisements reflect adolescents' ideal female images?", *Journal of Consumer Marketing*, Vol. 31 No. 3, pp. 170–176.

Rice, F.P. and Dolgin, K.G. (2005), *The Adolescent: Development, Relationships, and Culture*. 11th edn. Pearson, Boston.

Strauss, A.L. (1987), *Qualitative Analysis for Social Scientists*. Cambridge University Press, Cambridge.

Tobin, D.D., Menon, M., Menon, M., Spatta, B.C., Hodges, E.V.E. and Perry, D.G. (2010), "The intrapsychics of gender: A model of self-socialization", *Psychological Review*, Vol. 117 No. 2, pp. 601–622.

Chapter 10

Children and Advertising

Kara Chan and Anqi Huang

Introduction

Children are a special segment of the audience. The Communications Authority (2013) stated that television advertising aimed at children must not result in harm to children physically, mentally or morally. Furthermore, the advertising format and contents must not take advantage of the credulity and sense of loyalty of children. The public shows much concern about the effects of advertising on children. Many controversial advertisements that received complaints, as reported in Chapter 5, were considered unsuitable for children. Do children understand advertising? Do they put trust in advertising? With the prevalence of product placement that blends advertising and content, are children able to identify the selling intent of product placement? This chapter reviews results of recent studies about children and youths' understanding of advertising in general and social marketing communication. Children and youths' interpretation of two government publicity campaigns on green living and food waste reduction were used as case studies to illustrate factors that contribute to effective communication to children.

Understanding of Public Service Advertisements among Children

Social marketing uses the principles and processes of commercial marketing to promote socially beneficial behavior change (Evans, 2006). Because nearly all societies are keen to socialize new members (i.e. their children), children are a major target audience for social marketing. Social marketing usually involves the promotion of abstract ideas rather than concrete products and services, thus, it is natural to ask if children understand these messages. At what age will they begin to be interested in social marketing communication? How does this interest develop with time? What forms of social marketing communication appeal most to children? This chapter attempts to answer these questions.

Children's Responses to General Advertising and Public Service Advertising

Most researchers in developmental psychology agree that a child's ability to acquire cognitive reasoning progresses through a series of distinct stages (John, 1999; Piaget, 1970; Selman, 1980). Based on Piaget's (1970) stage theory of cognitive development and Selman's (1980) stage theory of social development, John (1999) proposes a model of consumer socialization. The model proposes that children learn to become a consumer through the perceptual stage (ages 3–7), the analytical stage (ages 7–11) and the reflective stage (ages 11–16). Using John's (1999) theoretical framework and empirical evidence from a survey of 1,758 children in China, Chan (2014) summarizes children's responses to television advertising at different stages.

At the perceptual stage, children do not have a clear understanding of the persuasive intent of advertising. They are usually aware that advertising wants them to buy the product featured in the commercial or tell their parents about it. However, they seldom have a clear picture about why television stations broadcast these messages (for example, some young children think that the commercials appear on television in order to give the audience a break from watching the program). Also, for the most part, they believe that advertising is mainly true. Furthermore, they often have strong views about advertising, whether positive or negative. The advertising appeals they like the best are humor and animations.

At the analytical stage, over a third of children are able to understand that advertising promotes products. Unlike the previous age group, most children in the analytical stage perceive that only about half of the advertising is true. Again, they do not have strong views about advertising; some still like it a lot, but others now have more neutral views on it. Also, while these children still enjoy funny ads and animated ads, they now begin to show an appreciation for public service advertisements, which the majority of them perceive as being more meaningful than other advertisements. Comparatively speaking, children at this stage have a more sophisticated understanding of advertising than children at the previous stage.

When children reach the reflective stage, most of them are able to identify the persuasive intent of advertising. Like children at the previous stage, children at the reflective stage perceive that half of the television commercials are truthful. However, by now most of them have become desensitized: they neither like nor dislike television advertising, and they are no longer interested in animated ads. But they still love funny advertisements. Furthermore, most of them show an appreciation for public service advertising, such as social service advertisements about environmental protection, which they still believe is meaningful (Chan, 2014). Notice that as children progress through the stages of the model their understanding and liking of public service advertisements also increases.

A study using face-to-face interviews with a structured questionnaire was conducted among 448 children aged 5–12 in Hong Kong (Chan, 2000). It was found that by ages 7–8, children were beginning to understand what advertising was and were aware of the persuasive intention of television advertising. These results provide empirical support for John's (1999) model of consumer socialization. The deciding factor in the interviewees' responses to advertisements was the entertainment element. The study showed a few television commercials to respondents and asked them to recall the key messages of the commercials. Two of these commercials were public service advertisements. The first was developed by the Electrical and Mechanical Services Department to promote liquefied petroleum gas as a cleaner form of energy for taxis by featuring taxi drivers who claimed that gas fuel would create a better environment for pedestrians. Less than one third of the respondents were able to demonstrate full understanding of the advertisement. Some reported that the advertisement was about the use of unleaded fuel, while some misunderstood it to be an advertisement advocating that drivers turn off their engines when their vehicles were not in use. Chan (2000) attributed the confusion to the fact that children were unfamiliar with driving or choice of fuel.

Chan (2000) found that public service advertisements were able to communicate well with younger children when they were presented in a child-friendly manner. A television public service advertisement produced by the Civic Education Committee about human rights reported an overall 63% of full understanding among all respondents and 27% of full understanding among children studying in kindergarten or primary 1 (equivalent to grade 1 in the U.S. system, ages 6–7). This advertisement featured an animated girl and an animated boy. The girl said that she wanted to be a doctor when she grew up. When the boy said that she could not be a doctor, the girl replied that if she had the competence, she could make it. The voice-over reassured the audience that boys and girls both have the right to choose their occupation. The closing scene showed a boy and a girl with an equals sign between them. Chan (2000) suggested that a straightforward narration and a concrete example of how human rights were being challenged contributed to the successful communication to the target audience (Chan, 2000).

A qualitative study was conducted to examine older children and youths' perceptions of public service advertisements in Hong Kong (Chan, 2010). In this study, thirty-two Chinese adolescents aged 14–16 were recruited to participate in a face-to-face interview. Most interviewees reported that they distinguished between public service advertisements and commercial advertisements mainly through the ad's persuasive intent. They perceived that public service advertisements were messages with no intention of making money, while advertisements for goods and services were messages for profit. Some interviewees also perceived that public service advertisements were educational, informative and meaningful in nature. Government departments, non-profit organizations and charity groups were identified by the interviewees as major sources of social marketing communication. When asked what these messages want people to do, most of the interviewees reported that these messages want people to follow the featured actions or to adopt the advocated attitudes. In general, these young consumers demonstrated a positive attitude toward public service advertisements, and most of them believed these messages. Most of them reported that their trust was based on the credibility of the government as a source of communication. Some believed these messages because they perceived that these messages were meaningful. Three interviewees reported that they believed these messages because the messages were close to what they saw in their daily lives. However, a few interviewees did not believe the public service advertisements because they found the persuasive messages exaggerated or unrealistic. One interviewee in particular criticized a public service advertisement advocating that "learning is not about getting high scores". Based on her own experience, she believed that the point of education was to compete with others and move ahead by getting good scores. She concluded that the government was telling lies (Chan, 2010).

The study also found that young people paid attention to details of public service advertisements. They were most interested in the characters portrayed in the advertisements, the scripts and the story, the celebrities featured, the music and the slogan. They also liked some of the public service ads because of the entertainment value, personal relevance, creativity and visuals. For instance, one interviewee enjoyed an advertisement with the slogan "Love your teeth, start flossing" that featured Ah Sa (of the group Twins) with a giant tooth. He found it creative, trendy, easy to remember and thought it had good sound effects (Chan, 2010).

When asked about advertising executions often used in public service ads on television, interviewees most frequently reported use of celebrities, slice-of-life dramas and slogans. An interviewee recalled without effort six celebrities who appeared in a public service ad, including three popular local singers and two prominent government officials. However, not all persuasive campaigns were appreciated by children and youths. Interviewees in a study to examine two government television advertisements promoting green living reported mixed views (Chan and Chang, 2013). The majority of the thirty-seven interviewees reported that they found the green living ads enjoyable, refreshing and visually stimulating. However, some interviewees found the same two ads unrealistic, irrelevant and unimpressive. Chan and Chang (2013) suggested that to encourage the young target audience to practice the desired behavior using public service advertisements, the social marketers should use visual images, music and appealing characters to evoke desirable emotions and to arouse a sense of personal relevance. According to them, the social message would also need to spell out how to achieve the advocated end-state; only when the audience is empowered with the perceived competence would they be motivated to carry out the specified behavior (Chan and Chang, 2013).

A recent study was conducted to examine Hong Kong children's understanding and comprehension of public service advertisements broadcast on TV in October 2013. A sample quota of thirty-one children aged 7–12 studying in primary 2 to 6 were personally interviewed. Two APIs (Announcements in the Public Interest) were shown to the interviewees. In the first API on drug abuse, serious consequences of sniffing thinner and abusing cough medicine such as rotten teeth and loss of bladder control were shown. The API featured children aged around 10–12 as its central characters. The voice-over of this API says:

> Not only can she not walk straight...Not only does she break out in cold sweats...Not only has her pulse rate shot up...Not only is she slow to react ... Not only are her teeth rotting...But her brain is also damaged. Do you still want to abuse thinner and cough medicine? Stand firm! Knock drugs out! (Information Services Department, 2010)

The other API included in the study was about social inclusion. The API featured characters of different races, ages and genders. The API urged the public to respect different values and lifestyles. The API featured five characters including a man, a girl dressed in fashionable clothing, an older man and an older woman. They were being kind and nice to one another. The script of this API was as follows:

> Man: "Respect—it's easy. Mutual understanding and accommodation."
>
> Indian girl: "We all think differently but accept each other for who we are".
>
> Pop girl: "Trendy style—no problem!"
>
> Old man: "Thank you, young man! And they don't mind if I'm a little clumsy".
>
> Wife: "It's best when people truly understand me".
>
> Voice-over: "Want to be respected? Try respecting others first".
>
> Old woman: "Don't mind me when I laugh out loud!" (Information Services Department, 2013d)

This public service advertisement obviously was not targeting children as its narration was adult-oriented. Interviewees were asked to report the key message of these two advertisements. They were also asked to describe the differences between these public service messages and advertisements of a commercial nature such as an advertisement for toothpaste or an advertisement for candy.

Results indicated that children's understanding of the social message on anti-drug API was much higher than that of the social message of the API on social inclusion. Among the thirty-one interviewees, twenty-three were able to identify the key message of the anti-drug API. They reported that illegal drugs are harmful to bodies, and that people should not take drugs. Seven of them had a partial understanding of the anti-drug abuse API. They remarked that people should not take medicine too casually. One interviewee was not able to identify the key message of the API. On the other hand, only twelve of the thirty-one interviewees were able to identify the key message of the social inclusion API. They reported that people should show respect to one another. A further seventeen interviewees had a partial understanding of the API. Some of them perceived that the message advocated respecting seniors. The remaining two interviewees were unable to discern the key message of the API.

The significant gap between the understanding of the two APIs can be attributed to several factors. Firstly, the anti-drug abuse messages were concrete and direct, while the social inclusion message may seem vague and fragmented to children. Secondly, the anti-drug API featured child characters throughout and would be more likely to attract the attention of children and youths. The social inclusion API featured six adults and was less likely to appeal to a young audience. Thirdly, some interviewees reported that they received similar messages about drug abuse from parents and school teachers. A few interviewees mentioned that the API on drug abuse had been shown at their schools. However, none of the interviewees reported that they were exposed to social inclusion messages at home or at school.

Furthermore, it was found that children distinguish social messages and commercial messages based on the intention of the messages as well as the execution strategies of the advertisements. Out of thirty-one interviewees, twenty reported that public service advertisements attempted to teach, educate, change attitudes or evoke action, while commercial messages were about promoting products to make money. Another eight interviewees distinguished between the two types of messages by their styles. Some interviewees commented that commercial messages were funny while public service advertising was longer, scarier, closer to daily life and less entertaining. The remaining three interviewees were unable to tell the difference between the two types of persuasive messages.

Big Waster and the Food Wise Hong Kong Campaign

Cartoon characters and jingles are often used in public service advertising to appeal to children. In this section, we feature a successful social marketing campaign that used such methods and captured the hearts of children. With its immensely popular cartoon character, Big Waster, the Food Wise Hong Kong Campaign is considered as one of the most successful social marketing campaigns developed by the Hong Kong government (Information Services Department, 2013c). As a wealthy society, Hong Kong generates large amounts of food waste. Statistics shows that food makes up 40% of the municipal solid waste that goes to the landfills every day (Information Services Department, 2013b). Most of this food waste is generated by households, while the rest comes largely from the commercial sector (Information Services Department, 2013b). The Food Wise Campaign was developed to promote public awareness of food waste in the community. It encourages Hong Kong people to think before they buy or order food.

A central character, Big Waster, (Figure 10.1) and a thirty-second television commercial with a rap song were designed. The Big Waster had a giant drooling head, a pair of broad eyes and a tiny body with a narrow waistline. It is used to represent individuals who purchase more food than they can stomach. Many children enjoy the ad and can recite the entire rap song. Some children even created their own dance to go with the song. According to the creative director who shot the advertisement, "The Big Waster is not a bad guy. It just has some bad habits". The creative director remarked that the audience finds it easy to identify with the Big Waster. This is because many Hong Kong people have thrown away expired food simply because they bought too much food at the supermarket (Information Services Department, 2013a).

Figure 10.1
Big Waster Poster

Source: Food Wise Hong Kong Campaign of the Environmental Protection Department.

The lyrics of the rap song read:

Rapper: "Your eyes are bigger than your stomach

               You're a big Waster!

               Hey, you can't finish

               Why order so much, man

               Leftovers are such a waste!

               Yo! Yo!

               So many dishes

               Who's gonna finish them?

               All this food into the rubbish bin

               What a waste!"

Backing: "Don't waste, don't waste"

Rapper: "Buy, buy, buy

               All the food expires

               Then, bye, bye, bye

               It's all thrown away!

               Order only portions you can finish

               Buy only what you need

               Please be conscious

               Stop the waste

               Everything is precious

               Let's be food wise!" (Food Wise Hong Kong, 2014)

Figure 10.2

Conceptual Model Showing How Public Service Advertising Works

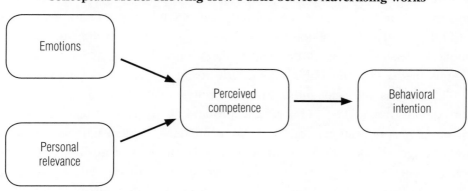

Source: Chan and Chang (2013).

The Big Waster's visual image, the rap song, and the light-hearted approach have won wide acceptance for the advertisement, especially among children. The ad's slogan, "Think before you buy food; think before you order food", has become a popular saying. To extend the impact of the campaign, the fictional character visited schools and was heartily welcomed (Information Services Department, 2013a).

Using Chan and Chang's (2013) conceptual model of social marketing we have the analysis represented in Figure 10.2.

The Big Waster and the rap song together create fun, excitement and a slight sense of mockery. The ad uses real-life situations in which food wastage occurs to create a sense of relevance. Also, the central message encouraging the reduction of food waste does not involve a high level of skill or competency to grasp. These three factors together contributed to the positive reception of the Big Waster advertisement among children and youths.

The Making of Public Service Advertising in Hong Kong

Most public service advertisements in Hong Kong are created with the assistance of the Information Services Department. In this section, we discuss the process of the creation of public service advertisements and how the creative process may affect communication with children and youths.

The Information Services Department, a department of the Hong Kong Government, is responsible for providing a communication link between the government and the people through newspapers, television, radio, magazines and other media (Information Services Department, 2014). It aims to enhance public understanding of government policies, decisions and activities through various media content, publicity and advertising. It has four divisions: local public relations, publicity and promotions, public relations outside Hong Kong and administration. The publicity and promotions division is responsible for government publications, promotional campaigns, advertisements, creative and design work and government photography (Information Services Department, 2014). It serves as the government's publicity adviser, serving various government departments and bureaus in designing and executing local publicity campaigns (Information Services Department, 2014).

In Hong Kong, the public service advertising handled by the Information Services Department has a special name, "Announcements in the Public Interest", or "APIs" for short. They provide information that the public needs to know (Wong, 2006). The production of each API is funded by government departments or bureaus. These messages are related to issues of public concern such as health, safety, social welfare, legal obligations, availability of public resources and changes affecting environmental factors. They are directly related to government policy or operational objectives (Information Services Department, 2013c). The design and production of APIs are normally contracted out to private advertising and media companies. The Information Services Department works closely with other government departments, working groups and committees in designing campaign themes and execution strategies (Wong, 2006). Information Services Department personnel are involved in the preparation of documents inviting quotations, selecting ad agencies for production, liaising with client bureaus and departments on production logistics, management of the approval process and allocation of airtime for broadcasting the APIs (Information Services Department, 2013c). Among the mass media, television is considered the most effective medium for delivering messages to the public (Wong, 2006). Hong Kong's licensing regulations oblige the three local free television licensees and two local commercial analog radio broadcasters to broadcast one minute of APIs every hour free of charge. With the free airtime, APIs on television are known to make a significant social impact (Chan, 2010).

As of 2015, there are eighteen different publicity campaigns broadcast in the television media. Table 10.1 (Information Services Department, 2015) lists these in alphabetical order. Among them, at least thirteen are of concern to children and youths. However, most such publicity campaigns do not employ age segmentation strategies. In other words, it is rare to find a publicity campaign developed on a single key message but with different executions,

Table 10.1

The Hong Kong Government's TV Publicity Campaigns

Campaign	Title or slogan of advertisement targeting children and youths
Anti-drugs*	Anti-drugs 2015 (Quit drugs now)
Basic law and constitutional development	
Civic Education	
Clean Hong Kong*	Let's keep Hong Kong clean
Fight crime*	Mind your belongings
Education*	Respect our teachers
Environmental protection*	Waste less! Rinse and recycle glass bottles
Family*	Family education (modelling)
Fire prevention*	Countryside protection and hill fire prevention
Health and hygiene*	Exercise every day with your family
Home safety and building management	Lift safety
Hospitality	
Information technology*	GovWiFi (security)
Intellectual property rights*	Don't sell counterfeit and pirated goods over the Internet
Labor relations, employment and occupational safety*	Youth employment and training program
Road safety and transport*	Pay attention. Cross the road with care
Volunteering*	Volunteering — new attitude to life
Others	

*Campaigns with children and youths as one of the target groups

(Information Services Department, 2015).

each aimed at a different age segment. Take the promotion of social inclusion ideas among children and youths as an example. In recent years, there has been an influx of school children from mainland China. Some schools also have students of non-Chinese races. Many children therefore have daily encounters with classmates from different cultures. It is important to foster mutual understanding and respect among schoolchildren. Therefore, there is a need to introduce the idea of social inclusion among children. The public service advertisement in place is not sufficient to cater to the cognitive level and tastes of children. In the government's audit report, the Information Services Department was criticized for its lack of yardsticks to measure the effectiveness of the publicity campaigns in terms of awareness, attitude/behavioral change and participation. Some publicity campaigns did not set any performance targets to measure the effects of communication (Audit Commission, 2001).

Conclusion

Children have a good understanding of public service advertisements in Hong Kong. They can identify the key messages of the public service advertisements which use straightforward and child-friendly narration. However, audience research indicates that not all public service advertisements communicate well with youths and children. Hong Kong citizens in general and children and youths in particular are responsive to creative stories, funny characters and social issues which have a high personal relevance. There is a need for social marketers to measure the effectiveness of public service advertisements using interviews or surveys. These social messages will be more effective when they are discussed or elaborated in detail in the family or at school.

Acknowledgements

Reprinted from: *Social Marketing: Global Perspectives, Strategies and Effects on Consumer Behavior*, "Understanding of public service advertisements among Chinese children", pp. 109–120, copyright (2015), K. Chan and A. Huang with permission from Nova Science Publishers, Inc.

References

Audit Commission (2001), "Management of government publicity programmes", available at: http://www.aud.gov.hk/eng/pubpr_arpt/subj_intgs.htm (accessed on June 9, 2014).

Chan, K. (2000), "Hong Kong children's understanding of television advertising", *Journal of Marketing Communications*, Vol. 6 No. 1, pp. 37–52.

Chan, K. (2010), *Youth and Consumption*. City University of Hong Kong Press. Hong Kong.

Chan, K. (2014), "International research on advertising and children", in Cheng, H. (Ed.), *The Handbook of International Advertising Research*, Wiley Blackwell, Oxford, pp. 414–433.

Chan, K. and Chang, H.C. (2013), "Advertising to Chinese youth: A study of public service ads in Hong Kong", *Qualitative Market Research*, Vol. 16 No. 4, pp. 421–435.

Communications Authority (2013), "Generic code of practice on television advertising standards", available at: http://www.coms-auth.hk/filemanager/common/policies_regulations/cop/code_tvad_e.pdf (accessed on July 9, 2015).

Evans, W.D. (2006), "How social marketing works in health care", *British Medical Journal*, Vol. 322, pp. 1207–1210.

Food Wise Hong Kong (2014), "Good practice guide", available at: http://www.fooodwisehk.gov.hk/en/resources.php (accessed on June 9, 2014).

Information Services Department (2010), "Anti-drug 2010 (Harm of abusing thinner and cough medicine)", available at: http://www.isd.gov.hk/eng/tvapi/10_ac136.html (accessed on June 9, 2014).

Information Services Department (2013a), "Big Waster sends eye-opening message", available at: http://www.news.gov.hk/en/categories/environment/html/2013/11/20131108_135340.shtml?pickList=highlight (accessed on June 9,2014).

Information Services Department (2013b), "Food Wise Hong Kong campaign launched" (with photos), available at: http://www.info.gov.hk/gia/general/201305/18/P201305180667.htm (accessed on June 9, 2014).

Information Services Department (2013c), "Public service advertising — TV APIs", *Guest lecture by Brett Free and Pamela Chan*, Hong Kong Baptist University, 4 November.

Information Services Department (2013d), "Respect different values, embrace different views", available at: http://www.isd.gov.hk/eng/tvapi/13_ce204.html (accessed on June 9, 2014).

Information Services Department (2014), "Publicity and promotions", available at: http://www.isd.gov.hk/eng/pub.htm (accessed on June 9, 2014).

Information Services Department (2015), "TV announcements", available at: http://www.isd.gov.hk/eng/tvapi.htm (accessed on December 31, 2015).

John, D.R. (1999), "Consumer socialization of children: A retrospective look at twenty-five years of research", *Journal of Consumer Research*, Vol. 26, December, pp. 183–213.

Piaget, J. (1970), "The stages of the intellectual development of the child", in Mussen, P.H., Conger, J.J. and Kagan, J. (Eds.), *Readings in Child Development and Personality*, Harper and Row, New York NY, pp. 291–298.

Selman, R.L. (1980), *The Growth of Interpersonal Understanding*. Academic Press. New York NY.

Wong, W.S. (2006), "Political ideology in Hong Kong's Public Service Announcements", in Chan, K. (Ed.), *Advertising and Hong Kong Society*, The Chinese University Press, Hong Kong, pp. 55–76.

Chapter 11

Advertising Medical Services

Kara Chan, Lennon Tsang and Vivienne Leung

Introduction

In past decades, the global rise in aging and economic globalization has challenged the status quo of health-care systems in many countries (Aspalter et al., 2012). Global aging is the result of two fundamental demographic forces: rising longevity and falling fertility (Peterson, 2002). Hong Kong's population is experiencing an aging trend. The proportion of individuals aged 65 and over is expected to increase from 15% in 2014 to 36% in 2064 (Census and Statistics Department, 2015). With an aging society, the public need for health care and medical services will increase. Hong Kong's medical system is a mix of private and public professional practices, with significant differences in the costs involved. In recent years, regulations for professional services, including medical legal services, were relaxed to allow medical practitioners to advertise in selected media. This chapter reviews public attitudes toward professional advertising. It also reports the results of a survey on public perceptions of medical advertising and the perceived social impact of such advertisements.

Public Attitudes toward Professional Advertising

The percentage of the global population aged over 65 has been estimated to increase from 8% in 2010 to 16% by 2050 (Haub, 2011). Improvements in health for seniors will allow them to live longer and therefore accrue more health-care costs (Goldman et al., 2005). This suggests an increasing demand for health-care services in the long run. This demographic trend will increase the demand for medical as well as health-care services. As a result, the medical costs to be borne by individuals and public funding by governments will also increase dramatically (Peterson, 1999).

A comparative study of health-care systems in Europe and Asia found that those in Asia are characterized by a high degree of preventive services and policies, combined with the use of traditional medicine. Governments in East Asia control health-care systems to a great extent and are very cost-conscious (Aspalter et al., 2012).

There are mixed views on whether health-care services should be made private. Proponents of private care say it will reduce waiting lists in the public system. Opponents say private markets will drive prices up to enable health providers to make profits (Davidson, 2012). Despite the differing opinions, the need for private health-care services has undoubtedly been increasing over the past decades. The rising costs of medical care may threaten the trust between medical health providers and patients. A survey of patients in the U.S. found that respondents with high medical bills have less trust in their physicians and have a more negative opinion of the thoroughness of the medical care they receive from their physician. Exposing patients to higher medical costs could lead to greater skepticism and less trust in physicians' decision-making skills, thereby making health-care delivery less effective (Cunningham, 2009).

Privatization of health-care systems leads to the need for health providers, including hospitals and medical practitioners, to promote their services. Advertising is one of the marketing communication channels to promote services. There has long been a call to relax advertising rules against the advertising of certain professions and regulations for different types of professionals including accountants, lawyers and physicians all over the world (Miller and Waller, 1979; Hite et al., 1990). Attitudes toward professionals advertising varied significantly among professionals and the general public. Studies in the 1970s showed that professionals disliked advertising and most professionals expressed worries that such advertising would tarnish the public image of their professions (Shimp and Dyer, 1978). A survey reported that advertising by medical professionals was perceived more negatively by medical practitioners than by the general public (Hite and Billizzi, 1986; Caruana and Carey, 1997). It also found that consumers desired informative advertising from professionals, especially during the period of prohibition on professionals' advertising when such services relied heavily on word-of-mouth for promotion (Hite et al., 1990).

A consumer survey found that professionals such as accountants, lawyers and doctors in Hong Kong generally enjoy a highly favorable public image. Respondents considered professional advertising useful in providing information about services and fee structures. They perceived that advertising by professionals would not jeopardize this favorable image. However, they noted that advertising by professionals would increase the cost of professional services (Au, 1997). Another qualitative study found that interviewees generally believed that advertising legal services is helpful as it makes the legal profession seem more approachable and transparent. However, interviewees considered that lawyers advertising using price appeal could be misleading. Interviewees also worried that the advertising of legal services would encourage the use of litigation as the preferred means of solving disputes (Chan et al., 2012).

Medical Professionals in Hong Kong and Advertising Regulations

In Hong Kong, there were 13,726 medical practitioners registered as of December 2015 (Information Services Department, 2016). The number of doctors per thousand people was 1.9, which was significantly lower than that of the U.K. (2.8 in 2013), the U.S. (2.5 in 2011), Japan (2.3 in 2010) and Singapore (2.0 in 2013; The World Bank, 2015). The Medical Council of Hong Kong was established under the Medical Registration Ordinance. The Council is responsible for enforcing the registration and professional discipline of all medical practitioners in Hong Kong. The objective of the Council is to maintain a high standard of professional conduct and to uphold trust in the competence and integrity of the medical profession (The Medical Council of Hong Kong, 2009). In the past, medical professionals were not allowed to advertise in Hong Kong (Au, 1997). In fact, according to the *Code of Professional Conduct for the Guidance of Registered Medical Practitioners* published by the Medical Council, medical practices should not be promoted as a commercial activity (The Medical Council of Hong Kong, 2009). The Council believed that advertising medical care as no more than a commercial activity would undermine public trust in the profession and eventually diminish the standard of medical care (The Medical Council of Hong Kong, 2009).

In view of the increasing demand for private medical services, the Medical Council relaxed the regulations on medical practice promotion in 2008. Publication of service information in four print media, namely newspapers, magazines, journals and periodicals, was permitted (The Medical Council of Hong Kong, 2009). Not many medical doctors advertised. In 2011, the advertising expenditure spent on health services was HK$435,817,000 (admanGo, 2012). Most of the advertisers were hospitals, clinics, laboratories or health-care groups. Individual medical doctors accounted for only 1% of this advertising expenditure.

A Study Examining Public Attitudes toward Advertising by Medical Professionals

A study was conducted to investigate the public's attitudes toward advertising by medical professionals. The main objectives of the study were:

- to investigate consumers' attitudes toward advertising by medical professionals;

- to examine if attitudes toward advertising by medical professionals vary among different demographic groups; and

- to examine if consumers with a high knowledge about the current regulatory framework and consumers with a low knowledge have different attitudes toward advertising by medical professionals.

The questionnaire used in the study was adapted from a previous study on attitudes toward professional advertising (Au, 1997). Additional statements were added by modifying those from a previous qualitative study on attitudes toward advertising by lawyers (Chan et al., 2012). The questionnaire had three sections, including "Attitudes toward advertising by medical professionals", "Attitudes toward medical professionals" and "Perceived impact of advertising by medical professionals". All the statements were measured on a five-point scale with one indicating "disagree strongly" and five indicating "agree strongly". Medical professionals were defined as all types of medical doctors and dentists who treat human patients. Following the attitudinal statements, respondents were asked in which media medical professionals in Hong Kong were allowed to advertise now. Respondents were asked to choose from a list of nine media including newspapers, radio and television. A new variable was added, labeled "Knowledge of advertising regulation". The variable was set to one if respondents were able to observe correctly that medical professionals were allowed to advertise in both newspapers and magazines. These respondents were labeled as having a high knowledge of the current regulatory framework. Otherwise, the variable was set to zero, with these respondents labeled as having a low knowledge of the current regulatory framework. Finally, demographic variables including age, sex, education, housing type, occupation and household income were collected. The study was conducted in Chinese.

In view of the unavailability of a suitable sampling frame, a quota sampling survey of Hong Kong residents aged 20 or above was conducted. Students studying research methods at Hong Kong Baptist University were asked to invite others to fill in an online questionnaire. At least one male and one female adult in the age groups of 20–29, 30–39, 40–49 and 50 or above were recruited by each student. Altogether 1,403 online questionnaires were received. Among these, 1,297, about 92%, were completed.

The demographic profile of the respondents is presented in Table 11.1. There were roughly equal proportions of males and females. The majority of them were aged 20–29. More than half of them had post-secondary or university education. Among them, 61% were coded as having a low knowledge of the current regulatory framework on advertising by medical professionals.

Table 11.1

Demographic Profile of Respondents (N=1,297)

Demographic	Number	Percentage
Sex		
Female	635	49.0
Male	662	51.0
Age		
20–29	547	42.2
30–39	258	19.9
40–49	267	20.6
50 or above	225	17.3
Education		
Primary or below	73	5.6
Secondary school	504	38.9
Post-secondary or university	720	55.5
Monthly household income		
HK$9,999 or below	222	17.1
HK$10,000–HK$19,999	412	31.8
HK$20,000–HK$39,999	440	33.9
HK$40,000 or above	223	17.2
*Knowledge level of the current regulatory framework**		
Low	786	60.6
High	511	39.4

*Knowledge level of the current regulatory framework was based on whether the respondent correctly chose newspapers and magazines as the media that allowed advertising by medical professionals.

Attitudes toward Medical Professionals and Advertising by Medical Professionals

The respondents' attitudes toward advertising by medical professionals are summarized in Table 11.2. Four out of ten statements had mean scores that differed significantly from the midpoint of 3.0. In other words, consumers in general did not have strong views about the remaining six out of ten attitudinal statements. The four statements on which consumers had strong views were about the quality of information contained in advertisements by medical professionals. Respondents showed an appreciation for the useful

Table 11.2

Respondents' Attitudes toward Advertising by Medical Professionals

Statements	Mean[a]	SD	t-value (mean=3)
It is proper for medical professionals to advertise	3.02	0.90	0.8
I would like to see advertising by medical professionals	2.98	0.93	-0.8
Advertising by medical professionals would be a useful means of informing potential consumers about services and specialties	3.28	0.92	11.0***
Advertising by medical professionals would be more deceptive than other forms of advertising	3.15	0.90	5.9***
The public would be provided with useful information through advertising by medical professionals	3.36	0.82	15.9***
I would like the services (if needed) of medical professionals who advertise	3.04	0.93	1.4
I worry about misleading and exaggerated information in advertising by medical professionals	3.72	0.93	28.0***
I think advertising by medical professionals should focus on individual doctors or dentists	3.05	0.96	1.8
I think advertising by medical professionals should focus on the contribution of the whole team of doctors or dentists of the same medical group	3.05	0.92	1.8
I believe a greater use of advertising by medical professionals would improve the quality of their services	2.96	1.04	-1.5

[a] All variables are measured on a five-point scale with 5 being "strongly agree" and 1 being "strongly disagree"

*p<.05; **p<.01; ***p<.001.

information about services and specialties of medical professionals provided by advertisements. However, they expressed worries that some advertisements by medical professionals might be deceptive or exaggerated. Respondents in general did not express strong views about whether medical professionals should advertise or whether their advertisements should put emphasis on individual doctors or a team of doctors.

Respondents' attitudes toward medical professionals are summarized in Table 11.3. Compared with their attitudes toward advertising by medical professionals, respondents expressed much stronger views in their attitudes toward medical professionals. Six out of seven statements had mean scores that differed significantly from the mid-point of 3.0. Respondents reported that they had a highly favorable image of medical professionals. They expressed an intention to deal with reputable medical professionals rather than those offering low fees. Respondents expressed the view that medical professionals who advertised did not inspire them with confidence. They reported that they would be suspicious of medical professionals who advertised. They disagreed with the statement that medical professionals who advertised were more trustworthy. They did not have more confidence in medical professionals who advertised. They also did not believe in a price-quality connection for medical professionals.

The different impacts of advertising by medical professionals as perceived by respondents are summarized in Table 11.4. Respondents expressed much stronger views concerning the potential impact of advertising by medical professionals than they did toward advertising by medical professionals. All seven statements had mean scores that differed significantly from the mid-point of 3.0. Among all twenty-four attitudinal statements tested in the study, the highest mean score of 3.81 was reported for the statement "Advertising would lead to an increase in prices of medical professional services as the advertising costs would be passed on to the clients". This indicates that a majority of the respondents believed that they would need to pay more for medical services if medical professionals advertise more. Again, respondents showed an appreciation of the informative content of advertising by medical professionals. This can be seen from their belief that the medical profession would be more transparent with advertising, and that the public would gain knowledge of the qualifications of medical professionals through advertising. Respondents perceived that advertisements by medical professionals would save the public time and effort in locating medical services. They also believed

Table 11.3
Respondents' Attitudes toward Medical Professionals

Statements	Mean[a]	SD	t-value (mean =3)
I presently have a highly favorable image of medical professionals	3.57	0.80	25.8***
In general, my image of medical professionals would be less favorable as a result of advertising	2.99	0.90	-0.3
It is better to deal with reputable medical professionals than one who offers the lowest price	3.51	0.96	19.1***
I believe medical professionals who advertise are in a better position financially and should be more trustworthy	2.87	0.93	-5.0***
I have more confidence in medical professionals who advertise	2.85	0.92	-5.9***
Medical professionals who charge a higher price will provide better quality services	2.91	1.01	-3.3***
I would be suspicious of medical professionals who advertise	3.35	0.84	14.8***

[a] All variables are measured on a five-point scale with 5 being "strongly agree" and 1 being "strongly disagree"
*p<.05; **p<.01; ***p<.001.

Table 11.4
The Impact of Advertising by Medical Professionals as Perceived by Respondents

Statements	Mean[a]	SD	t-value (mean=3)
Advertising would lead to an increase in prices of medical professional services as the advertising costs would be passed on to the clients.	3.81	0.88	33.4***
Advertising would increase the quality of medical professional services through competition.	3.07	0.89	3.0**
Advertising would help consumers make more intelligent choices between medical professionals.	3.05	0.87	2.1*
Advertising helps the public to understand the qualifications of medical professionals.	3.29	0.87	11.8***
Advertising by medical professionals would benefit only quacks and incompetents.	3.13	0.83	5.8***
Advertising by medical professionals would reduce the time and effort spent finding a suitable medical professional.	3.26	0.84	10.9***
Advertising would increase the transparency of the medical profession.	3.34	0.92	13.5***

[a] All variables are measured on a five-point scale with 5 being "strongly agree" and 1 being "strongly disagree"
*p<.05; **p<.01; ***p<.001.

that advertising would introduce competition and, as a result, the quality of medical services would improve.

Comparison between Attitudes toward Advertising by Professionals and toward Television Advertising in General

Respondents' favorable image of medical professionals and their appreciation of the information in medical advertisements were similar to the findings of Au's (1997) study. (His study included attitudes toward advertising by accountants, doctors and lawyers.) However, there were two differences between the findings of the current study and Au's. First, respondents in the current study believed that the quality of medical professional services would increase through competition while respondents in Au's (1997) did not believe so. Second, respondents in the current study were of the opinion that advertising by medical professionals would help consumers to make more intelligent choices, while respondents in Au's (1997) study held neutral views on the issue.

Respondents' attitudes toward advertising by medical professionals were similar to public attitudes toward television advertising in general (Chan, 2006). The function of using advertising to spread information about medical professionals was well received by the respondents, while many believed it would not offer buying confidence.

A strong and deeply rooted belief about the economic cost of advertising was reflected in the current study as well as Chan's (2006) study. Similar to our current finding, the statement in Chan's (2006) study with the highest mean among the perceived consequences of advertising was "Television advertising increases the cost of products" (mean=3.7).

Attitudes toward Advertising by Medical Professionals among Different Demographic Groups

Sex and household incomes of respondents did not particularly correlate with attitudes toward advertising by medical professionals. Only one or two statements out of twenty-four registered statistical differences.

The age variable demonstrated significant influence on attitudes toward advertising by medical professionals. Nine out of twenty-four attitudinal statements showed significant age group differences. Respondents aged 20-29 agreed most that advertising by medical professionals would be more deceptive than other forms of advertising. They worried the most about misleading advertisements by medical professionals. They were more likely to agree that advertising would lead to higher prices. They disagreed the most that medical professionals who advertise are more trustworthy. They disagreed the most that medical professionals who charge higher prices would provide better service. They agreed the most that it is better to deal with reputable doctors than doctors offering the lowest price. In other words, younger respondents were more skeptical of advertising by medical professionals than older respondents. In addition, respondents aged 50 or above disagreed most that it was proper for medical professionals to advertise. They also had the least favorable image of medical professionals.

The education variable also demonstrated significant influence on attitudes toward advertising by medical professionals. Half of the twenty-four attitudinal statements showed significant differences between education groups. Respondents with primary or lower education levels had the most favorable attitudes toward advertising by medical professionals. They agreed the most that it is proper for medical professionals to advertise and that they would like to see such advertisements. They felt most strongly that these advertisements would be useful in informing consumers about services and specialties and said they would use the services of medical professionals who advertise. They agreed most with the statement that advertising would help consumers make intelligent choices regarding medical services. Respondents with post-secondary education demonstrated the strongest skepticism toward advertising by medical professionals. They worried the most about misleading information in these advertisements. They did not believe that allowing medical professionals to advertise would improve the quality of the service. They did not believe that medical professionals who advertise are more trustworthy. They had the highest levels of agreement with the statement that it is better to deal with reputable doctors than those offering the lowest price. They showed the least confidence in medical professionals who advertise. They believed most strongly that advertising would lead to an increase in prices of medical services.

Older respondents and respondents of a lower educational level were found to be less skeptical toward advertising by medical professionals. This may be because older respondents and respondents of lower educational levels have a higher need for medical services. Reliance on the service may make them less skeptical.

Attitudes toward Advertising by Medical Professionals by Levels of Knowledge

Altogether ten out of twenty-four attitudinal statements showed significant difference in mean scores between the two groups. Table 11.5 summarizes

Table 11.5

Attitudes among Respondents with a High or Low Knowledge Level of the Regulatory Framework on Advertising

Statements	Knowledge level[a]		
	Low	High	t-value
It is proper for medical professionals to advertise	2.94	3.14	-3.8***
Advertising by medical professionals would be a useful means of informing potential consumers about services and specialties	3.20	3.41	-4.1***
The public would be provided with useful information through advertising by medical professionals	3.31	3.45	-3.1***
It is better to deal with reputable medical professionals than one who offers the lowest price	3.46	3.59	-2.4***
Advertising would lead to an increase in prices of medical professional services as the advertising costs would be passed on to the clients	3.73	3.94	-4.4***
Advertising would increase the quality of medical professional services through competition	3.03	3.14	-2.1***
Advertising would help consumers make more intelligent choices between medical professionals	3.01	3.12	-2.3***
Advertising makes the public more aware of the qualifications of medical professionals	3.21	3.40	-3.8***
Advertising by medical professionals would reduce the time and effort spent finding a suitable medical professional	3.19	3.36	-3.5***
Advertising would increase the transparency of the medical profession	3.28	3.44	-3.1***

[a] All variables are measured on a five-point scale with 5 being "strongly agree" and 1 being "strongly disagree
*p<.05; **p<.01; ***p<.001.

the mean scores of the two groups for statements with significant differences. In general, respondents with a high level of knowledge of the regulatory framework on advertising media demonstrated more positive attitudes toward advertising by medical professionals than those with a lower knowledge level. Respondents with a high knowledge level were more appreciative of the information value of advertising by medical professionals. They were also more likely to believe the impact of advertising by medical professionals would be positive. This suggests that skepticism about advertising may arise from lack of knowledge of advertising practices.

Social Implications of the Study

Advertisers should design communication messages that are in line with consumers' attitudes and beliefs. According to the findings of the study, in advertising medical services, medical professionals should put emphasis on providing service users with relevant information of their services, expertise and qualifications to assist their information search. They should refrain from using price appeal. The public generally believes that advertising costs will be transferred to service users. It is believed that enhancing buying confidence through advertising by medical professionals is difficult. Medical professionals may consider a careful selection of credible media as well as the adoption of a professional and non-aggressive advertising tone in enhancing user confidence in their advertising messages.

Conclusion

To conclude, public attitudes toward advertising by medical professionals were mostly favorable. Respondents reported that advertising by medical professionals provides people with information about the services and qualifications of practitioners. However, respondents were worried about misleading information in these advertisements. They believed strongly that advertising by medical professionals would lead to an increase in the price of services. Younger respondents and respondents with higher education were more skeptical toward advertising by medical professionals. As this is the first study to examine consumers' attitudes toward advertising by medical professionals in a Chinese context, the information yielded is useful for medical practitioners in designing their advertising messages and for professional media bodies and policymakers to make informed decisions on the regulation of such advertising.

Acknowledgements

Part of this chapter was published in Chan, K., Tsang, L. and Leung, V. (2013), "Consumers' Attitudes toward Advertising by Medical Professionals", *Journal of Consumer Marketing*, Vol. 30 No. 4, pp. 328–334.

References

admanGo (2012), "Advertising expenditure by product category in 2011", available at: www.admanGo.com.

Aspalter, C., Uchida, Y. and Gauld, R. (Eds.) (2012), *Health Care Systems in Europe and Asia*. Routledge. Abingdon, Oxon.

Au, A.K.M. (1997), "Consumers' attitudes toward professional advertising in Hong Kong", *Services Marketing Quarterly*, Vol. 15 No. 2, pp. 41–53.

Caruana, A. and Carey, C. (1997), "The attitude toward advertising by medical practitioners and the general public: Some evidence from Malta", *Management Research News*, Vol. 20 No. 9, pp. 39–47.

Census and Statistics Department. HKSAR Government (2015), "Press release: Hong Kong population projections 2015-2064", September 25, available at http://www.censtatd.gov.hk/press_release/pressReleaseDetail.jsp?charsetID=1&pressRID=3799 (accessed on April 11, 2016).

Chan, K. (2006), *Advertising and Hong Kong Society*. The Chinese University Press, Hong Kong.

Chan, K., Leung, V., Tsang, L. and Yip, T. (2012), "An exploratory study of consumers' attitudes toward advertising of legal professionals in Hong Kong", *Asian Journal of Business Research*, Vol. 2 No. 2, pp. 70–86.

Cunningham, P.J. (2009), "High medical cost burdens, patient trust, and perceived quality of care", *Journal of General Internal Medicine*, Vol. 24 No. 3, pp. 415–420.

Davidson, S. (2012,), "Private v public health care: No simple policy", *The Drum Opinion on ABC News*, February 22, available at: http://www.abc.net.au/unleashed/3842776.html (accessed on December 10, 2012).

Goldman, D.P., Shang, B., Bhattacharya, J., Garber, A.M., Hurd, M., Joyce G.F., Lakdawalla D.N., Panis, C. and Shekelle P.G. (2005), "Consequences of health trends and medical innovation for the future elderly", *Health Affairs*, Vol. 24, pp. 5–17.

Haub, C. (2011), "World population aging: Clocks illustrate growth in population under age 5 and over age 65", available at: http://www.prb.org/Articles/2011/agingpopulationclocks.aspx (accessed on December 10, 2012).

Hite, R.E. and Bellizzi, J.A. (1986), "Consumers' attitudes toward accountants, lawyers, and physicians with respect to advertising professional services", *Journal of Advertising Research*, Vol. 26 No. 3, pp. 45-54.

Hite, R.E., Fraser, C. and Bellizzi, J.A. (1990), "Professional service advertising: The effects of price inclusion, justification, and level of risk", *Journal of Advertising Research*, Vol. 30 No. 4, pp. 23–31.

Information Services Department, HKSAR Government (2016), "Hong Kong: The facts — Public health", available at: http://www.gov.hk/en/about/abouthk/factsheets/docs/public_health.pdf (accessed on April 11, 2016).

Miller, J.A. and Waller, R. (1979), "Health care advertising: Consumer vs. physician attitudes", *Journal of Advertising*, Vol. 8 No. 4, pp. 20–29.

Peterson, P.G. (1999), "Gray dawn: The global aging crisis", *Foreign Affairs*, Vol. 78 No. 1, pp. 42–55.

Peterson, P.G. (2002), "The shape of things to come: Global aging in the twenty-first century", *Journal of International Affairs*, Vol. 56 No. 1, pp. 189–210.

Shimp, T.A. and Dyer, R.F. (1978), "The views of the legal professional toward legal service advertising", *Journal of Marketing*, Vol. 42 No. 3, pp. 74–81.

The Medical Council of Hong Kong (2009), "Code of professional conduct for the guidance of registered medical practitioners", pp. 15–23, available at: http://www.mchk.org.hk/Code_of_Professional_Conduct_2009.pdf (accessed on June 22, 2015).

The World Bank (2015), "Data by country: Physicians per 1,000 people", available at: data.worldbank.org/indicator/SH.MED.PHYS.ZS (accessed on June 22, 2015).

Chapter 12

Advancing Social Causes through Video Games

Vincie Pui Yuen Lee

Introduction

Publicity and advertising play an essential role in the promotion of a healthy lifestyle and educate the public on how to maintain a healthy lifestyle. Many health advertisements seek to advance people's understanding of the risks and consequences of particular health issues, provide them with a better understanding of diverse illnesses, help the public assess their lifestyle and persuade and influence people to pursue healthy behavior (Naidoo and Wills, 2009). Health advertising in Hong Kong has widely adopted mass media, such as TV commercials and posters to send health messages to the public. This chapter argues that video games are becoming significant in promoting health. We suggest that the interactive nature of playing a video game surpasses traditional communication media (such as TV and print media) by engaging players in the health communication process. In this chapter, we first explore the growing popularity of the video game culture among Hong Kong's youth. We then investigate the use of video games for health communication in both commercial and public sectors. A particular genre of video games promoting healthy behavior, namely health games, will be discussed. This chapter supports its argument with findings from an empirical study of Hong Kong teenagers' experiences playing health games.

The Digital Generation

Increasingly, the use of communication technologies is viewed as important in informing the public of health concerns (Kreps et al., 1998). New communication technologies, such as the Internet and mobile phones, have been widely adopted for promoting health concerns to the general public in recent decades (Kreps et al., 1998). They are especially useful in Hong Kong, where young people do not spend much time watching TV, but they do browse the Internet frequently and use mobile devices for everyday communication. According to the Communications Authority of Hong Kong, in 2014 the estimated Internet users' penetration rate reached 73%, and 96% of smartphone users accessed the Internet daily multiple times. Young people use mobile phones and the Internet to search for information, contact people and for entertainment, such as playing video games. The Internet and mobile devices are considered an indispensable part of people's lives.

The popularity of high technology devices, such as tablets and smartphones, and the increasing speed of broadband Internet access have allowed video game-playing to become a popular activity among the youngsters in Hong Kong. Teenagers are fond of playing video games because they find them entertaining and challenging. According to Wang et al. (2014), some teenagers spend up to three hours every day playing video games. Video games provide a new advertising opportunity for marketers who are keen to communicate with a young audience. The notion of utilizing video games for health advertising to young people is, therefore, promising. Various genres of video games (e.g. action games, adventure games, fighting games, puzzle games and role-playing games) have been introduced by different game developers.

There are many ongoing game projects and research activities about health games. Most of them focus on education; for instance, they educate people about food and nutrition (e.g. *Pyramid Pile Up*), build attention training (e.g. *Inside and Outside, Bird Watching*) or encourage physical exercise (e.g. *Active Life Outdoor Challenge*). However, limited research is available on understanding how video games could be used for public service promotion and for persuasive purposes.

Health Promotion in Hong Kong

Health promotion is broadly defined as the process of enabling people to increase control over, and to improve, their health. It is a planned process to create awareness of specific health issues and to encourage individuals to act on, or respond to, a health message (Kiger, 2004). Health promotion focuses on increasing the awareness of health issues, such as disease prevention and quality of life, and eventually aims to change people's behavior and lifestyle (Simon-Morton et al., 1998). Many health communication activities seek to advance people's understanding of the risks and consequences of particular health issues, provide them with a better understanding of diverse illnesses, help them to assess and alter their lifestyle and make decisions to facilitate healthy behavior. Creating, gathering and sharing health information is important in health promotion because they are essential in guiding behavior and decisions (Kreps, 1998). In other words, it is essential to design persuasive messages and communicate through salient communication channels to the target audience in order to achieve successful health promotion.

Hong Kong stands out among wealthy megacities in that Hong Kong people are increasingly concerned about their health. The Information Services Department (ISD) is in control of producing diverse TV Announcements in the Public Interests (APIs) for the Department of Health in Hong Kong (see Chapter 13). Health messages in Hong Kong cover diverse health topics, such as the prevention of cancer, obesity, anti-smoking and alcohol and drug abuse, the latter aimed at teenagers. Because of the free-of-charge airtime available, TV is the major medium used by the government for promoting health messages to youngsters in Hong Kong. The Narcotics Division of the Security Bureau, specifically tasked to combat the problem of drug abuse in Hong Kong, together with the ISD, has produced APIs promoting anti-drug messages to teenagers and adults. TV announcements produced in 2013 and 2014 used the theme of friends, which reminded young people not to be tempted by friends to try drugs, and the theme of seeking help early in 2014, which aimed to encourage people with drug problems to seek help early.

Video Game-Playing Culture Among Teenagers

Playing video games, both on consoles and online, is popular among children and teenagers, and is regarded as "an immensely popular form of entertainment" (Towne et al., 2014). The video game industry has continued to grow around the world and has generated significant revenue in recent years. According to the Entertainment Software Association's (ESA) report in 2014, the video game industry grew globally 9.7% annually from 2009 to 2012. In Hong Kong, the revenue generated from video games has continuously increased, and it reached HK$2 billion in 2015 (Newzoo, 2015). This tremendous growth makes it one of the largest creative industries in Hong Kong (Hong Kong Monthly Digest of Statistics, March 2014). Furthermore, there has been an increasing number of both younger age game-players and game-playing time in recent years. For instance, the Hong Kong Internet Use and Online Gamer Survey (Fung, 2013) showed that the number of online game-players aged 9–15 has increased significantly. They spent four days per week on average, ninety minutes per day, playing video games. According to Wang et al. (2014), nearly 50% of children in Hong Kong play video games every day. In their survey, one-third of the respondents spent up to three hours per day playing video games on weekdays; the others spent more than one hour on video game-playing on weekends. Over two-thirds of primary and secondary school students in Hong Kong use digital screen devices for offline and online activities every day. They indicated that playing video games was a popular activity for relieving pressure from the overload of homework (Department of Health, 2015). According to Wang and his colleagues (2014), a growth in younger aged video game-players has been found in recent years, with the youngest game-players being only 2 years old. About 19% of preschool students in Hong Kong indicated that they play video games daily for an average of twenty-seven minutes per day. Furthermore, this study found that 23% of secondary school student participants spent more than three hours on video games each day on weekdays, and 37% spent more than three hours on video games each day on weekends (Wang et al., 2014).

Video games bring both entertainment and educational benefits for health communication (Schott et al., 2006). Some studies (e.g. Blumberg et al., 2013) have demonstrated that playing video games has beneficial effects on psychological and physical health. Previous research has suggested that video games enable youngsters to learn about values and change behavior (Lieberman, 2009) as well as enhance their knowledge and skills as players in social groups (Thompson, 2010). The rapid development of interactive digital technology of video games has advanced health communication, by encouraging passive recipients to become active players (Shan et al., 2015). Other benefits of the interactive nature of video games include providing an engaging experience in the communication process, the delivery of tailored health information to the audience (Beratarrechea et al., 2014) and helping to avoid onset of some health problems (Centers for Disease Control and Prevention, 2015). Lieberman (2001) has suggested that video games would be a powerful channel that could benefit the young generation, not only for entertainment, but also for communicating health values to change their daily habits and behavior.

Advergames for Commercial Promotions

One type of video games for communication are "advergames". An advergame is a digital game designed to promote a specific idea and service with a "fun to play" game. Advergames benefit from the use of persuasion knowledge, which helps to achieve a desirable outcome without delivering an explicit promotion cue (Terlutter and Capella, 2013). For instance, BMW commissioned a game based on *GT Legends*, a sports car racing game, to promote a new car model in 2008. Advergames are usually free of charge and can be easily downloaded on digital devices on different platforms. Advergames are a new form of advertising compared to traditional non-interactive advertising, such as TV advertising and printed advertising (Winkler and Buckner, 2006). The aim of advergames is to entertain the audience (Lee and Youn, 2008) and deliver a subtle message at the same time (Nairn and Fine, 2008). The key to delivering a message in an advergame is not to deliver a factual message explicitly (Nairn and Fine, 2008), but to let the audience "play with" the subtle message that has been built into the game design and to engage them in the playing process (Lee and Youn, 2008). During the process of advergame-playing, it is expected that the players will be influenced by the game content and playing experience, resulting in a positive attitude toward the brand or product. The aim of advergames is to change the thought process of its players.

In previous studies of advergames, researchers were interested in studying players' attitudes toward brands, brand consciousness, game and product congruity, brand image and brand recall. Relatively little is known about how advergames may be used for health communication. There is a need to understand how video games are used for communication in both commercial and non-commercial sectors.

Non-Commercial Video Games

The use of non-commercial advergames in health communication can help promote public health policy and evoke social awareness on certain health issues (Dietz et al., 2009; Harris et al., 2009; Skiba, 2008). Both audiences of commercial advergames and publicity advergames are susceptible to persuasion by an immersive game experience (Orji et al., 2013; 2014). However, the degree of impact on different types of audiences varies; for example, children are highly susceptible to persuasion via advergames due to their limited cognitive capacity (Dias and Agante, 2011; Folkvord et al., 2013). Thus, health advergames designed for children should achieve a desirable outcome (Bogost, 2007).

Currently, there is limited knowledge of planning interactive health communication technology (Skinner et al., 2006), especially for promoting public health policies and awareness to young people. The planning of digital health games involves a thorough understanding of digital game design and the health communication process in the game.

Health Games: A Video Game Genre for Health Promotion

Advergames for public services announcements are categorized as a particular type of health game, distinct from games for training, exercising and educational purposes (Sawyer and Smith, 2008). A health game is a genre of "serious games", which involve the use of video games for purposes other than mere entertainment (Blackman, 2005; Thompson, 2010). In other words, an advergame as a form of health game will have a specific mission to promote public health policy, increase social awareness about disease control and encourage healthy behavior. Health games have received considerable attention from the public and academics in recent years. For instance, research on health games (Lieberman, 2001; Orji et al., 2013) claimed that digital health games have assumed a growing importance in improving players' understanding of health care and behavior. The U.S. Government has sponsored research on the use of digital games to improve health and health care across a number of important areas such as food safety, nutrition and obesity, HIV prevention, early pregnancy and tobacco usage by organizing a series of Game for Health Conferences since 2010 (see http://gamesforhealth. org). Dias and Agante (2011) explored advergames and their influence on children's eating habits. There are also games designed to aid children in developing healthy long-term habits (e.g., good nutrition, hygiene, making healthy choices). For instance, *Sesame Street's Color Me Hungry* game teaches the importance of "eating your colors" by choosing appropriate fruit and vegetables. The game *Dance Dance Revolution* developed by Konami keeps children active for many hours to achieve physical fitness. The diversity of health games provide substantial health benefits to youngsters.

Health Game-Playing Experiences of Teenagers in Hong Kong

This section suggests some empirical findings to support the idea that video games could advance health communication to teenagers. We refer to a study about teenagers' experiences in playing a Hong Kong advergame, *The Drug Sensor*, which was designed with a specific anti-drug message. This study focused on understanding teenagers' game-playing experiences, and it aimed to advance our knowledge of designing video games for promoting health messages for the public.

Health Game Design

Anti-drug messages are embedded within the video game. It is a mission-completion game. Players have to prepare a beverage according to a customer's order in a given time. For instance, a player needs to prepare a drink with a mixture of orange, apple and pineapple juice if s/he receives a fruit punch order from a customer. If the player can finish preparing the

Figure 12.1

The Drug Sensor Video Game[1]

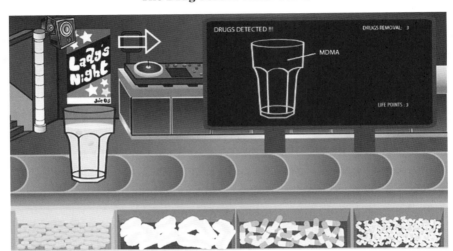

beverage within the given time, points are added to his or her income. An additional challenge embedded in the game is that gangsters randomly and secretly add harmful drugs, such as MDMA, to the beverages. The final challenge for the player is to use the drug sensor to test a beverage to find out if there are drugs in it. If drugs are found, the players have to identify them and stop the beverage from being delivered to a customer. The main mission for the player is to ensure that safe beverages are prepared for customers and to prevent drugs from reaching them. Points are deducted if the mission fails. When a player is playing the game, messages about the risks and consequences of drugs are conveyed to the player.

The Research Method

To explore young people's health game-playing experiences, an inductive inquiry approach was adopted. We interviewed thirty-six participants, aged 9–15, in Hong Kong in 2013. Eighteen of them were in primary school and

---

1. Interface designed by Kwong Ho Yin, a communication student at Hong Kong Baptist University.

eighteen in secondary school. The participants were selected by a snowball sampling method. Each participant was invited to play *The Drug Sensor* video game before being interviewed. The interviews were conducted with open-ended questions, and the participants were asked to talk about the video game and the game-playing process. The study focused on exploring participants' experiences of playing the game. All interviews were audio-taped and transcribed. Thematic analysis was used to generate the following four key game-playing experiences.

Health Game-Playing Experiences

We identified four key game-playing experiences. They are:

- the video game engages players' attention;

- the video game is highly interactive;

- the video game is thought-provoking;

- the video game advances social connectivity.

The Video Game Engages Players' Attention

The Drug Sensor game requires participants to consciously avoid gangsters who would try to put drugs in customers' beverages. Negative health consequences of drug taking are therefore communicated through players' engagement in the game. Some of the participants stated that avoiding drugs being put in the beverages helped them to understand the risk and consequences of drug taking. They realized that drugs are "harmful to our health" and "could make us sick". While they were playing the game, they had to take an active role in receiving health messages. The game environment enabled players to construct health concepts including anti-drug sentiments through understanding the risks and consequences of the drugs they encountered. Furthermore, some participants observed that they found the game "fun" and "interesting", and these feelings enhanced their positive attitudes toward the health message embedded in the game. We found that health messages about the risks and consequences of drug taking were well delivered and received by the participants.

The Video Game is Highly Interactive

This video game is highly interactive. It provides players with rich audio and video stimuli. Players are given a mission to accomplish; i.e. they have to find out about the drugs being added to the beverages within a limited time. The interactive content of the video game encourages players to respond in real-time and be involved in a simulated drug problem. This contrasts with the impact of traditional publicity, wherein the audience passively receives the anti-drug messages. While participants in this study were playing, they said, "I have to take action immediately", and "Oh! I failed to discover them, and I lost the game". The interactive nature of the video game helps players to stay vigilant in the simulated environment. The instant feedback and responses during the game playing gives the participants confidence to act upon and interact with the circumstances that they face. The rewards and points in the video game reinforce the players' anti-drug sentiments. King (2012) claimed that the interactive procedure of a health game engages the audience's cognitive process in healthy behavior and consequently advances health knowledge. Various interactive elements in video games advance the delivery of the advertised message and steer the players toward healthy choices.

The Video Game is Thought-Provoking

The ultimate aim of developing health communication video games is to change people's behavior regarding health issues. In this study, we discovered that challenging the game-players by putting them in a stimulating and dangerous situation, could motivate the players. The game uses red to emphasize dangerous situations; for example, when a player has given a lot of beverages with drugs to the customers. The visual effects highlight the consequences of taking drugs. Players supported avoiding drugs. The game made the players think. For instance, one player said, "You have to help yourself in real life", while another said, "Don't think we are too naïve!" This shows that the game is thought-provoking for players, which may help change their behavior.

The Video Game Advances Social Connectivity

Some participants said that they wanted to share the game and their experiences with their classmates and friends. Some said that they would like to share with others the information they had learnt. We believe that the sharing culture of teenagers nowadays plays an essential role in spreading health messages by word of mouth. Some participants remarked that the health game has the potential to generate communication among peers on this topic. We believe that video games could not only encourage the sharing of health messages with young people, but also advance social connectivity, thus building a supportive atmosphere to achieve a healthy lifestyle. Social interaction is useful in creating positive social pressure and providing support to a peer group, which could encourage healthy behavior in the long run (Fraser and Spink, 2002).

Conclusion

Video games have significant advantages in promoting healthy behavior. In recent years, video games have received considerable attention as a powerful form of commercial promotion and education media. The video game is also a new form of advertising compared to traditional non-interactive advertising. In particular, we discovered that the video game has some unique characteristics that could outperform traditional media. In this chapter, we have discussed the popularity of the video game-playing culture and how advergames are used by marketers in a commercial context. Possessing many distinctive characteristics, video games may play a role in delivering health messages to the public. We showcased some insights from children and teenagers' game-playing experiences and outlined how video games could be used in promoting health messages to them. We shared a case study of young participants' experiences of playing *The Drug Sensor* game to demonstrate the benefits of video games in delivering anti-drug messages. By combining the interactive nature of digital media with important messages, video games can be a great communication and education medium for the promotion of healthy behavior. Further research is needed to study the information processing of messages in video games by children and adolescents and the strategies that should be applied to health game design in order to enhance their persuasive effects.

References

Beratarrechea, A., Lee, A.G., Willner, J.M., Jahangir, E., Ciapponi, A. and Rubinstein, A. (2014), "The impact of mobile health interventions on chronic disease outcomes in developing countries: A systematic review", *Telemedicine and e-Health*, Vol. 20 No. 1, pp. 75–82.

Blackman, S. (2005), "Serious games ... and less!", *ACM Siggraph Computer Graphics*, Vol. 39 No. 1, pp. 12–16.

Blumberg, F.C., Altschuler, E.A., Almonte, D.E. and Mileaf, M.I. (2013), "The impact of recreational video game play on children's and adolescents' cognition", *New Directions for Child and Adolescent Development,* Vol. 139, pp. 41–50.

Bogost, I. (2007), *Persuasive Games: The Expressive Power of Videogames*. MIT Press, Cambridge. MA,

Centers for Disease Control and Prevention (2015), "Preventive health care", Gateway to Health Communication and Social Marketing Practice, available at: http://www.cdc.gov/healthcommunication/toolstemplates/entertainmented/tips/preventivehealth.html (accessed on October 23, 2015).

Department of Health (2015), "Report of advisory group on health effects of use of internet and electronic screen products", Department of Health, Government of HKSAR, available at: http://www.studenthealth.gov.hk/english/internet/report/files/e_report.pdf (accessed on October 18, 2015).

Dias, M. and Agante, L. (2011), "Can advergames boost children's healthier eating habits? A comparison between healthy and non-healthy food", *Journal of Consumer Behaviour*, Vol. 10 No. 3, pp. 152–160.

Dietz, W.H., Benken, D.E. and Hunter, A.S. (2009), "Public health law and the prevention and control of obesity", *Milbank Quarterly*, Vol. 87 No. 1, pp. 215–227.

Folkvord, F., Anschütz, D.J., Buijzen, M. and Valkenburg, P.M. (2013), "The effect of playing advergames that promote energy-dense snacks or fruit on actual food intake among children", *The American Journal of Clinical Nutrition*, Vol. 97 No. 2, pp. 239–245.

Fraser, S.N. and Spink, K.S. (2002), "Examining the role of social support and group cohesion in exercise compliance", *Journal of Behavioral Medicine*, Vol. 25 No. 3, pp. 233–249.

Fung, A. 馮應謙 (2013), "香港青少年與網絡遊戲 [Youth and online games in Hong Kong]", *Journal of Youth Studies*, Vol. 16 No. 1, pp. 43–55.

Harris, J.L., Brownell, K.D. and Bargh, J.A. (2009), "The food marketing defense model: Integrating psychological research to protect youth and inform public policy", *Social Issues and Policy Review*, Vol. 3 No. 1, pp. 211–271.

Hong Kong Monthly Digest of Statistics, (March 2014) "Feature Article: The Cultural and Creative Industries in Hong Kong", *Census and Statistics Department*, Hong Kong Special Administrative Region.

Kiger, A.M. (2004), *Teaching for Health*. Churchill Livingstone. Edinburgh.

King, S. (2012), "The interactive indulgence: The use of advergames to curb childhood obesity", *The Elon Journal of Undergraduate Research in Communications*, Vol. 3 No. 2, pp. 1–3.

Kreps, G.L., Bonaguro, E.W. and Query, J.L. (1998), "The history and development of the field of health communication", in Jackson, L.D. and Duffy, B.K. (Eds.), *Health Communication Research: A Guide to Developments and Directions*, Greenwood Press, Westport, CT, pp. 1–15.

Lee, M. and Youn, S. (2008), "Leading national advertisers' uses of advergames", *Journal of Current Issues and Research in Advertising*, Vol. 30 No. 2, pp. 1–13.

Lieberman, D.A. (2001), "Management of chronic pediatric diseases with interactive health games: Theory and research findings", *The Journal of Ambulatory Care Management*, Vol. 24 No. 1, pp. 26–38.

Lieberman, D.A. (2009), "Designing serious games for learning and health in informal and formal settings", in Ritterfeld, U., Cody, M. and Vorderer, P. (Eds.), *Serious Games: Mechanisms and Effects*, Routledge, New York, pp. 117–130.

Naidoo, J., and Wills, J. (2009), *Foundations for Health Promotion*. 3rd edn. Elsevier Health Sciences, Kidlington.

Nairn, A. and Fine, C. (2008), "Who's messing with my mind? The implications of dual-process models for the ethics of advertising to children", *International Journal of Advertising*, Vol. 27 No. 3, pp. 447–470.

Newzoo (2015), "Top 100 countries by game revenues", available at: https://newzoo.com/insights/rankings/top-100-countries-by-game-revenues/ (accessed on October 12, 2015).

Orji, R., Mandryk, R.L., Vassileva, J. and Gerling, K.M. (2013), "Tailoring persuasive health games to gamer type", *Proceedings of the SIGCHI Conference on Human Factors in Computing Systems in Paris*, France, April 27 – May 2, Association for Computing Machinery, New York, NY, pp. 2467–2476.

Orji, R., Vassileva, J. and Mandryk, R.L. (2014), "Modeling the efficacy of persuasive strategies for different gamer types in serious games for health", *User Modeling and User-Adapted Interaction*, Vol. 24 No. 5, pp. 453–498.

Sawyer, B. and Smith, P. (2008), "Serious games taxonomy", paper presented in the Serious Games Summit at the Game Developers Conference, San Francisco, CA, February 2008.

Schott, B.H., Seidenbecher, C.I., Fenker, D.B., Lauer, C.J., Bunzeck, N., Bernstein, H., Tischmeyer, W., Gundelfinger, E.D., Heinze, H. and Duzel, E. (2006), "The dopaminergic midbrain participates in human episodic memory formation: Evidence from genetic imaging", *The Journal of Neuroscience*, Vol. 26 No. 5, pp. 1407–1417.

Shan, L.C., Panagiotopoulos, P., Regan, Á., De Brún, A., Barnett, J., Wall, P. and McConnon, Á. (2015), "Interactive communication with the public: Qualitative exploration of the use of social media by food and health organizations", *Journal of Nutrition Education and Behavior*, Vol. 47 No. 1, pp. 104–108.

Simon-Morton, D.G., Calfas, K.J., Oldenburg, B. and Burton, N.W. (1998), "Effects of interventions in healthcare settings on physical activity or cardiorespiratory fitness", *American Journal of Preventive Medicine*, Vol. 15 No. 4, pp. 413–430.

Skiba, D.J. (2008), "Emerging technologies center: Games for health", *Nursing Education Perspectives*, Vol. 29 No. 4, pp. 230–232.

Skinner, H.A., Maley, O. and Norman, C.D. (2006), "Developing internet-based eHealth promotion programs: The Spiral Technology Action Research (STAR) model", *Health Promotion Practice*, Vol. 7 No. 4, pp. 406–417.

Terlutter, R. and Capella, M.L. (2013), "The gamification of advertising: Analysis and research directions of in-game advertising, advergames, and advertising in social network games", *Journal of Advertising*, Vol. 42 No. 2–3, pp. 95–112.

Thompson, D., Baranowski, T. and Buday, R. (2010), "Conceptual model for the design of a serious video game promoting self-management among youth with type 1 diabetes", *Journal of Diabetes Science and Technology*, Vol. 4 No. 3, pp. 744–749.

Towne, T.J., Ericsson, K.A. and Sumner, A.M. (2014), "Uncovering mechanisms in video game research: Suggestions from the expert-performance approach", Frontiers in Psychology, Vol. 5, available at: http://www.ncbi.nlm.nih.gov/pmc/articles/PMC3939770/ (accessed on October 12, 2015).

Wang, C.W., Chan, C.L., Mak, K.K., Ho, S.Y., Wong, P.W. and Ho, R.T. (2014), "Prevalence and correlates of video and internet gaming addiction among Hong Kong adolescents: A pilot study", The Scientific World Journal Vol. 2014, available at: http://www.hindawi.com/journals/tswj/2014/874648/ (accessed on October 12, 2015).

Winkler, T. and Buckner, K. (2006), "Receptiveness of gamers to embedded brand messages in advergames: Attitudes toward product placement", *Journal of Interactive Advertising*, Vol. 7 No. 1, pp. 37–46.

Chapter 13

Political Advertising and Public Service Advertisements

William Dezheng Feng

Introduction

As introduced in Chapter 10, the Information Services Department is responsible for the coordination of the design and execution of local publicity campaigns. The broadcast media are obliged to carry one minute of these publicity messages, known as announcements in the public interest (APIs), every hour. These messages are therefore prominent in society. Various approaches can be used to study APIs. This chapter introduces a sociolinguistic approach to examine the rhetorical features, argumentation strategies and visual images in the API texts. The term "text" does not just refer to language or utterances, but includes the totality of resources for meaning-making (e.g. the images, utterances, music and so on in television APIs). Meaning-making in this sense refers to the process by which people make sense of events. A semiotic theory for analyzing the texts is discussed and its application to the analysis of anti-drug APIs is elaborated. The social semiotic analysis of API discourse provides a useful complement to the mainstream content analysis and reception studies by modelling the complex meaning-making process in an explicit way.

Different Approaches for Analyzing APIs in Hong Kong

Following the global trend, the mode of governance in Hong Kong has been changing from top-down authoritative enforcement to a softer approach through education and promotion. Against this backdrop of political change, public service advertising and public communication campaigns have come to play an increasingly important role in Hong Kong. Nowadays, public service advertisements (PSAs) can be seen everywhere in Hong Kong. Posters on environment protection, health advice, drug abuse, public security and other social issues can be found on the streets and in bus stations, shopping malls and school campuses. In addition, APIs, a term used to refer to PSAs on television and radio (Wong, 2006), are broadcast several times daily on all channels.

In spite of the significance and breadth of PSAs, there are few studies in Hong Kong from the perspective of either communication or linguistic studies. Researchers include Kara Chan (e.g. Chan and Tsang, 2011; Chan and Chang, 2013; Chan and Huang, 2015), Wendy Wong (e.g. Wong and Cuklanz, 2000a, 2000b; Wong, 2006) and a handful of others (e.g. Cheng and Leung, 2014). Kara Chan mainly works from the perspective of reception, using surveys to understand the interpretation or the effects of the PSAs. For example, Chan and Tsang (2011), through a survey of 570 secondary school students, found that respondents' attitudes toward advertisements advocating healthy eating have a high positive correlation with their attitudes toward healthy eating. In comparison, the approach adopted by Wendy Wong and colleagues relies mainly on qualitative discourse analysis. For example, Wong (2006) provided a thorough sociopolitical analysis of the human rights campaign before 1997 and the basic law promotion campaign after 1997 and found that the former provided information which the audience needed to know for their benefit, while the latter delivered information which the authorities deemed the audience ought to know in order to promote a pro-China political ideology.

Due to the lack of research in this field, our understanding of PSAs in Hong Kong, including how they are designed and whether they are effective, is quite limited. Some fundamental questions remain unanswered or require further investigation:

- what are the features of PSA texts (rhetorical features, argumentation strategies, use of images, characters, etc.) in Hong Kong?

- what types of appeals are designed? What are the mechanisms/ strategies of persuasion?

- how do Hong Kong people react to different textual features and persuasive strategies of PSAs? How should the effects of PSAs be measured?

- what do PSAs reveal about the sociocultural reality of Hong Kong? What are the cultural and ideological values hidden in advertisements?

These questions summarize the objectives of different approaches to PSA research. Question 1 is the concern of linguistics, semiotics and discourse analysis; question 2 falls into the intersection of discourse studies, social psychology and communication research; question 3 is the concern of the mainstream reception studies in communication research; and question 4 is mainly addressed by social theories and cultural studies. Complementing other chapters in this book, the main aim of this chapter is to address question 1, that is, to introduce a linguistic/semiotic theory to disentangle the complexity of PSA texts. As "text" serves both as the carrier of appeals and cultural values and as the stimuli of audience reception, a systematic understanding of PSA text is essential to answering all the other questions.

PSAs as Multimodal Discourse: A Social Semiotic Model

PSAs have stimulated considerable interest in communication studies over the last three decades, in the United States and elsewhere. Among these studies, the features and effectiveness of PSA messages have been a central concern from approaches such as content analysis (e.g. Freimuth et al., 1990; Paek et al., 2010) and audience research (e.g. Lang et al., 2000; Dillard and Peck, 2000; Dillard and Ye, 2008). Compared with recipient-oriented empirical research, the linguistic and semiotic analysis of PSA discourse has attracted much less attention. However, although not widely adopted in PSA research, there is extensive literature on the language of advertisements (e.g. Leech, 1966; Vestergaard and Schroder, 1985; Cook, 1992; Gorddard, 1998). In recent years, with the development of multimodal discourse analysis, studies on visual images in print and television advertisements have proliferated (e.g. Cook, 1992; Forceville, 1996; Cheong, 2004; Feng and Wignell, 2011). For example, Cook (1992) provided a detailed description of language (words, phrases and style), paralanguage, pictures, etc. of advertising discourse; Forceville (1996), by extending conceptual metaphor theory to print advertisements, developed a framework of pictorial metaphors and discussed their roles in persuasion; Feng and Wignell (2011) analyzed the representation of intertextual voices and the roles of different kinds of social activities in TV commercials.

To explicate the complex semiotic features in PSAs, in particular in television APIs, we need powerful analytical tools. In analyzing moving images, Bateman and Schmidt (2013, p. 32) argued that "we can ill afford to approach them without the powerful analytic tools that an appropriate semiotics provides". The "appropriate semiotics" they referred to are systemic functional semiotics (or social semiotics) (Halliday and Matthiessen, 2004), and in this section, I will lay out the key tenets of the theory.

The Semiotic Strata

Systemic functional theory was developed to model both language and social context as semiotic systems realizing one another. In this model (simplified), "context" includes "context of culture" (e.g. social values, cultural norms and ideology) and "context of situation" (i.e. the activities that are going on, the social relations that are involved and the channel of communication used), while "language" involves word forms/grammar (i.e. words and their roles in combination) and discourse semantics (i.e. meaning of texts) (Halliday and Mathiessen, 2004), as represented in Figure 13.1. The premise of this model is that language use is a kind of social activity, through which we understand and construct social realities. This social activity does not refer to the things we do without language (like eating or walking), but the things we can do with language or other semiotic systems (e.g. explaining, persuading and entertaining), which are termed as "registers". At a higher level, these activities are carried out with specific social purposes and reflect the author's stance

Figure 13.1

Semiotic Strata and PSA Discourse

The social realm { Context of culture .... Social values

Context of situation .... Social activities (registers)

The semiotic realm { Discourse semantics .... Meanings in PSAs

Words and grammar .... Semiotic resources in PSAs

and attitude, as well as the general values and ideology of society. Moving down to the semiotic realm, social activities are constructed by the meanings of sentences and texts (discourse semantics). Moving further down, these meanings are generated by language (words and grammar) and semiotic resources such as color, camera angle, the actors' appearance, clothing, actions, etc. in multimodal discourses like television APIs.

This model is particularly pertinent for the investigation of ads and Hong Kong society, as it explicitly spells out the dialectic relation between social elements (i.e. social values, purposes and activities) and linguistic/semiotic elements, recognizing that the social is realized through the semiotic and the semiotic reflects the social. In terms of PSAs in Hong Kong, on the one hand, the aims of PSAs can be realized through PSA texts; on the other hand, through analyzing PSA texts, we can understand the social reality of Hong Kong.

Activity Types and Register Hybridization

For many activity types (e.g. persuading and explaining), the register for another activity (e.g. narrating and entertaining) is borrowed, which results in register hybridization. A typical example would be using the activity of telling a story (with the purpose of entertaining) in the activity of advertising (with the purpose of promoting the product). To account for such hybridity in PSAs, Matthiessen's (2014) register typology is drawn upon. This typology is adapted into seven primary activities that language or other semiotic resources can perform: expounding (explaining phenomena, as in science textbooks or academic articles), reporting (recording or chronicling events, as in news reports), recreating/narrating (storytelling, as in novels or movies), sharing (exchanging personal experiences or opinions, such as in gossip and discussions), recommending (advising or persuading the audience, as in advertisements and reference letters), exploring (questioning, arguing or reasoning, as in debates) and enabling (explaining procedures, as in recipes and manuals).

For advertising discourse, which belongs to the recommending register, direct propaganda is used less and less nowadays as advertisers borrow various other registers to enhance their persuasive power while trying to reduce their commercial nature. As a result, advertisements have become a parasite discourse (Cook, 1992), borrowing styles from all kinds of discourse types (e.g. science, fine art, gossip) which belong to registers such as expounding, recreating and sharing. The modelling of registers can be used in diachronic analysis (e.g. the change of register profile of anti-drug APIs for the 1950s to the 2000s) or cross-cultural analysis (e.g. the registerial difference between anti-drug APIs in Hong Kong and the U.S.). We will discuss what registers are represented in anti-drug APIs in Hong Kong later in the chapter.

Attitudinal Meanings and Their Construction

As explained above, social activities are constructed through the meaning of language and other semiotic resources. Due to space constraints, this chapter focuses only on attitudinal meaning, which was developed as a subtype of interpersonal meaning (Martin and White, 2005). Attitude includes values of emotional response (affect), values by which human behavior is socially assessed (judgment), and values which address the aesthetic qualities of objects and entities (appreciation). Affect is further categorized into inclination, happiness, security and satisfaction. Judgment can be divided into social esteem, which involves sub-categories of normality (how usual/special someone is), capacity (how capable/powerful someone is) and tenacity (how resolute/dependable someone is); social sanction, which is concerned with veracity (how truthful someone is) and propriety (how ethical someone is).

Table 13.1

Categories of Attitude

Category	Subcategory
Affect	+/-Inclination
	+/-Happiness
	+/-Security
	+/-Satisfaction
Judgment	+/-Normality
	+/-Capacity
	+/-Tenacity
	+/-Veracity
	+/-Propriety
Appreciation	+/-Reaction
	+/-Composition
	+/-Valuation

Source: Martin and White (2005).

Appreciation is formulated in terms of the entity's aesthetic impact, including reaction (is it interesting, attention grabbing, etc.), composition (is it balanced, coherent, well organized, etc.) and valuation (is it valuable, original, etc.). All these values have a positive/negative valence: "+" is used to mark positive attitudes and "−" is used to mark negative attitudes in analysis. The system is shown in Table 13.1.

In terms of how attitudinal meaning is constructed (by words and grammar), Martin and White (2005) distinguish between inscribed attitude (direct) and invoked attitude (indirect). Inscribing means that attitude is directly constructed through the attitudinal lexicon, such as "happy", "sad", "good" and "bad", while invocation refers to cases where only the fact is represented (e.g. "I got the job" to invoke happiness; "He won seven Olympic medals" to invoke capacity; "She donated all her money to the orphanage" to invoke morality). Acknowledging both inscribed and invoked attitude allows for cross-coding among affect, judgment and appreciation (Martin and White, 2005, p. 67). For example, when a drug addict is judged as being weak and ugly, the negative valuation of drugs is also invoked. More importantly, it is also possible to incorporate non-linguistic resources in attitude representation. For example, luxury accessories can invoke the judgment of wealth, and the depiction of certain events can invoke our perception of the characters' emotions or attributes.

Case Study: Modelling Register and Attitudinal Meaning in Anti-Drug APIs

Since the 1990s, the Hong Kong government has promoted research on preventive education and publicity, and hundreds of projects have been implemented. A previous project that provided detailed analysis of anti-drug APIs was the Assessment and Audience Utilization of Hong Kong Anti-drug APIs Project, funded in 1998 and completed in 2000 (Wong and Cuklanz, 2000a). Wong and Cuklanz (2000b) reported on the persuasive strategies in APIs before 1992 (e.g. the invocation of the Opium Wars) and after 1992 (e.g. the use of metaphors and testimonials). In what follows, I will provide a brief survey of the corpus of APIs using the framework introduced in the previous section. The corpus of our analysis is composed of the thirty-nine anti-drug APIs, which can be easily found on the website of the Information Services Department (http://www.isd.gov.hk/eng/api_more.htm#ad) and YouTube.

Modelling Register Profile

To get an overall picture of the registers, an Excel spreadsheet with each API as a row and each of the seven registers in Matthiessen's (2014) register typology as a column was created. Then we watched the APIs and ticked the box if a certain register was present. Some typical examples of the registers are illustrated as follows:

- Sharing: "The gang leader picked me, asked me to deliver heroin. I was scared to carry it on the streets…One day, some plainclothes policemen tapped me on my shoulder. Right then I knew I could not go back". (Dealing with the Devil, 2009)

- Expounding: "Ketamine is not just a drug; it's a recipe for misery!

Hallucination, memory loss, can't control your bladder, heart problems...!" (Harm of Abusing Ketamine, 2011)

- Narrating: (Visual narrative) Orientation: Two high school students are chased by several young adults. Complication: The young adults catch them and try to give them drugs. Resolution: One of the students throws the pills on the ground and steps on them. (Run, 2010)

- Exploring: "Would he go through hell for you? Or is he giving you hell? Is your buddy covering your back? Or is he stabbing you in the back? ...Hold it! You don't have to prove your friendship and love by taking drugs!" (Friends, 2013)

- Recommending: "Stop putting it off; seek help now. Many people and organizations can help. Don't hide yourself." (Seek Help Early, 2014)

- Enabling: Helpline: 186 186 WhatsApp/WeChat 98 186 186 Narcotics Division, Security Bureau Action Committee Against Narcotics www.nd.gov.hk (Quit Drugs Now, 2015)

By counting the occurrences of these registers, we can observe some interesting patterns. First, recommending and enabling registers are obligatory elements in all cases, suggesting that the primary purpose of APIs is to persuade citizens to quit or avoid drugs. Recommending is typically realized by imperative sentences (e.g. "Knock drugs out"; "Don't hesitate, report the drug abusers"), while enabling is typically realized by call-and-visit information (e.g. telephone number and website). Second, in no API do recommending and enabling occur alone; instead, they are always preceded by other registers, leading to the registerial hybridity introduced earlier. The registers form a schematic, or a generic structure of [sharing/expounding/exploring/narrating]^[recommending]^[enabling]. Third, among the registers, sharing is the most frequently used, mostly in cases where a drug abuser shares his/her experience and feelings. As the number of teenage addicts has increased in recent years, the APIs now focus more on personal stories of young drug addicts than objective explanations about the harm of drugs, which can engage teenagers' attention and empathy more easily. Sharing is followed by expounding, which mostly involves voice-over explanations of the harm

Table 13.2

The Distribution of Registers in Anti-Drug APIs

Register	Frequency
Sharing	15
Expounding	12
Exploring	7
Narrating	5
Recommending	39
Enabling	39

of drugs. Two other registers found in the corpus are exploring (presenting options for the audience to think about and choose) and narrating (telling real or fictional stories of drug addicts). The overall distribution is shown in Table 13.2.

Modelling Attitude Profile

The types of affect, judgment and appreciation represented in the APIs play an important role in influencing audiences' attitudes toward drug abuse. The present analysis is guided by the following four questions:

- whose attitude and toward whom/what?

- what type of attitude is represented (using the categories of Table 13.1)?

- is the attitude positive or negative?

- is the attitude inscribed or invoked, and is it constructed by language or visual image, or both?

These were laid out as columns in the Excel spreadsheet, and their occurrence was annotated. First, in terms of the appraiser (the person whose attitude is being discussed), the most striking feature of the APIs in the corpus is the predominance of voice-overs who evaluate drug addicts and the harm of drugs (in the expounding and exploring registers) through the

Table 13.3
Examples of Attitude in Anti-Drug APIs

API text	Affect	Judgment	Appreciation
I was devastated	-Happiness		
When my son was sent to jail because of taking drugs.	-Happiness, t	-Propriety, t (of his son)	
I didn't have time to look after him	-Satisfaction, t	-Propriety, t	
Drug treatment and rehabilitation centers help those in need to start a new life!			+Valuation, t
Not only are her teeth rotting…But her brain is also damaged	-Security, t (fear from the audience)	-Normality, t -Capacity, t	-Valuation, t (of drugs)
If you are a heroin addict, you are ignored and rejected by your former friends!	-Happiness, t	-Propriety, t (by friends)	-Valuation, t (of heroin)

firm, authoritative voices of experts. In the sharing register, in most cases, teenage/young adult drug addicts share their negative emotions and negative judgments of themselves. Targets of this attitude mostly belong to two types, namely, drug addicts and drugs, but in a few cases, parents, friends and viewers in general are also evaluated. In what follows, we will see how they are evaluated.

The way attitude is annotated is illustrated in Table 13.3 ("t" is used to mark invoked attitudes). From these few random examples, some observations can be made. (a) Most attitudes are negative, including negative affect of drug abusers and their families, negative judgment of drug abusers, and negative appreciation of the effect of drug. These can invoke from the viewer negative affect (e.g. fear), negative judgment of drug abusers and negative appreciation of drugs, so as to persuade them to stay away from drugs. (b) Most attitudes are invoked by describing the facts of drug abuse and its consequences (e.g. sent to jail, teeth rotting, ignored by friends). These facts are perceived to be real and reliable, and may be more engaging and more effective in influencing

Table 13.4

Distribution of Attitude in Anti-Drug APIs

	Positive		Negative		Total
	Inscription	Invocation	Inscription	Invocation	
Affect	6	11	26	68	111(35%)
Judgment	7	12	10	69	98 (31%)
Appreciation	0	9	22	76	107 (34%)
Total		37 (12%)		279 (88%)	316 (100%)

viewers than just expressing subjective opinions. Moreover, these facts can invoke multiple attitudes; that is, two or all of the three categories. For example, "My son was sent to jail" invokes "my" sadness and the bad behavior of "my son", while "Her teeth rotting (because of drugs)" can invoke viewers' negative judgment of her (ugly), fear and negative attitude toward drugs. This pattern is supported by the analysis of all attitudinal meanings of the corpus, as shown in Table 13.4.

We can see from Table 13.4 that the overall pattern confirms that of Table 13.3, with more negative than positive attitudes, more invocations than inscriptions. It also shows that there is an equal distribution of affect, judgment and appreciation, which is a well thought-out configuration for effective persuasion, working on pathos, ethos and logos. It is noteworthy that there are a number of positive attitudes, which typically occur in two situations, before taking drugs and after rehabilitation. For example, "Once our family was very happy; it was like paradise. But when I found out my son was taking drugs, I felt like we were in hell.", and "I used to take drugs, everything was a mess...Then I decided to go to a Methadone detoxification center. Now I have started working and my family members are happy for me", illustrate these two cases respectively. The contrast between positive and negative effectively constructs the consequence of drug abuse (i.e. turning a happy life miserable) and the effect of rehabilitation (i.e. starting a new life), which is important for discouraging drug abuse and encouraging rehabilitation.

Figure 13.2

Examples of the Visual Construction of Attitudinal Meaning

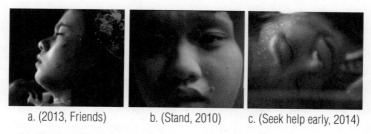

a. (2013, Friends)   b. (Stand, 2010)   c. (Seek help early, 2014)

Source: Information Services Department, Narcotics Division, Security Bureau.

In terms of attitude construction, it is also important to note the role of visual images. The attitudes, especially affects, and to some extent, judgments, are co-constructed by both language and images. These images mostly show emotional suffering (negative affect) and biological (sometimes social) problems and failures (invoking negative judgment). Figure 13.2 illustrates some examples. The images can significantly enhance the impact on viewers (grabbing their attention, invoking fear, etc.). Moreover, they are also more effective in persuading as the attitude (the emotions of drug abusers, and hence the harm of drugs) is not imposed on viewers through telling them (echoing the majority of invocations in Table 13.4), but is shown to them vividly, allowing viewers to come up with their own attitudes. This is a vital aspect of visual persuasion, because people are more easily persuaded by meanings they construct themselves (Jeong, 2008).

Conclusion

This chapter set out to provide an alternative approach to analyzing PSA texts, and in particular APIs in Hong Kong, which is also applicable to print and television advertisements in general. Among the theoretical tools provided, the semiotic strata can model the dialectic relation between advertising and society; the register typology enables us to examine the social activities that language and images are used for (e.g. expounding, sharing, recommending) and to elucidate the phenomenon of register hybridization; the attitude framework allows us to see how drug abusers and drugs are evaluated and how the patterns of attitude contribute to persuasion. Then, I analyzed the register and attitude profiles in the corpus of anti-drug APIs in Hong Kong. The analysis provides new understanding of the creative choices in the designing of APIs. The semiotic approach emphasizes that all meanings are constructed by making choices. Elucidating the choice systems, of which this chapter is a preliminary demonstration, can provide an explicit metalanguage for teaching the complex mechanisms of meaning-making in advertisements. However, it should be pointed out that due to space constraints, only a very small part of social semiotic tools have been introduced.

Although the analysis focuses on the micro-level textual details, it should be emphasized that text analysis should not be isolated from broader social and communicative concerns, as explained in Figure 13.1. First, text is the result of specific social communicative purposes, and a detailed understanding of text can reveal the social reality and how the communicative purposes are realized (e.g. the dominance of teenage characters reveals the social reality of teenage drug abuse, the purpose of discouraging drug abuse is realized by the representation of negative attitudes). Second, micro-text analysis is supportive of other approaches to advertising research in understanding social change, cultural difference, persuasive effect and so on. For example, by analyzing the registers and attitudes of APIs (or other advertisements) from the 1950s and 2000s, or from Hong Kong and the Unites States, we can systematically show the diachronic change and cultural differences, which can then be explained by social and cultural theories. The advantage of the semiotic framework is that it provides more systematically organized content parameters and grounds our interpretations of social cultural differences firmly on the explicit analysis of their carriers, namely, texts, so that subjectivity can be reduced and inter-analyst reliability can be increased. For reception analysis, we can investigate audience reaction to PSAs with different registerial and attitudinal features/configurations (cf. Morgan et al., 2003). Therefore, we conclude with the hope that different approaches can be integrated in disentangling the complexity of advertisements and the even more complex relationship between advertising and society.

Acknowledgements

The research for this chapter was supported by the Central Research Grant, The Hong Kong Polytechnic University (Project No.: G-YBCC).

References

Bateman, J. A. and Schmidt, K.H. (2013), *Multimodal Film Analysis: How Films Mean*, Routledge, London.

Chan, K. and Chang, C. (2013), "Advertising to Chinese youth: A study of public service ads in Hong Kong", *Qualitative Market Research: An International Journal*, Vol. 16 No. 4, pp. 421–435.

Chan, K. and Huang A. (2015), "Understanding of public service advertisements among Chinese children", in Evans, W.D. (Ed.), *Social Marketing: Global Perspectives, Strategies and Effects on Consumer Behavior*, Nova Science Publishers, New York, pp. 109–120.

Chan, K. and Tsang, L. (2011), "Promote healthy eating among adolescents: A Hong Kong study", *Journal of Consumer Marketing*, Vol. 28 No. 5, pp. 354–362.

Cheng, K. and Leung, V. (2014), "Reinforcing gender stereotypes: A critical discourse analysis of health-related PSAs in Hong Kong", *American International Journal of Social Science*, Vol. 3 No. 3, pp. 36–48.

Cheong, Y.Y. (2004), "The construal of ideational meaning in print advertisements", in O'Halloran, K.L. (Ed.), *Multimodal Discourse Analysis*, Continuum, London, pp. 163–195.

Cook, G. (1992), *Advertising Discourse*. Routledge, London.

Dillard, J.P. and Peck, E. (2000), "Affect and persuasion: Emotional responses to public service announcements", *Communication Research*, Vol. 27 No. 4, pp. 461–495.

Dillard, J.P. and Ye, S. (2008), "The perceived effectiveness of persuasive messages: Questions of structure, referent, and bias", *Journal of Health Communication*, Vol. 13 No. 2, pp. 149–168.

Feng, D. and Wignell, P. (2011), "Intertextual voices and engagement in TV advertisements", *Visual Communication*, Vol. 10 No. 4, pp. 565–588.

Forceville, C. (1996), *Pictorial Metaphor in Advertising*. Routledge, London.

Freimuth, V.S., Hammond, S.L., Edgar, T. and Monahan, J.L. (1990), "Reaching those at risk: A content-analytic study of AIDS PSAs", *Communication Research*, Vol. 17 No. 6, pp. 775–791.

Gorddard, A. (1998), *The Language of Advertising: Written Texts*. London, Routledge.

Halliday, M.A.K. and Matthiessen, C.M.I.M. (2004), *Introduction to Functional Grammar*. 3rd edn. Routledge, London.

Jeong, S.H. (2008), "Visual metaphor in advertising", *Journal of Marketing Communications*, Vol. 14 No. 1, pp. 59–73.

Lang, A., Zhou, S., Schwartz, N., Bolls, P.D. and Potter, R.F. (2000), "The effects of edits on arousal, attention, and memory for television messages: When an edit is an edit can an edit be too much?" *Journal of Broadcasting & Electronic Media*, Vol. 44 No. 1, pp. 94–109.

Leech, G. (1966), *English in Advertising*. London: Longman.

Martin, J.R. and White, P.P.R. (2005), *The Language of Evaluation, Palgrave Macmillan*. New York. NY.

Matthiessen, C.M.I.M. (2014), "Appliable discourse analysis", in Fang, Y. and Webster, J.J. (Eds.), *Developing Systemic Functional Linguistics: Theory and Application, Continuum, London*, pp. 138-208.

Morgan, S., Palmgreen, P., Stephenson, M., Hoyle, R. and Lorch, E. (2003), "Association between message features and subjective evaluations of the sensation value of anti-drug public service announcements", *Journal of Communication*, Vol. 53 No. 3, pp. 512–526.

Paek, H., Kim, K. and Hove, T. (2010), "Content analysis of antismoking videos on YouTube: Message sensation value, message appeals, and their relationships with viewer responses", *Health Education Research*, Vol. 25 No. 6, pp. 1085–1099.

Vestergaard, T. and Schroder, K. (1985), *The Language of Advertising*. Blackwell. New York. NY.

Wong, W.S. (2006), "Political ideology in Hong Kong's public service announcements", in Chan, K. (Ed.), *Advertising and Hong Kong society*, Chinese University Press, Hong Kong, pp. 55–76.

Wong, W.S. and Cuklanz, L. (2000a), "Assessment and audience utilization of Hong Kong's APIs", *grant project final report to the Action Committee Against Narcotics*, Hong Kong Government.

Wong, W.S. and Cuklanz, L. (2000b), "The myths of Chinese images revisited: Persuasive strategies in Hong Kong anti-drug public service announcements", *in National Association of African American Studies and National Association of Hispanic and Latino Studies: 2000 Literature Monograph Series Proceedings of Annual Conference*, Houston, TX, pp. 271–298.